D0984840

THE CONFIDENCE
OF
BRITISH PHILOSOPHERS

STUDIES IN THE HISTORY
OF
CHRISTIAN THOUGHT

EDITED BY

HEIKO A. OBERMAN, Tübingen

IN COOPERATION WITH

HENRY CHADWICK, Oxford
EDWARD A. DOWEY, Princeton, N.J.
JAROSLAV PELIKAN, New Haven, Conn.
BRIAN TIERNEY, Ithaca, N.Y.
E. DAVID WILLIS, San Anselmo, California

VOLUME XVII

ARTHUR QUINN
THE CONFIDENCE
OF
BRITISH PHILOSOPHERS

LEIDEN
E. J. BRILL
1977

THE CONFIDENCE

OF

BRITISH PHILOSOPHERS

An Essay in Historical Narrative

BY

ARTHUR QUINN

LEIDEN
E. J. BRILL
1977

ISBN 90 04 05397 2

Copyright 1977 by E. J. Brill, Leiden, The Netherlands

PRINTED IN THE NETHERLANDS

"Many shall run to and fro; and knowledge shall be increased."

The Book of the Prophet Daniel, 12:4

TABLE OF CONTENTS

PREFACE

I intend the narrative that follows as an essay in humanistic history. Much of what I mean by "humanistic" in this context has been suggested in a recent work on eighteenth-century British humanism by Paul Fussell.

> The Humanist is convinced that man's primary obligation is the strenuous determination of moral questions; he thus believes that inquiries into the technical operations of the external world ("science") constitute not only distinctly secondary but even irrelevant perhaps dangerous activities.

Traditionally history has been in this sense a humanistic discipline, perhaps even the humanistic discipline *par excellence*. This is no longer so; hence the need for an explanatory preface.

Serious historians of the present day generally prefer, in Lord Acton's phrase, to "treat History as a progressive science." They are concerned almost exclusively, and at times brilliantly, with the technical operations of history. And the best of these historians, as Arnold Toynbee aptly put it, "will be remembered among the famous Western engineers"; their historiographical feats will "rank with our stupendous tunnels and bridges and dams and liners and battleships and skyscrapers." To perform such feats, they have had to shy away from, or even studiously to avoid, moral discriminations. A man like Hitler or an institution like slavery the truly scientific historian must consider indifferently, as if an historical phenomenon like any other.

Such a habit of mind, however dangerous it might appear to the humanist, is perhaps inevitable in those who value, above all else, accuracy. Moral discriminations do not seem amenable to exact research in the way that mere technical operations do; a moral norm, unlike a scientific hypothesis, does not seem susceptible to empirical testing. Therefore, when viewed from the artificial perspective of science, humanistic writing takes on a peculiarly inconsequential character. And so the humanistic literary critic Wayne Booth feels obliged to defend even a Shakespeare from the charge of inconsequence, so deeply has the scientific paradigm come to dominate judgment.

> Though Shakespeare seems, when looked at superficially, to "have no beliefs", though it is indeed impossible to extract from the plays any

one coherent philosophical or religious or political formulation that will satisfy all readers, it is not difficult to list innumerable norms which we must accept if we are to comprehend particular plays, and some of these do run throughout his works. It is true that these beliefs are for the most part self-evident, even commonplace—but that is precisely because they are acceptable to most of us. Shakespeare requires us to believe that it is right to honor our fathers, and that it is wrong to kill off old men like Lear or grind out the eyes of old men like Gloucester. He insists that it is always wrong to use other people as instruments to one's own ends, whether by murder or slander, that it is good lo love, but wrong to love selfishly, that helpless old age is pitiable, and that blind egotism deserves punishment. . . . Such a list of persistent norms is surprisingly similar to the norms derived from other really great authors, as well as those found in many very mediocre ones. Certainly to work in accordance with such universals is not enough to make an author great. But to accept them in the works where they are pertinent is a fundamental step before greatness can be experienced.

Booth's apologia helps clarify the task of a humanistic author, at least as I understand it. He endeavors to assist his readers to discover perhaps, but certainly to exercise and thereby to strengthen, their moral intuitions. He does so on the presumption that his own moral intuitions and those of his readers, both present and future, are the same. He can find a warrant, if not a proof, for this presumption, in the endurance of a Shakespeare.

Now I can indicate more plainly what I mean when I say that I have tried to write a humanistic history. To write a successful humanistic history is to use historical materials (accurate to the best technical estimates of the day) to illumine presumably self-evident moral truths in a deeply affecting way. The characteristic novelty one experiences in reading an enduring work of humanistic history derives from neither the historical materials nor the moral norms considered separately. The novelty derives from the deeply affecting way in which the two are brought together, the way the norms are incarnated and thereby constellated.

Humanistic histories are often accused of being popular, rhetorical, and sententious by those proud of histories that are esoteric, indifferent, and amoral. These accusations are accurate, only they should be perceived as praise.[1]

The narrative that follows is about pride, by reputation the deadliest of the seven deadly sins. It details how pride in its purest, most beguiling form, pride of the spirit, corrupts men and leads them and

those that follow them to grief. It is a story not significantly different
from that told in *Genesis*, and re-told in John Milton's *Paradise Lost*.
It is a sententious story, and yet one that can scarcely be told too
often.

I have told it with respect to modern philosophy. In fact, I have
told it more than once, trying to weave together into a single narrative
different variations of this story. And I have tried as much as possible
to let the stories speak for themselves, without didactic intrusions. I
have tried to trust my readers' intuitions.

Of course, this is not to say that the narrative is entirely without
artifice. In particular, the four major parts of the narrative are held
together by obviously artificial means. They all happen to be about
British philosophical movements; each successive movement happens
to be in some sense a response to the one that preceded it; the rise
and fall of the Newtonian philosophy happens to provide a temporal
frame for the four-part narrative considered as a whole.

I would not pretend that the unity evoked by these means was
anything but artificial. Nonetheless, I would like to believe that
beneath this artificial unity stands a deeper, more natural one. I
would like to believe that the parts of my narrative are related like
the stanzas of a lyric poem, a poem such as Wallace Stevens' "On
the Road Home."

> It was when I said,
> "There is no such thing as the truth,"
> That the grapes seemed fatter.
> The fox ran out of his hole.
>
> You . . . You said,
> "There are many truths,
> But they are not parts of a truth."
> Then the tree, at night, began to change,
> Smoking through green and smoking blue.
> We were two figures in a wood.
> We said we stood alone.
>
> It was when I said,
> "Words are not forms of a single word.
> In the sum of the parts, there are only the parts.
> The world must be measured by the eye";
>
> It was when you said,
> "The idols have seen lots of poverty,
> Snakes and gold and lice,
> But not the truth";

> It was at that time, that the silence was largest
> And longest, the night was roundest,
> The fragrance of the autumn warmest,
> Closest and strongest.

Striking about this poem is its unabashed thematic repetition, how each stanza both grows out of what preceeded it and yet deepens our comprehension of the whole. And if the poet succeeds, it is because the metaphors finally take on a luminous life of their own, constellating.

As I look back upon my narrative, the unity I would most like it to have is a unity given to it by its metaphors, metaphors held in common with Milton and the Old Testament. I did not impose these metaphors, but found them in the words of the philosophers, who at those times were perhaps speaking better than they knew.[2]

My narrative, nonetheless, does have a more material relevance for the series Studies in the History of Christian Thought than the metaphors. While the narrative does show the persistence of biblical metaphors in some avowedly non-Christian philosophical movements, it also shows the persistence of a biblical view of history. Most of the thinkers in these movements believed in what the prophet Daniel called "the time of the end." However, they did not just believe in it (as any good Christian must); they were confident they would be its proud makers.

Soon after the collapse of the Puritan Commonwealth, and just before he was to begin writing his most enduring poetry, a humbled John Milton concluded, "Known only to the Father is the hour and day of the end." To this wise saying I would only wish to add, "And also the century."

PROLOGUE

Philosophers in pursuit of first principles often appear, even to fellow philosophers, to be off on a quixotic quest.

Bertrand Russell, perhaps the most famous British philosopher of his day, once began a series of lectures, "Philosophy, from the earliest times, has made greater claims and achieved fewer results than any other branch of human learning. Ever since Thales said that all is water, philosophers have been ready with glib assertions about the sum total of things; and equally glib denials have come from other philosophers ever since Thales was contradicted by Anaximander."

With such admissions being made periodically by philosophers themselves, no wonder many outside philosophy have given up any hope for its reformation. So radical a departure from the past must appear to be congenitally precluded.

Nevertheless, most philosophers, prominent among them many proclaimers of the futility and hubris of previous philosophy, have not permitted the past to limit their own aspirations for the future. For instance, the very lecture of Russell quoted above continued, "I believe that the time has now arrived when this unsatisfactory state of things can be brought to an end." Bertrand Russell was condemning his predecessors only to introduce his own personal claim to have discovered ultimate philosophical principles.

The true nature of philosophy had been discovered at last. A handful of philosophers, in particular Russell and his philosophical confidantes, now knew the correct method for philosophizing, and were consequently beginning to give final solutions to perennial philosophical problems. It was, Russell said, "an achievement surpassing all that has hitherto been accomplished by philosophers." Our intellectual hopes would be satisfied, Russell said, "more fully than former ages could have deemed possible for human minds."

Russell was confident that this achievement in which he shared was unprecedented in the long history of western philosophy. Whether or not it was unprecedented, his confidence that it was did not itself lack precedents. Such confidence had been seen since the earliest times of philosophy. In fact, this confidence had ample precedents even within the relatively brief span of British philosophy.

Since the seventeenth century almost every generation of British philosophers (to say nothing of the philosophers of other nations) has made claims as great as those Russell made. Such confidence appears to be a most deeply rooted feature of western philosophy, transcending as it does all schools and all times.

The following are but four instances of this confidence, one originating in each of the past four centuries of British philosophy. Saved until last will be that shared and enjoyed by Bertrand Russell himself.

PART I

GRAVITY

INTRODUCTION

In his family garden, near Woolsthorpe, Lincolnshire, in 1665 or 1666, Isaac Newton, home temporarily from Cambridge University, discovered the principle of gravity.

Newton was home waiting out a plague. The Great Plague, the worst since the Black Death, ruled London, and threatened to spread that rule throughout Britain. To help prevent this, the universities, including Cambridge, were closed. But nothing, it seemed, or no one save God, could help London. There alone almost one hundred thousand were counted dead; and few survivors would have thought that any number could measure the evil marked by the mass trench graves.

Just before the plague began, John Milton, as if by divine providence, had finished an epic theodicy. *Paradise Lost* would justify the ways of God to man; it would explain how death and discord had come to rule the world.

> "O Sacred, Wise, and Wisdom-giving Plant,
> Mother of Science, Now I feel the Power
> Within me clear, not only to discern
> Things in their Causes, but to trace the ways
> Of highest Agents deem'd however wise."

Satan had just tasted the forbidden fruit to show Eve how beneficent it was.

> "Queen of this Universe, do not believe
> Those rigid threats of Death; ye shall not Die:
> How should ye? by the Fruit? it gives you Life
> To Knowledge: By the Threatner? look on mee,
> Mee who have touched and tasted, yet both life,
> And life more perfect have attain'd than Fate
> meant mee, by venturing higher than my Lot."

The desire for knowledge, the desire for what Satan called the God-like fruit, this desire, Milton would have us believe, is the source of all man's suffering.

Milton at least presented his case at an appropriate time. What better instance of that suffering than the Great Plague, what better instance of that desire than Isaac Newton?

And, if Newton's discovery of gravity was but a ritual of man's first disobedience, then it had an appropriate setting—Newton in a garden, temporarily preserved from the death all around, Newton in a garden staring at an apple.[1]

An account in Newton's own words of the circumstances of his discovery has not survived. What has survived is a report by an old friend, William Stukeley, of a conversation he had with Newton the year before the great man's death. During the dinner they had together, the aged Newton's thoughts turned to his childhood home. He wished, he said, to spend his last days in the place of his childhood. He asked his friend to try to buy a home there for him. (Stukeley subsequently did try, but unsuccessfully; and Newton died in London, far from the countryside of Lincolnshire.) It was after dinner that Newton began to reminisce about his great discovery.

> The weather being warm, we went into the garden and drank tea, under the shade of some apple trees, only me and himself. Amidst other discourse, he told me, he was just in the same situation, as when formerly, the notion of gravitation came into his mind. It was occasion'd by the fall of an apple, as he sat in a contemplative mood. Why should the apple always descend perpendicularly to the ground, thought he to himself. Why should it not go sideways or upwards, but constantly to the earth's centre? Assuredly, the reason is, that the earth draws it. There must be a drawing power in matter: and the sum of the drawing power in the matter of the earth must be in the earth's centre, not in any side of the earth. Therefore does this apple fall perpendicularly, or towards the centre. If matter thus draws matter, it must be in proportion of its quantity. Therefore the apple draws the earth, as well as the earth draws the apple. That there is a power, like that we here call gravity, which extends itself thro' the universe.
> And thus by degrees he began to apply this property of gravitation to the motion of the earth and of the heavenly bodys, to consider their distances, their magnitudes and their periodical revolutions; to find out, that this property conjointly with a progressive motion impressed on them at the beginning, perfectly solv'd their circular courses; kept the planets from falling upon one another, and dropping all together into one centre: and thus he unfolded the Universe. This was the birth of those amazing discoveries, whereby he built philosophy on a solid foundation, to the astonishment of all Europe.

Newton had unfolded the world; he had placed philosophy on a solid foundation at last. This was the interpretation widely accepted by the time of Newton's death—this, and not that invited by Milton's poetry. After his death, the British poet Alexander Pope proposed as his epitaph:

Nature and Nature's Laws lay hid in Night:
God said, *Let Newton be*! All was Light.[2]

Isaac Newton the man might have died, but his unfolding of the world survived him. And, according to oral tradition, so did the very apple tree under which that unfolding began. After Newton's death, this tree was reverenced as a relic, a symbol of his undying achievement, and mankind's achievement through him. The tree stood as if a reassurance that the world of nature, and perhaps that of man himself, was governed by rational principles. Newton under this very tree had discovered one such principle, and had thereby discovered that such principles are to be discovered. The tree made the immortality of Newton's discovery palpable.

Newton's apple tree survived the eighteenth century. However, as it aged, it became less and less stable. Its branches had to be propped up to help it survive, but it did survive. It was still standing in the early nineteenth century when the famous French astronomer Pierre Simon Laplace is supposed to have said, "There could be only one Newton, for there is only one universe to discover."

Even after the tree itself had been blown over in a windstorm a little more than a century after Newton's own death, his principle survived. His principle remained so vital late in the nineteenth century that the famous British biologist Thomas Henry Huxley could confidently write, "It is no use to talk to me of analogies and probabilities. I know what I mean when I say I believe in the law of inverse squares, and I will not rest my life and my hopes upon weaker convictions."

And even in the mid-twentieth century, when the principle itself seemed to have been unrooted, no other than Albert Einstein, himself famous for having laid Newton's principle to rest, could write, "Fortunate Newton, happy childhood of science!"[3]

CHAPTER ONE

THE CAMBRIDGE PLATONISTS
(to 1661)

When Isaac Newton first came to Cambridge as a student in 1661, the University, like Britain itself, was adjusting to the new order of things. To the last Parliament before the Civil War of the 1640's, Cambridge had sent Oliver Cromwell himself. Now Cromwell was dead, and so was the Puritan Commonwealth over which he had ruled. The commonwealth in the service of which Milton had worked himself blind had run its course, and now the monarchy had been restored.

At Cambridge University, by 1661, a new group of thinkers had asserted itself. This group professed faith in God and confidence in reason, and sometimes more than implied that these really were the same thing. As one of them said, "To go against *Reason*, is to go against *God*; it is the self-same to do that which the Reason of the Case doth require; and that which God Himself doth appoint: Reason is the Divine Governor of Man's Life; it is the very Voice of God."

In the 1660's, despite the Restoration, many were shocked at such an exaltation of reason. In 1662 one of the admirers of these Cambridge thinkers felt the need to publish a pamphlet in defence of them, "A Brief Account of the New Sect of Latitude-men." In particular, S. P., as the author of the pamphlet discreetly called himself, was concerned with defending them from the charge of "hearkening too much to their own Reason."

> And now let no Man accuse them of hearkening too much to their own Reason, since their Reason steers by so excellent a Compass, the antient Fathers and Councils of the Church. For Reason is the Faculty, wereby a Man must judge of everything; nor can a Man believe any thing except he have some reason for it, whether that Reason be a Deduction from the Light of Nature, and those Principles which are the Candle of the Lord, set up in the Soul of every man that hath not wilfully extinguish'd it; or a Branch of Divine Revelation in the Oracles of Holy Scripture; or the general Interpretation of genuine antiquity, of the Proposal of our own Church consentaneous thereto, or lastly the Result of some of all of these: For he that will rightly make use of his Reason, must take all that is reasonable into

consideration. And it is admirable to consider how the same Conclusions do naturally flow from all these several Principles; and what in the faithful Use of the Faculties that God hath given, Men have believ'd for true, doth excellently agree with that Revelation that God hath exhibited in the Scripture, and Doctrine of the antient Church with them both. Thus the Freedom of our Wills, the universal Intent of Christ's Death, and Sufficiency of God's Grace, the Conditions of Justification, and many other Points of the like nature, which have been almost exploded in these latter degenerate Ages of the World, do again begin to obtain, with different Persons upon different accounts: some embrace them for their Evidence in Scripture, others for the concurrent Testimony of the primitive Church for above four hundred years; others for the Reasonableness of things themselves, and their Agreement both with the Divine Attributes, and the easy Suggestions of their own Minds. Nor is there any Point in Divinity, where that which is most antient doth not prove the most rational, and the most rational the antientist; for there is an eternal Consanguinity between all Verity: and nothing is true in Divinity, which is false in Philosophy, or on the contrary; therefore what God hath join'd together let no Man put asunder.

The members of this new sect understood, as few had, that the evidence of Scripture, the evidence of History, and the evidence of Philosophy all point to the same conclusions. These conclusions may have been lost in degenerate ages, but they had been known in the most ancient times, and were being recovered at the present. To recover these fully, reason need be given full latitude. According to S. P., the men of the new sect understood this, and they had in the process returned Christianity "to her old loving nurse the Platonick philosophy." [1]

Cambridge Platonism, as this new sect came to be called, had surprising roots in Cambridge. Both its original leader, Benjamin Whichcote, and almost all the prominent members were educated at the most Puritan of the Cambridge colleges, Emmanuel. Emmanuel College had, in fact, been established in the late sixteenth century to foster Puritan thought. It had been founded by Sir Walter Mildmay, Chancellor of the Exchequer to Queen Elizabeth. Queen Elizabeth is supposed to have challenged him on this subversive act, "Sir Walter, I hear you have erected a Puritan foundation." "No, madam," Mildmay replied, "far be it from me to countenance anything contrary to your established laws; but I have set an acorn, which, when it becomes an oak, God alone knows what will be the fruit thereof."

Benjamin Whichcote had graduated from Emmanuel College in

1629, and in 1633 he became a fellow. In 1644 the Puritan parliament presented him with the office of Provost (or master) of King's College, Cambridge. (The previous Provost was judged too sympathetic to the overthrown monarchy.) And finally, in 1655, at the height of Cromwell's commonwealth, Benjamin Whichcote was appointed Regius Professor of Divinity. His academic career seemed, from the outside, entirely tied to the Puritan cause, with its fundamentalist Christianity, and its emphasis upon faith instead of reason.

However, in the 1650's Whichcote's preaching became an object of concern for his Puritan colleagues. Whichcote had begun to preach that reason was the very voice of God. With this, the stricter Puritans could not agree.

Reason for them was the voice not of God, but of man's fallen nature. Had not St. Paul warned, "Take heed lest any man spoil you through philosophy and vain deceit"? Had not even that pagan Socrates known that "to search out what the gods have not chosen to reveal must be displeasing to them"? Had not, in fact, our first father, Adam, fallen, and we with him, because he had presumed to forbidden knowledge?

The spokesman for Whichcote's concerned Puritan friends was Anthony Tuckney, Whichcote's former tutor at Emmanuel, and now its Master. Tuckney exchanged with Whichcote a series of letters in which he tried to convince his old student that he was straying dangerously far from the purity of Christian doctrine. But Whichcote was unpersuaded. The rationality of Christian doctrine he would never eschew. He would not ever have to choose between philosophy and religion, reason and faith, Athens and Jerusalem. Of that he was certain. He wrote to Tuckney:

> Sir, though I dearly love you in my relation to you, and highly honour you for your own worth, yet cannot I out of respect to you, give up so noble so choice a truth, so antidotical against temptation, so satisfactory, so convictive, so quietive, in so full confirmation to my mind of the truth of the Christian religion. Sir, this knowledge, God being merciful to me, I will keep til I die, not out of wordly design, but out of love to my soul.

So Benjamin Whichcote continued to preach his choice, antidotical, satisfactory, quietive, fully confirmed truth. In this preaching, his favorite text was *Proverbs*, Chapter 20, Verse 27, "The spirit of man is the candle of the Lord." The Spirit of God is the Lord of Nature. Man's spirit, in a lesser reflected sense lord over his body, could

illumine this providence of God, could illumine it through understanding it, could illumine it and thereby reverence it. The light of
reason is not opposed to the Divine Light, its Source; reason is the
reflection in man of the Divine Light. Religion is the purest expression
of reason. On this subject, Whichcote could frame his own proverbs.
"There is nothing so intrinsically rational as religion." "To go against
reason is to go against God." [2]

Benjamin Whichcote continued to preach his truth at Cambridge
until 1662, when he was removed from the University, not by Puritan
divines, but by the restored Monarch. Politically, if not theologically,
Whichcote was one of the Puritan party. He had been made head of
King's College to replace a royalist. Now all Cambridge was to be
royalist once again. Men like Whichcote and Tuckney were removed.

The removal of Whichcote was not a serious blow to Cambridge
platonism. By 1660, he was no longer the leader of the group, and
neither King's nor Emmanuel was any longer its college center.
During the 1650's the leadership had passed to somewhat younger
hands, Ralph Cudworth, himself educated at Emmanuel under
Whichcote, and Henry More.

More, alone of the Cambridge platonists, had not been educated
at Puritan Emmanuel. Rather he had been educated, and then made
fellow, at Christ's College, Milton's own college. In 1654 Cudworth
was made master of this college. (Cudworth, despite his appointment
during the Puritan reign, and even despite personal connections with
Cromwell himself, somehow survived the purge of Puritans—a
Latin ode by Cudworth celebrating the restoration of the Monarch
may have helped.) So Christ's Church by 1660 had become the
center of Cambridge platonism.

And if it had a new center, it also had a new defense. Whichcote
had defended the use of reason directly, proclaiming his own piety
and attesting how beneficial reason had been in its cultivation. Now
at Christ's Church a subtler defense was discovered, one that should
have particularly vexed the Bible-citing Puritans.

The master at Christ's Church when Henry More was first made
fellow, and probably his tutor before, was Joseph Mede. Mede's
academic specialty was the divining of Biblical prophecies. There
are numerous signs of the stature he had gained in this specialty.
His most general work on *The Book of Revelations*, entitled *The Key to
Revelations*, went through a number of editions. (It was still in print

in the nineteenth century.) A work by another author on *Revelations*—
this one a narrow study of the significance of St. John's use of
the number 666—bore a preface written by Mede attesting to its
competence. The preface to yet another seventeenth century work
on *The Book of Revelations*, this one written decades after Mede's
death, contained perhaps the highest compliment. Its author felt
compelled to respond to the widely held opinion that no new work on
Revelations was needed since its meaning had already been made clear
by Joseph Mede.

The author of this new work was Henry More. More had acquired
Mede's taste for finding the fulfillment of Biblical prophecies in the
subsequent histories of Europe. These fulfillments demonstrated, for
both Mede and More, that the Bible was divinely inspired and that
history was divinely governed.

The younger man, moreover, discovered a use for Biblical prophecy
of which Joseph Mede was innocent. More argued that seventeenth-
century men could use reason fully in matters of religion because of a
vision given to the prophet Daniel. In this vision Daniel was told that
near the end of time godly men will use reason in matters of religion.
More argued that seventeenth century men could use reason in
matters of religion because this must be the prophesied time.

> That which some have noted, if not complained of, (though how
> justly I will not take upon me to judge) that the Age we live in is
> *Seculum Philosophicum*, a Searching, Inquisitive, Rational, and Philo-
> sophical Age, is a truth so plain that it cannot be hid; but was foreseen
> many and many Ages agoe by the Prophet *Daniel*, or rather foretold
> him by the glorious Angel that appeared unto him on the banks of
> the great River *Hiddekel*, *That many shall run to and fro, and knowledge
> shall be increased*: That this should happen at *the time of the End* (Daniel
> 12, verse 4). And I think it is manefest that we are even at the end of
> that time . . . . And therefore it is to me no wonder that men have
> been and are still so inquisitive after the truth of things.

This is from *The Apology of Dr. Henry More*, in which More was
trying to defend himself from the charge of hearkening too much
to his own reason, and of being too inquisitive after the truth of
things not intended for mere men to know. More found his best
defense on the banks of the great river Hiddekel. The above passage
continued:

> Wherefore that there might be a "turning unto Righteousness"
> as well as "a running after Knowledge" (Daniel 12, verse 3), and that
> the pretence to a real skill in Philosophy might be no prejudice to

any ones Faith and Persuasion of the Truth of Christian Religion, I did set my self seriously and freely to search also into the most rational grounds of all such Philosophical Speculations as could any way pretend to have any moment for either the corroborating or enervating any Principle of Faith, or what Truths are recorded in the Holy Scriptures. And now to make my report after a most diligent and anxious Inquisition, and as free, I think, as any man possibly can make, I can *ex animo* avow to all the world, *that there is no real clashing at all betwixt any genuine Point of Christianity and what true Philosophy and right Reason does determine* or allow, but that . . . there is a perpetual peace and agreement betwixt Truth & Truth, be of what nature or kind so ever; and that they are blind *Superstitionists* and superficiary *Philophasters* that imagine any such digladation betwixt true Philosophy and real Christianity.

The superficial philosophers, the philophasters (a name of More's own coinage) themselves evidence that we were in the time of the end. Daniel had been told that during this time "many shall be purified and made white, and tried; but the wicked shall do wickedly and none of the wicked shall understand; but the wise shall understand." And so, during this time when men could finally come to understand their religion through reason, some, the evil ones, will use their reason to becloud, to besmirch, even to betray their God.

To be sure, atheism, and its concomitant denial of divine providence, had almost always been present in the world. It was present in varying degrees in pagan writing. Some would find a denial of providence in the fatalism of the most ancient Greek poet, Homer.

As with green leaves, so fareth with men;
Some fall with the wind, others grow in their place.

The benighted Homer had failed to see that human history had a direction, a purpose, an end, which transcended the passing of seasons and lives. Homer, nonetheless, could be tolerated. He presented his views by default; he saw nothing better. There was, however, a more virulent form of atheism that had been transmitted to the seventeenth century from ancient times, an aggressive, mocking atheism which sought to prove that no providence governed the world, that the world was merely an accidental collection of atoms.

This was the materialist philosophy of Democritus and Epicurus which Lucretius in his *De Rerum Natura* had set to poetry in order to beguile the unwary—and in the time of the end, more and more were being beguiled. The Cambridge platonists seem to have agreed that within their own lifetime, such atheism had significantly increased, particularly in the 1650's.

In the 1640's the Cambridge platonists wrote little specifically
against atheism. Henry More, for instance, had been content to
answer the poetic impiety of Lucretius poetically. He described
Lucretius' inspiration as:

> that foul love
> That crept from dismal shades of night and quill
> Steeped in sad Styx, and fed with stinking gore
> Sucked from corrupted corse, that God and men abhor.
> Such is the putrid muse, Lucretius,
> That fain would teach souls all mortal be:
> The dusty atoms of Democritus
> Certes have fallen into thy feeble eye,
> And thee bereft of perspicacity.

Such denunciations might well serve as an expression of a commonly
held contempt for any enemy long dead, but they were not going to do
battle with his arguments once they lived again. And in the 1650's
they did live again. In 1650 Thomas Hobbes published his *Leviathan*.
Just as Lucretius had centuries earlier, Hobbes declared the very idea
of an incorporeal substance to be a contradiction in terms. Just as
Lucretius had centuries earlier, Hobbes declared religion to be
derived from fear of the unknown, not love of the known.

So in the 1650's More began to argue, too. In book after book,
almost all of which went through more than one edition, he tried
to refute the materialism of the atomists—*An Antidote against Atheism*
(1652); *The Immortality of the Soul* (1659); *Divine Dialogues . . . concerning the attributes of God and his providence in the World* (1668); *Enchiridion metaphysicum: or a succinct and lucid dissertation on incorporeal beings*
(1671).

Puritans like Tuckney, if they had followed the course of Cambridge
platonism, could well have felt vindicated by all this activity. The
only antidote to atheism was faith. The platonists were discovering
for themselves what the Puritans had known all along—reason was
a slippery tool. It was easy to claim that religion was the most rational
of things, that all religious beliefs could be proven by man's natural
light. It was another to make good this claim when it was challenged
by the irreligious.

A man had to determine such things in his own heart, with the
help of God. Fallen reason is of no help. Even many of the ancient
pagans knew this. They knew, from their own experience, that Babel
was natural man's fallen fate. And they knew that reason, given full
reign, only increased the confusion. Had not the Roman Cicero,

whom the platonists themselves professed to admire, observed that nothing is so absurd that it has not been defended by some philosopher? If Cicero was right, and the history of philosophy but presents such a chaos of outlandish extremes, is it not the height of pride to think that you can bring order? Pride and foolishness?

Who in seventeenth century Europe knew better the ancient thinkers than Michel de Montaigne? Yet Montaigne, as much as he admired the pagan classics, eschewed such philosophical aspirations as the Cambridge platonists professed. Montaigne wrote, "Certainly philosophy is no other than sophisticated poetry." And those who insisted upon finding more in philosophy Montaigne had warned that "the opinion of knowledge is a plague on the mind." And the symptom of such a plague was just the feverish activity in which More himself was engaged.

Henry More should realize that all this activity, all this effort to rise above his natural station, will come to nought. More should follow the advice that Milton's Adam received from the angel Raphael shortly before Adam, too, presumed to more knowledge than was his to have. The angel advised Adam not

> "To ask, nor let thine own inventions hope
> Things not reveal'd, which the invisible King,
> Only omniscient, hath supprest in Night,
> To none communicable in Earth and Heaven:
> Anough is left besides to search and know.
> But knowledge is as food, and needs no less
> Her Temperance over Appetite, to know
> In measure what the mind may well contain,
> Oppresses else with Surfiet, and soon turns
> Wisdom to Folly, as Nourishment to Wind."[3]

A Puritan like Milton could feel secure in such an admonition. He could find many allies, even among the irreligious. Moderation in philosophy was taught not only by revelation. It was taught by wordly wisdom itself, especially when informed by the historical evidence of past philosophical futility.

The platonists, however, would not concede that the historical evidence weighed against their confidence—historical evidence, that is, properly understood. When properly understood, history was as much on their side as was revelation. This was implied by S. P., in his defense of the Cambridge platonists, when he wrote that they had discovered "that which is most antient doth prove most rational, and the most rational the antientist." His readers might have thought he meant by "antientist" the oldest doctrines of the church, Christianity in all its pristine purity. The platonists, however, intended to claim more than this.

One could recover not just the pristine purity of Christianity; one could also recover the pristine purity of Greek philosophy. Just as the Babel of medieval Christianity could be dispelled by a study of the earliest church, so the Babel of pagan philosophy could be dispelled by the study of the earliest Greek philosophy. And just as there was a single true religion on which all the earliest Christians agreed, so there was a single true system of the world on which all the earliest philosophers agreed.

The difficulty in recovering this original philosophy was that the original philosophers, because of the imperfections of those to whom they spoke and wrote, were often purposely obscure, clothing their doctrines in allegories, much as Our Lord, when speaking to the multitude, clothed his in parables. This was as it should be. As More put it in one of his letters, "It is just with God that the foulness of mens mindes are a barr to them from the truth."

Nevertheless, the time of the end was now near, the time when many shall run to and fro and knowledge shall be increased. Just as the Protestants had recovered the purity of Christianity from its centuries of corruption, so the Cambridge philosophers, and others like them, were recovering the purity of the primal philosophy from its corruptions.

These corruptions of philosophy no more impugn the original philosophy than do the corruptions of Christianity impugn it. And the history of philosophy certainly proves, rather than disproves, the legitimacy of man's aspiration for first principles. It demonstrates that once, long ago, man did possess just these principles. It shows how all other philosophies were but derivations, devolutions from this original philosophy.

Thus, all these later philosophies were not the Babel they seem. They all had some of the primal truth. Ralph Cudworth himself put the situation most generally. He even expressed the matter in an allegory, as was the wont of the primal philosophers; but, living as he did in the seventeenth century, Cudworth made the meaning of the allegory clear.

> All great errors have ever been intermingled with some truth. And indeed, if falsehood should appear alone into the world in her own true shape and native deformity, she should be so black and

horrid that no man would look upon her; and therefore she hath always had an art to wrap up herself in a garment of light, by which means she passed freely disguised and undiscerned. This was elegantly signified in the fable thus: Truth at first presented herself to the world and went about to seek entertainment; but when she found none, being of a generous nature, that moves not to obtrude herself upon unworthy spirits, she resolved to leave earth, and take her flight for heaven: but as she was going up, she chanced, Elijah-like, to let her mantle fall; and falsehood, waiting by for such an opportunity, snatched it up presently, and ever since goes about disguised in Truth's attire.

So even the followers of Lucretius had a part of the truth. They did understand the material principle of nature; they were just mistaken in their belief that this one principle could account for all.

The complete recovery of the original philosophy in its pristine form was Henry More and Ralph Cudworth's ultimate aim. More had the quicker pen. He could engage the materialists in polemic, showing them the inadequacy, the incompleteness of their system of the world. Cudworth, for his part, said, "They are not always the best men who blot the most paper." And while More was making his polemical points, Cudworth was quietly, slowly reconstructing the original philosophy, hoping eventually to present it beyond all polemic.

In the 1650's, the publication of the first part of Cudworth's *The True Intellectual System of the World*, as it was to be called, was still decades off. Nevertheless, the work of recovery had advanced sufficiently that both More and Cudworth knew this true system in outline. This system was most purely preserved by Plato and his followers. They as much as anyone had been responsible for preserving it down to the present day, when the Cambridge platonists would help make it the common possession of all men of good will.

Of the allegories through which the original philosophy was obscurely conveyed, Cudworth thought perhaps that of Pan, the god of nature, playing on his pipes (or harp) was the best. It represented best the dualism that was the foundation of the original philosophy. Pan represented the active, unifying principle of the world, the spiritual principle, ultimately God. The pipes represented the passive, divisive principle of the world, the material principle, ultimately atoms. How are these two principles related to form the whole system of the world? Pan plays his pipes, and his music tells us that the material is governed and made harmonious by the spiritual.

The history of philosophy, when properly understood, proclaims the truth of this primal system which is at once its Edenic beginning and its blissful end. The wordly wisdom which urges us to forgo the highest aspirations of reason is, when the history of philosophy is properly understood, but a myopia. Of such discretion, the blessed near the time of the end have no need. The plague of uncertainty is passing.

Moreover, the historical relationship between the original philosophy and divine revelation is one of harmony, not competition. It is not without reason that platonic philosophy has been the loving nurse of Christianity. The original philosophy could be traced back from Plato to Pythagoras and Thales, and from them to a mysterious "Phoenician" named "Mochus." And from whom did Mochus get the true system of the world? Here Ralph Cudworth, who besides being Master of Christ's College was also University Professor of Hebrew, had a startling answer. "Mochus" could have been, and undoubtedly was, but a Greek corruption of the Hebrew "Moses." The original philosophy had come to the Greeks from the Hebrews, and ultimately from God Himself. The system of the world taught by the most ancient philosophy is the same system taught by the most ancient revelation. It is the system taught by *Genesis* itself, once its allegory is understood.

This was a truth too important to await Cudworth's systematic demonstration. In 1658 the facile More produced *Conjectura Cabbalistica: or Conjectural Essay of Interpreting the Mind of Moses in the Three First Chapters of Genesis*. The Cabbala, as he explained in his "Preface to the Reader," was the interpretation of the Pentateuch which Moses had recieved from the mouth of God. This Cabbala did not survive in its purity. Now More felt the time was ripe to reconstruct what must have been in it. More's reconstruction of the Cabbala was dedicated to the man who perhaps would become the English Moses by speaking to them the most profound truths, and perhaps by leading them to a philosophical promised land, "the Eminently Learned and truly Religious, Dr. Cudworth."

On the title page More placed two Biblical quotations. The first, from the thirty fourth chapter of *Exodus*, reported allegorically that Moses in writing the Pentateuch had to write allegorically: "And when Aaron and all the People of Israel saw Moses, behold, the skin of his Face shone, and they were afraid to come nigh him. Wherefore Moses, while he spake unto them, put a Veil on his Face." The

second, from the tenth chapter of *Matthew*, not only foretold
the time when the meaning of the most obscure of revelations will
be known, but also advised Christians to strive for that day: "There
is nothing covered, that shall not be revealed; and hid, that shall
not be known. What I tell you in Darkness, speak you in Light;
and what you hear in the Ear, that preach you on the House-tops."

Now was the time of the light, the time to speak without veils,
the time which was the fulfillment of Moses' own time. As if to
emphasize the oneness between himself and Moses, as if to emphasize
that More was now saying to a time which could understand what
Moses had said long ago to one that could not, More wrote about
Genesis as if he himself were its author.

> Our design being to set out the more conspicuous parts of the
> external Creation, ... there are two notable Objects which present
> themselves to our Understanding, which we must first take notice
> of, as having an universal influences upon all that follows: and these
> I Symbolically decypher, the one by the name of Heaven and Light;
> for I mean the same thing by both these terms; the other by the name
> of Earth.

That was the beginning of More's explanation of the first chapter of
Genesis.

The light, of course, is for More the actual existence of the spiritual
principle, capable of governing the darkness. The earth, the darkness,
is itself only the possibility of the existence of the material principle.
The material, passive principle could now exist because the spiritual,
active principle which was to govern it already existed.

In such a way, More gradually deciphered the meaning of *Genesis*,
an allegorical meaning which was identical to the meaning of the
allegories of the most ancient philosophers. The work of creation
each day was interpreted as the bringing together of the spiritual
and the material, the active and the passive. "And the union of the
Passive and Active principles was the First day's Work." "And the
union of the Passive and Active Principle was the sixth day's work." [4]

This, then, was the state of Cambridge philosophy when Newton
arrived as a new undergraduate in 1661. Although lesser members
of the Cambridge group, like S. P., were still answering objections
against the very pursuit of philosophy itself, More and Cudworth
had progressed to more important tasks.

The Bible, especially *Daniel*, proved that this was the time when knowledge would be increased. History showed that it would be increased by recovering the original philosophy, so long buried in myth and allegory. Although the Bible assured that this recovery would be successful, this was not to say that the labor of recovery itself would be easy. It would take a man with the historical erudition and philosophical perspicacity of a Ralph Cudworth to do so; and even him it would take a lifetime. Nonetheless, the recovery had begun; nothing could stop it now.

CHAPTER TWO

THE CAMBRIDGE PLATONISTS AND ISAAC NEWTON
(1661-87)

Isaac Newton, when he entered Cambridge, was probably already aware of the Cambridge philosophers, at least of Henry More. He had been prepared for Cambridge at Grantham Grammar School. Two who oversaw that preparation—and Newton had lodged with the family of one—had themselves studied with the most famous graduate of the Grantham school, Henry More. Not surprisingly, in the earliest of Newton's surviving undergraduate notebooks he cites "the excellent Dr. More."

Newton was citing More's *The Immortality of the Soul*, published only two years before Newton's arrival at Cambridge. One of the most important aspects of this work, besides its refutation of materialism, had been More's discussion of the French philosopher, René Descartes.

In the years when More himself was an undergraduate, Descartes had tried to discover the ultimate philosophical principles. He announced his success in 1637 in his *Discourse on Method*. In the early sections of this work, Descartes was at pains to portray himself as someone fully aware of all the arguments against such an enterprise. He told his readers, "I had been taught, even in my College days, that there is nothing imaginable so strange or so little credible that it has not been maintained by one philosopher or other." And he confided in them, "Seeing that it [philosophy] had been cultivated for many centuries by the best minds that have ever lived, and that nevertheless no single thing is to be found in it which is not subject of dispute and in consequence which is not dubious, I had not enough presumption to hope to fare better there than other men had done."

Nevertheless, fare better he did, at least by his own estimate. He fared better, he thought, because he had discovered how to apply to the perennial problems of philosophy the kind of indisputable reasoning for which mathematics was famous. Much to his professed surprise, Descartes found he could demonstrate with mathamatical certainty the existence of a perfectly benevolent God, and also the existence of an immortal human soul.

Henry More was one of the first in Britain to recognize the importance of what Descartes was trying to do. More's estimate of Descartes
was more complex than his estimate of any other contemporary
philosopher. Cudworth, More would praise; Hobbes, he would
mock; but Descartes was not so simple. Of Descartes, More was
both an admirer and a critic.

More did believe that Descartes provided the best treatment of the
material side of the true philosophy. In 1662, after surveying his own
work to recover the original philsosphy, More concluded,

> It is there very evident to me, that the ancient Pythagorick or
> Judaick Cabbala did consist of what we now call Platonism and Carte-
> sianism, the latter being as it were the Body, the other the Soul of the
> Philosophy. . . . And therefore I do not a little please myself in that
> I have made some progress towards the resuscitating of that ancient
> and venerable Wisdom again to life, and bringing together, as it
> were, of the Soul and Body of Moses, first investing him, or cloathing
> him with the Covering of his own most sacred text.

More had made enough progress to see the limitations as well as
the strengths of the Cartesian philosophy. Superficially Descartes
might appear to have resuscitated Moses himself. Descartes had, after
all, both defended the dualism of spirit and matter, and affirmed such
corollaries of the dualism as the existence of a providential God and
the immortality of the human soul. And he had tried to give all his
demonstrations the certainty of geometry. Nonetheless, More knew
enough of the ancient and venerable wisdom to know that Descartes
had, in a most fundamental respect, failed in his design.

This failure derived from Descartes' very characterizations of
matter and spirit. The characterizations were related to one another
through geometry. Descartes identified matter with the geometrical,
the object of geometry. Whatsoever is extended, is material. Spirit,
on the other hand, he identified with whatever thinks, and, for him,
the paradigm of thought was geometry. So spirit understands geometrically, and matter is understood geometrically—the material
is the perfect object for the spiritual. This, however, did not satisfy
Henry More.

The spiritual was, in Descartes' system, no longer the lord of the
material. Descartes, for instance, had difficulty explaining how the
soul influenced the body. He had difficulty because he had reduced
the spiritual to being merely an observer of the material. Pan was
to listen appreciatively while his pipes played, but they could play

whether he listened or not. So in what sense could the tune or the pipes be said to be his? And, if they were not under his control, might he not be under theirs? Might he not simply be just another of the apparent harmonies produced by the blind meanderings of atoms?

More believed that once the existence of the spiritual principle was questioned, Descartes would be helpless to defend it. If all rational demonstrations were about geometrical objects, extended objects, then how could the existence of a non-extended substance ever be demonstrated?

It could not. And this, for More, had a clear implication. If only that which was extended could be demonstrated to exist (which was certainly so), and if spiritual beings do exist (which they certainly do), and if God intended that men of good will, at least seventeenth-century men of good will, should know all that is (which He certainly did), then spiritual substances must be extended. In a letter to Descartes shortly before he died, More summed up his complaint quite simply: "You define matter or body in too general a manner as extension. For all existing realities, even God, must be conceived as extended."

For this reason, More in *Immortality of the Soul*, *The Divine Dialogues*, and the *Enchiridion Metaphysicum*, while attacking the atheists, also attacked the Cartesian identification of the material with the spatial.

> It is not at all proved, that Matter and Extension are reciprocally the same, *as well every thing extended Matter, as all Matter extended*. This is but an upstart conceit of this present Age. The ancient Atomical Philosophers were as much for a Vacuum as for Atomes.

The atheistic atomists, such as Lucretius, had proclaimed the existence of both the atoms and the void in which they move. Henry More believed this admission of a void into the purportedly materialistic universe of the atomists provided a sufficient basis for the reassertion of the importance of the spiritual principle. Empty space was not empty space, but rather the spirit of the world.

By what power are the parts of a solid body held together? By what power is iron drawn towards the poles of a magnet? By what power are falling bodies drawn towards the earth? By what power are the planets maintained in their paths around the sun? Certainly not by the power of a passive, material extension. Do these phenomena not argue for the existence of an active spirit which imposes upon the material world its rational harmony? Does not even our understanding of material phenomena through geometry presuppose the existence of such a spirit? All our measurements of nature—of sizes, of shapes, of motions—presuppose the existence of an absolute, perfect, unchanging, immovable space—a single space which penetrates throughout the whole of the world, and gives that world its geometrical, its rational unity? And does not this space, existing as it does prior to all matter, itself imply "the existence of some real Being thereunto appertaining, which therefore must be concurrent with the *Essence* of *God*, and cannot but be a Spirit because it pervades the Matter of the Universe"? In the void, the existence of which even Lucretius admitted, More had discovered an active substance, a spirit in which the whole world lives, and moves, and has its being. He had discovered the Lord of Creation.

> This infinite and immobile being which is so certainly discerned in the nature of things will appear not just real but divine once we have enumerated those divine names and titles which are suitable to it. These titles and names themselves will create the confidence that this to which so many splendid attributes belong cannot itself be nothing. These attributes which follow belong properly only to the Metaphysical Prime Being. One, Simple, Immobile, Eternal, Complete, Independent, Existing for Itself, Existing Through Itself, Necessary, Immense, Uncreated, Unbounded, Incomprehensible, Omnipresent, Incorporeal, Permeating and Encompassing all Things, Existing by its own Essence, Actual Being, Pure Act. There are no fewer than twenty epithets by which the divine Deity is wont to be described which harmonize most exactly with this infinite internal place which we have demonstrated to exist in the nature of things.

Did not this characterization of space clarify the meaning of the ninetieth Psalm? "Lord thou hast been our dwelling place in all generations. Before the mountains were brought forth, or ever thou hadst formed Earth or the World, even from everlasting to everlasting thou art God."[1]

Of course, it was not quite so simple. Descartes and the materialists, as More well knew, had long ago devised responses to such objections as he was raising. They would not credit More's reasonings with the certainty of geometry.

More could not assume the burden of proof himself, they would say. He could not prove in the case of a single natural phenomenon that its explanation required more than matter alone. Matter alone, for example, could explain why bodies fall to the earth. Imagine the earth surrounded by a whirlpool of a weightless etherial matter, a vortex with the earth as its center. Any body thrown up into this whirlpool will inevitably be drawn back to earth.

A similar materialistic explanation could account for the harmonious motion of the planets. Now a far larger vortex had to be imagined, this one surrounding the sun and extending throughout the solar system. This whirlpool would tend to drag the planets toward the sun, unless the planets had enough motion of their own to counteract the whirlpool. If they had just enough to counteract it, but not enough to escape it, they would move relative to the sun much as they do now. By such hypotheses, philosophers could explain troublesome phenomena without resorting to spiritual interventions.

As for space, geometry did not need to presuppose it to be immaterial. All geometrical measurements are of matter. When we say that a body is moving we mean that it is moving relative to another body. More precisely, they are moving relatively to one another. This is a philosophically more precise way of speaking because to determine which body is, in fact, "really moving" is impossible. Moreover, upon reflection, the very idea of "real motion," like the idea of "pure space"—like any idea which tries to free geometry from its material foundations—is absurd, fraught with self-contradiction. After all, motion *is* the measurement of a relation, nothing more. An elementary knowledge of geometry would make this clear.

Despite these resources within the Cartesian position, the young Isaac Newton followed More in his rejection of the French philosopher. In an unfinished treatise he started about the time of his great discovery, Newton rejected Descartes' identification of space and matter as "repugnant to reason." And he followed More in his association of extension with spirit, and of space, considered as a whole, with God.

> No being exists or can exist which is not related to space in some way . . . space is eternal in duration and immutable in nature and this because it is the emanent effect of an eternal and immutable being. If ever space had not existed, God at that time would have been nowhere.

Newton, however, could rebut the Cartesian replies in a way that More could not. Henry More, knowing little geometry himself, was ill equipped to argue about its nature. He could, and did, claim that the mathematical description of motion presumed the existence of an ideal, spiritual space; but he could give no such a description himself. He could, and did, claim that the falling of a projectile, and the motion of the planets, implied an immaterial principle operating in nature; but he could not prove that the Cartesian whirlpools did not account for these as well.

Newton had the mathematical tools More lacked. He had gained these tools at Trinity College. Whatever the reasons for his choice of Trinity as his college—there seems to have been a family connection —the choice was a fortunate one. Trinity in 1660 had become the center of Cambridge mathematical activity. This was largely due to the efforts of one Isaac Barrow. In recognition of these efforts, in 1661 Barrow was made the first Lucasian Professor of Mathematics.

Barrow, while not usually numbered among the Cambridge platonists, did have important areas of agreement with them. Some passages from him read as if from Whichcote: for instance, "The proper work of man, the grand drift of human life, is to follow Reason, that nobel spark kindled in us from heaven." But the platonist with whom he had the greatest affinity was Henry More.

Like More, Barrow was an early admirer of Descartes' system. Like More, Barrow initially had some misgivings—in particular, Barrow thought, "He thinks unworthily of the Supreme Maker of things who supposes that he created just one homogeneous Matter, and extended it, blockish and inanimate, through the countless acres of space, and moreover, by the sole means of Motion directs these solemn games and the whole mundane comedy, like some carpenter or mechanic repeating and displaying *ad nauseam* his one marionettish feat." And, like More, Barrow had, by the time of Newton's matriculation at Cambridge, begun to repudiate the Cartesian system, and call for one that "is not based on arbitrary figments of the mind, does not take resort to insensible causes, does not feed the mind with chimera. . . nor whirl its fancies into giddiness."

Although Barrow himself never tried to supply this system, he did make some significant additions to the Cambridge philosophy; for instance, in his geometrical lectures (almost certainly attended by Newton), he argued that time, as well as space, had to be admitted as an immaterial absolute. Nevertheless, despite his mathematical competence, Barrow, who during the Commonwealth had suffered for his religious beliefs and who had been ordained a minister only a few years before he ascended to the Lucasian chair, does not seem to have been satisfied with teaching mere mathematics. In 1669, after a tenure of only six years, he resigned. A contemporary of Barrow explained his resignation as follows: "He had vowed at his ordination to serve God in the Gospel of his Son, and he could not make a bible out of Euclid, or a pulpit out of his mathematical chair—his only redress was to quit them both." So he quit them both, and Isaac Barrow subsequently became a famous preacher, and eventually was appointed Master of Trinity. He was succeeded in the Lucasian chair by a man of his own choosing, Isaac Newton.[2]

The system of the world which Isaac Newton eventually produced fulfilled many of the hopes of Cambridge philosophy. The world was governed by a force, gravity, which could not be the effect of a Cartesian vortex. The force acted across an immaterial space and during an immaterial time. The force sustained the beneficent harmony of the world.

This was the system of the world, the unfolding of which began, in the Newtonian account, with his discovery of gravity in 1665. But Newton initially chose to remain silent about his discovery. He did not make it public in the 1660's, or in the 1670's. The 1670's, in particular, was an unhappy time for Cambridge philosophy.

It should have been the happiest of times. In 1676 Ralph Cudworth finally published the first part of his *The True Intellectual System of the World*. Cudworth described this first part as "the propylaeum, or at least the first inner court of a vaster structure that was to have its penetralia"—the "propylaeum," the entrance to a temple; the "penetralia," the innermost recesses of a temple, where the sacred mysteries are preserved from the view of the unworthy.

No reader of the first part of Cudworth's system could doubt that the whole would be a vast structure. The propylaeum alone was almost one thousand folio pages. Therein all the arguments of the atheist and materialist were stated in their fullest, strongest form. And then they were refuted by irrefutable arguments, arguments which Cudworth could prove were in the possession of the most ancient thinkers. All this was the beginning of that which, when finished, would satisfy the highest longings of mankind, do justice to the beautiful harmony of the world, and give reverence to Him Who created it all—and, in the process, perhaps begin the final fulfillment of history.

The penetralia, however, were never revealed, for the propylaeum was not appreciated. Many readers felt that Cudworth's arguments against atheism and materialism never quite refuted those in favor.

Some even suspected that Cudworth had written his work as a covert defense of the very impiety he claimed to be refuting. They saw in his work subtle symptoms of the disease it purported to cure. This lack of appreciation left Cudworth, by all accounts, deeply disappointed. He responded to it with silence. He lived ten years after the publication of *The True Intellectual System of the World*, Part One, but he cast not another word before the world. The rest of the true system of the world, the inmost secrets of the penetralia, he left veiled. It was as if he had inferred that only he, and not the time, was ripe.[3]

Shortly before the first part of *The True Intellectual System* appeared, Isaac Newton's own public career as a philosopher began. He published his first work in 1672. This was the first of a series of papers on optics he submitted to the Royal Society of London.

The Royal Society had been chartered in 1662 by the recently restored Charles II for "improving Natural Knowlege." Although the leaders of this Society were primarily from Oxford and London, the Cambridge philosophers, More, Barrow, and Cudworth, were soon to be selected fellows. More and Cudworth could not have shared some of the other fellows' preoccupation with mechanical inventions. However, they did share fully the Society's more philosophical aspirations. And they must have applauded the preface to the 1671 volume of the Society's official publication, *Philosophical Transactions*. This appeared anonymously, giving the impression of an official statement from the Society as a whole. It was a defense of the Society from false accusations. One part of it, in particular, must have pleased the Cambridge philosophers.

> There are Some who seek all occasions to discourage our Industry. . . . Sometimes, to render it odious for Novelty, they call it contemptuously the New Philosophy when as yet perhaps themselves are not ignorant that tis so old as to have been the Discipline in Paradise and from the First of Mankind (who from observing the kinds and differences of animals gave them their Names); to have been practiced and countenanced by the Best of Men; Patriarchs and Prophets; oft times with Divine Assistances and Inspirations; giving them, that were successful therein, very eminent attributes of Glory, as in Noah, Moses, Solomon, Daniel, and others.

Newton's original optical papers were well received by the Society. Within a year he too had been made a fellow. Soon, however, Newton's optical work began to draw criticism, both from within the Society and from those who had read of this work in the Society's *Philosophical Transactions*. Newton's chief critic within the Society was its own salaried experimenter, Robert Hooke.

At first Newton tended to dismiss the criticism. He professed to be delighted with Hooke's criticism of his work, since it showed how strong in fact were his own arguments— "so acute an objector hath said nothing that can enervate any part of it." But, when the criticisms persisted, the tone changed. Newton began to see what happened to those who tried to speak the truth openly to the world. His critics questioned the accuracy of his experimental reports, they thought his work based on questionable hypotheses; Newton insisted on his own accuracy, and that his work was not hypothetical; those who thought so simply did not understand it.

Newton wrote to the secretary of the Royal Society, wanting to resign from the Society and withdraw altogether from public philosophising. "I intend to be no further solicitous about matters of Philosophy. And therefore I hope you will not take it ill if you find me ever refusing doing any thing more in that kind, or rather that you will favour me in my determination by preventing so far as you can conveniently any objections or other philosophical letter that may concern me."

At first he was coaxed into continuing but by 1676, the time of Cudworth's own withdrawal, Newton regained his resolve to give up public philosophising. "I will resolutely bid adew to it eternally excepting what I do for my private satisfaction or leave to come out after me." Newton did not publish again for over a decade. (It was, moreover, twenty five years before he published again in the *Philosophical Transactions;* and this paper was published anonymously.)

Henry More must have agreed with the younger man's decision. By 1676 he had himself decided to give up philosophy. During the 1670's, More had published little that was new. Most of his efforts were spent translating his complete works into Latin. A London admirer had left money so that the enduring truths of More would be clothed in an equally enduring language. More finished this task only after Cudworth had published all that was to be published of *The True Intellectual System of the World*. Henry More then decided that he had spent too much of his life in pursuit of philosophy.

In the preface to the first volume of his *Omnia Opera*, More repudiated philosophy. He declared that even on philosophical questions such as the immortality of the soul, "greater Certainty ... is to be drawn from the Scriptures rightly and completely understood, than from the clearest fountains of Philosophy." More only regretted that he had not realized this sooner. If he had, he believed it "would in greatest part have extinguish'd that so ardent Desire of Philosophizing, which seized me when I was very young."

Henry More apologized to his readers for the "sharpness and vehemence" of much of his writing in this first volume, inconsistent as it was with Christian humility. He concluded his preface by re-affirming his conviction that the time of the end shall truly come. "There shall be, there shall be most Certainly a Time, and that Day shall at length appear, when the Sun of Righteousness being arisen, Egyptian Mists and Darkness shall be dispersed."

The mists and darkness would certainly, most certainly, be dispersed one day. But were they being dispersed now? After his *Omnia Opera* was published, More returned to his biblical studies. In particular, he returned to the study of biblical prophecies.

Was this really the time of the end which had been foretold? Once again More searched the biblical and historical evidence. Once again he proved to himself that he was living near the beginning of the last age.

In 1680 More published his treatment of the chief New Testament prophecies, those of St. John. In 1681 he published his account of the chief Old Testament prophecies, those of the prophet Daniel: *A Plain and Continued Exposition of the Prophecies or Divine Visions of the Prophet Daniel, Which have or may concern the People of God whether Jew or Christian.*

Once again, More decided that the visions of Daniel gave the fullest signs for those who wished to know the time of the end. Of all the visions of Daniel, More was perhaps most interested in the final one during which Daniel was told: "Thou, O Daniel, shut up the words, and seal the book, even to the time of the end: many shall run to and fro, and knowledge shall be increased. . . .Go thy way, Daniel: for the words are closed up and sealed till the time of the end. Many shall be purified, and made white, and tryed: but the wicked shall do wickedly: and none of the wicked shall understand; but the wise shall understand."

The words that were to be closed up and sealed until the time of the end were the prophetic words of Daniel himself and the other apocalyptic prophets. These words had been closed to human under-standing, but More believed they were now being opened up. The

Protestant Reformation had made their meaning accesible. According to More, "the Vision of the Rising of the Whiteness was fulfilled in the late Blessed Reformation, there being thus no other Vision to predict it but this." Since this prophecy had finally been fulfilled, man must be entering the last stage of his prophesied history, the final stage of the struggle between the forces of light and those of darkness, between the forces of spirit and those of matter, between the forces of the Christ and those of the Anti-Christ—"after so many Principalities, Provinces, and Kingdomes had cast off the Pope in the late Blessed Reformation, what does this imply but that they were before in the hands of the Anti-christ, and that where the Pope has any Dominion it is *ipso facto* Anti-christ's Kingdome, and that on the contrary that all the Reformed parts of Christendome are the Kingdome of Christ."

As if to emphasize the most important prophecy of Daniel, the prophecy which was now coming true. More placed on the title page of his *Exposition*: "Daniel, chapter 12, verse 10: Many shall be purified and made white and tryed, but the wicked shall do wickedly, and none of the wicked shall understand; but the wise shall understand."

At the same time Henry More was deepening his understanding of Biblical prophecies, Isaac Newton was much engaged in Biblical studies. He corresponded on the interpretation of *Genesis*, explaining apparent natural philosophical flaws in Moses' presentation as merely accommodations to "ye vulgar." He searched the Old Testament prophecies for predictions of what had already come true. On the interpretation of these prophecies, Newton was particularly impressed with More's discoveries. Or so More himself wrote in 1680 to a friend who had inquired how much More and Newton agreed on "Apocalyptical Notions."

> I remember you either here at the time or at London before asked me about Mr. Newton and my agreement in Apocalyptical Notions. And I remember I told you both, how well we were agreed. For after his reading of the Exposition of the Apocalypse which I gave him, he came to my chamber where he seem'd to me not onely to approve my Exposition as coherent and perspicuous throughout from the beginning to the end, but (by the manner of his countenance which is ordinarily melancholy and thoughtfull, but then mighty lightsome and chearfull, and by the free profession of what satisfaction he took therein) to be in manner transported.

Newton did read More's work with care, as marginal annotations to his copy of More's *Exposition* still attest. He himself began to correspond with others about the prophetic books. Exactly when he wrote his own *Observations upon the Prophecies of Daniel and the Apocalypse of St. John* is uncertain (it was only published posthumously); but the basic research for it began about this time.

Newton's *Observations* differ little from More's *Exposition* in the basic interpretation of the significance of *Daniel*. Perhaps the most striking difference between More and Newton is the detail with which Newton described the Anti-Christ. He devoted more than thirty pages to showing the historical accuracy of the prophecy concerning "the King who did according to his will and magnified himself above every God and honored Mahuzzins."

This powerful king who magnified himself above every God was, of course, the Bishop of Rome. Who or what "Mahuzzins" were, was less obvious; Newton interpreted them as "the images and souls of dead men," which the Papists came to homage in ways befitting only God. So appalled was Newton at this defilement of the purity of Christianity, with its reverencing of relics and the like, that he devoted a whole chapter to narrating its spread throughout Christendom.

In most matters, Newton is in agreement with More. For instance, from the passage, "O Daniel, shut up the words and seal the book, even to the time of the end: Many shall run to and fro, and knowledge shall be increased," Newton inferred, "Tis therefore a part of this Prophecy, that it not be understood before the last age of the world; and therefore it makes for the credit of the Prophecy, that it is not yet understood. But if the last age, the age of opening these things, be now approaching, as by the great successes of later Interpreters it seems to be, we have more encouragement than ever to look into these things."

In short, Newton believed it is "to us and our posterity that those words mainly belong; 'In the time of the end the wise shall understand, but none of the wicked shall understand.' "[4]

In 1679, Robert Hooke himself tried to get Newton engaged once again in the improvement of natural knowledge. Hooke asked Newton, in particular, for "your thoughts of. . . compounding the celestial motions of the planets of a direct motion by the tangent and an attractive motion towards the central body." Newton was reluctant; as he put it in his reply to Hooke, "I have for some years last been endeavouring to bend myself from philosophy to other studies in so much that I have long grudged the time spent in that study unless it be perhaps at idle hours sometimes for a diversion." Nonetheless, he did continue to answer Hooke's letters for a couple of years before the correspondence lapsed.

Later, when Newton published his own system of philosophy, this correspondence proved to be an embarrassment, Hooke claiming that Newton had used his ideas without acknowledgement. The followers of Newton, following his example, dismissed this claim. Henry Pemberton, who assisted the elderly Newton as an editor, was typical when he wrote that Hooke's letters simply "gave occasion to his [Newton's] resuming his former thoughts."

According to Pemberton, in the 1660's Newton had been working with some measurements, crucial to the theory of gravity, which were inexact. Then in 1680, he used improved measurements. "Hereupon he composed near a dozen propositions relating to the motion of the primary planets around the sun."

None of these important propositions did Newton divulge in his correspondence with Hooke, nor did he take steps to have them published. He was, it appears, more interested in biblical prophecies about human history. Once again, however, the world, the same world which had daunted Cudworth and already had buffeted Newton, intruded.

By the 1680's there were a number of Royal Society Fellows who thought that the planets were held in their orbits by an attractive force inversely proportional to the square of the distance. They could not, however, make the difficult derivation of the orbits of the planets from this assumption. One of them, Edmund Halley, went to see if Newton could be of any help. Of course, by Pemberton's account, Newton had already derived the basic propositions of planetary motion years before. Nonetheless, Halley's visit by all accounts did provide the occasion for Newton to take up philosophical questions again.

With Halley's effusive encouragement, and deft coddling, Newton finally did make public his discoveries. In the Preface to *Philosophiae Naturalis Principia Mathematica* (as the soon to be famous book was entitled), Newton was gracious about the important if secondary role Halley had played.

> In the publication of this work the most acute and universally learned Mr. Edmund Halley not only assisted me in correcting the errors of the press and preparing the geometrical figures, but it was

3

through his solicitations that it came to be published; for when he
had obtained of me my demonstrations of the figure of the celestial
orbits, he continually pressed me to communicate the same to the
Royal Society, who afterwards, by their kind encouragement and
entreaties, engaged me to think of publishing them.

Halley, for his part, was fond of boasting in his later years that he
was the sly Odysseus who had coaxed the sullen Achilles to leave his
tent.

The *Principia* was published in 1687, shortly after the death of
Henry More. The everhopeful More died with one last work on his
desk. It was, however, too unfinished to be published. It was to be
called *The Cure for the World*.[5]

CHAPTER THREE

ISAAC NEWTON
(1687)

Since the ancients (as we are told by Pappus) made great account of the science of Mechanics in the investigation of natural things, and moderns, laying aside substantial forms and occult qualities, have endeavored to subject the phaenomena of nature to the laws of mathematics, I have in this treatise cultivated Mathematics so far as it regards Philosophy.

So began Newton's preface to his *Philosophiae Naturalis Principia Mathematica*, or *Mathematical Principles of Natural Philosophy*. Here he had to justify why he had narrowed his natural philosophy so that it covered only the mathematical principles and not all of them. Like a good Cambridge philosopher, he cited the authority of both the ancients and the moderns. However, he did not add that these were the people near the beginning and near the end of time. Neither did he so much as mention that he was himself actually hoping to recover the original philosophy. He could easily have mentioned this, since it was so; but he chose not to reveal that ambition.

Newton was going to be very careful. This was a work not just for Cambridge, but for the world. It was a work that was going to be read by the wicked as well as the wise. It was a work that was going to be read not only in London with its atheists, but also on the continent with both its atheists and reverencers of mahuzzins. With his work, the wise might be purified; but, with it also, the wicked would do wickedly. He would have to speak to this mixed audience, but he did not have to speak to it candidly. He would speak so the good would understand, and the rest would be vexed. He may have left his tent, but he had retained his veil.

The ancients considered Mechanics in a twofold respect; as rational, which proceeds accurately by demonstration, and practical. To practical Mechanics all manual arts belong, from which Mechanics took its name. But as artificers do not work with perfect accuracy, it comes to pass that Mechanics is so distinguished from Geometry that what is perfectly accurate is called Geometrical; what is less so, is called Mechanical. But the errors are not in the art, but in the artificers. He that works with less accuracy is an imperfect Mechanic, and if any could work with perfect accuracy, he would be the most perfect Mechanic of all.

"The most perfect Mechanic of all." All Newton's readers would know Who that was. And these readers might also think they saw the significance of this allusion to Him for the *Principia* as a whole. If Newton could demonstrate that the world was governed by perfect geometrical principles, then the existence of a Perfect Geometer was assured. Here the good would rejoice, and the wicked would prepare to fight. But the wicked had no one to fight against, for Newton merely passed over this allusion, without further comment. He had given his readers merely a glimpse, and then moved on to say that he was writing not about mechanics but about philosophy— and he does so using the royal "we."

> Our concern being not the arts but philosophy, our subject being not manual but natural powers, we consider chiefly those things which relate to gravity, levity, elastic force, the resistance of fluids, and the like forces, whether attractive or impulsive. And therefore we offer this work of mathematical principles of philosophy. For the whole burden of philosophy seems to consist in this, from the phenomena of motions to investigate the forces of Nature, and then from these forces to demonstrate the other phenomena.

"Whether attractive or impulsive"—once again, a passing phrase evoked an existing division between the good and the wicked. The whole Cartesian materialistic physics was based on the assumption that all material forces were impulsive—that is, communicated by contact. Henry More, of course, had tried to enumerate all those forces, like gravity, which he thought could not be reduced to mere impulsion, and hence must be ascribed to a spiritual agency. The Cartesians dismissed the arguments in favor of such forces as faulty, and dismissed the forces themselves as occult.

What was Newton implying on this controversial subject? He had in his very first sentence eliminated the occult from philosophy, and had done so in the name of mathematics. And yet here, less than a page later, just as he was about to describe the whole burden of philosophy, suddenly he was indifferent to whether these forces were impulsive or attractive. Here he was implying, or seeming to imply, that attractive as well as impulsive forces could be mathematically treated.

Of course, Newton did not say that directly. Nevertheless, the first section of his *Principia*, "Definitions," was constructed to persuade his readers that attractive forces were as much a legitimate part of the mathematical principles of natural philosophy as were impulsive forces.

Despite the indirection of the Preface, a reader could scarcely have begun the Definitions, while still underestimating the intentions of the book. He could not because between Newton's preface and the first of his definitions was placed an ode by Edmund Halley, an ode claiming that the book which followed was the greatest achievement of the human race, an achievement just the understanding of which made men like gods. The ode began:

> Lo! the laws that govern matter and the motions of the heavens,
> The Creator's computations are revealed before our eyes.
> Laws that God refused to violate at creation, when He laid
> Them as the world's foundations, that for ages it might stand.
> The innermost penetralia of the conquered heavens are
> revealed, the law which turns the farthest orbs is no longer hidden.

After surveying, in epic fashion, those great discoveries of Newton which revealed the inmost secrets of the heavenly penetralia, Halley then turned to exhort his readers.

> Those on whom
> Delusion casts its gloomy pall of doubt,
> Upborne now on the wings the genius lends,
> May penetrate the dwelling place of the gods,
> May scale the heights of heaven. O mortal men,
> Arise! And casting off your earthly cares,
> Learn ye the potency of heaven-born mind,
> Its thought and life far from the herd withdrawn.

According to Halley, those who first civilized mankind through codes of law did not "elevate the human race to such a height." Neither did those who first invented writing. Only by Newton's achievement had the human race been raised to its pinnacle. Once Halley's readers recognized this, there remained for him but to invite them to join in a song of praise to the man who made these discoveries, "NEWTON," that man thanks to whom "we are at last admitted to the banquet of the gods."

> You who take delight in nectar and the heavenly food,
> Sing with me the praise of him who
> opened the hidden vault of truth, NEWTON;
> Of him through whose pure heart and mind
> did Apollo cast his own radiant divinity, NEWTON.
> Nearer the gods no mortal may approach.[1]

In Newton's definitions, the movement to the divine banquet began quietly enough. Newton defined the quantity of matter, and the quantity of motion. His Cartesian readers could scarcely have been pleased with his definition of quantity of matter, since it was to be measured by weight. The possibility of a weightless matter, such as that which was supposed to compose the vortices, was one Newton refused to discuss. "I have no regard here for that medium, if such there be, that freely pervades the interstices of bodies," Newton wrote.

The Cartesians would probably have felt more at ease with Newton's definition of the inert force of matter, the third definition.

> *The* Vis Insita, *or Innate Force of Matter, is a power of resisting, by which every body, as much as in it lies, endeavours to persevere in its present state, whether it be of rest, or of moving uniformly forward in a right line.*
> This force is ever proportional to the body whose force it is and differs nothing from the inactivity of the Mass, but in our manner of conceiving it. A body, from the inert nature of matter, is not without difficulty put out of its state of rest or motion. Upon which account, this inherent force may, by a most significant name, be called Force of Inertia.

This was the innate force of matter—the force which, if adequate to all natural phenomena, would imply a materialist philosophy. This force manifests the inert nature of matter, its propensity for inactivity.

The third was the last definition with which most Cartesians could have felt at ease; for Newton, having defined the passive principle, began in the fourth definition to move toward the definition of the active.

> *An impressed force is an action exerted upon a body, in order to change its state, either of rest, or of moving uniformly in a right line.*
> This force consists in the action only, and remains no longer in the body, when the action is over. For a body maintains every new state it acquires, by its force of inertia only. But impressed forces are of different origins, as from Percussion, from Pressure, from Centripetal Forces.

For a Cartesian the fourth definition was almost acceptable. For him, impressed force had no other source than inertial force. Two moving bodies collided; each impressed its resistance to change on the other; the inertial state of each changed. The change of motion was simply the result of a conflict between inertias.

It was almost acceptable; however, the last sentence gave pause.

Impressed forces are not different origins. Percussion is the origin of all. For example, the pressure of compressed air might be explained as the result of the collisions of the many air particules against the sides of the container. Impressed forces which did not appear to be the result of collisions were perhaps the result of microscopic collisions, not directly visible.

Cartesians would have also offered a similar explanation of centripetal forces, if only they knew what centripetal forces were. However, they could not have known, for the word "centripetal" had never been used before. Once again, Newton was forcing his adversaries to defer an objection, this time their objection to attraction.

The Cartesians, ever since Newton had mentioned attractions in the preface, had been waiting to object that attractions were occult forces with no place in a rational natural philosophy. Material bodies simply cannot act at a distance on each other without material intermediaries; they cannot act across empty space. Newton knew the Cartesians were waiting, and, however much it vexed them, they were going to have to wait some more. Newton was not going to give them any attractions against which to object.

Attractions were physical forces, and Newton was only talking about mathematical forces. He would talk about forces which appeared to be attractions, and he would do so without trying to decide whether or not they were really attractions. A force which mathematically had all the properties of an attraction, Newton would call by the neutral mathematical name, "centripetal force." This he explained in his fifth definition.

A Centripetal force is that by which bodies are drawn or impelled, or any way tend, towards a point as to a center.

Cartesians could not object to this definition, could they? Newton was not deciding whether the bodies were being drawn, as by an attraction, or impelled, as by a vortex. His addition of the phrase "or any way tend" proclaimed his neutrality. Of course, in his explanation of this definition, he did have to mention that the centers toward which bodies tend are usually the centers of other bodies. This explanation began as follows.

> Of this sort is Gravity by which bodies tend to the center of the earth; Magnetism, by which iron tends to the loadstone; and that Force, whatever it is, by which the Planets are continually drawn aside from the rectilinear motions, which otherwise they would pursue, and made to revolve in curvilinear orbits.

Newton then proceeded to give a more extended explanation of this his fifth definition than he had to the previous four combined. He explained how the planetary force, whatever it was, appeared most nicely contrived. If it had been much smaller, it would not have been able to turn the planet around from its rectilinear course; and if it had been much larger, it would have pulled the planets out of their orbits.

Newton might not know what this planetary force was—could it be magnetism?—but he did know the problem it presented the mathematician. "It belongs to Mathematicians to find the force that may serve exactly to retain a body in a given orbit, with a given velocity, and *vice versa*, to determine the curvilinear way into which a body projected from a given place, with a given velocity, may be made to deviate from its natural rectilinear way, by means of a given force."

Newton might not know what this planetary force was. He did, however, use a suggestive example. He had his readers imagine a cannon ball being repeatedly shot off the top of a mountain, each successive time with a greater force. First it was projected with a blast that enabled it to travel two miles before it landed back on earth. Gradually it was projected with a greater and greater force until it finally completely circled the earth once before landing back. From this it was but a little step to have his readers imagine the projectile never falling back, but rather orbiting the earth indefinitely. And from this it was but a little step to have his readers consider the moon which does in fact orbit in just this way.

> And after the same manner that a projectile, by the force of gravity, may be made to revolve in an orbit, and go round the whole Earth, the Moon also, either by the force of gravity, if it is endued with gravity, or by any other force, that impels it towards the Earth may be perpetually drawn aside towards the Earth, out of the rectilinear way, which by its innate force it would pursue; and would be made to revolve in the orbit which it now describes: nor could the Moon without some such force be retain'd in its orbit.

Some readers might have felt that they were being led to identify the force of gravity with the force that held the moon, and by implication the planets, in orbit. But Newton, if challenged, could always claim his innocence. Of course, he had made his readers imagine the projectile gradually becoming the moon. However, once the projectile became the moon, did he not say explicitly that it might be another force which impels the moon toward the earth? If the reader drew unwarranted conclusions, was it Newton's fault?

However, it was not unwarranted conclusions, but unwarranted objections against which Newton was most on guard. After giving three more definitions concerning centripetal force, Newton paused to emphasize yet again that he was only interested in giving "a Mathematical notion of those forces, without considering their Physical causes and seats." Lest any readers still not appreciate the importance of this disavowal, he repeated it in more general terms.

> I ... use the words Attraction, Impulse, or Propensity of any sort towards a centre, promiscuously, and indifferently, one for another; considering those forces not Physically, but mathematically; Wherefore the reader is not to imagine that by those words I anywhere take upon me to define the kind, or the manner of any Action, the causes or the physical reason thereof, or that I attribute Forces, in a true and Physical sense, to certain centres (which are only Mathematical points) when at any time I happen to speak of centres as attracting or as endued with attractive powers.

This distinction between the mathematical and the physical would have vexed the Cartesians not just because it precluded their objection to attraction. Descartes had identified the material with the extended, the object of natural philosophy with the object of geometry; and he had thereby reduced both space and time to mere relations between objects. Newton's continual insistence upon the difference between the physical and the mathematical could only have led Cartesians to suspect that Newton was about to defend space and time as immaterial absolutes, much as More and Barrow had tried. For once, the Cartesians did not have to wait long to have their suspicions justified.

This Newton did in the very next section of Definitions. However, he did so in a way that could not have more vexed the Cartesians, if it had been devised just for that end.

Newton had decided to write the *Principia* in strict geometrical form. All the formal apparatus was there—definitions, axioms, lemmas, propositions, corollaries, scholia. The Cartesians, and those like them, had rejected attraction as an occult property, alien to the truly geometrical understanding of the world. When Newton represented this same attractive force as a governing principle of the world, she was to be impeccably dressed in geometrical finery. All the protocol was to be strictly observed, more strictly than it ever had been when the Cartesian vortex made its debut.

Definitions, axioms, lemma, propositions, corollaries, scholia—of
all these the scholia were decidedly the least important. They were
what an editor might add to his edition of a classical text. They were
there as assists, and were in no way essential to the argument. A
scholium was virtually an aside.

Newton chose to prove the reality of his absolutes, of space, time,
place, and motion, in a scholium. Not in a proposition or even a
definition, but in an aside, Newton showed that the world really
did move and have its being in a perfect, immaterial space and time.

The length of this scholium, however, belied the title he gave it.
The aside was longer than all the definitions together. Moreover,
Newton did apparently feel the need to explain why he had put all
this in a scholium. He did not include these notions under his definitions because space and time are known to all. Therefore, he did
not need to define them; he only needed to remove from them the
material blemishes which they had acquired in the minds of the
common folk. Or as Newton put it, "The vulgar conceive those
quantities under no other notions but from the relation they bear to
sensible objects. And thence arise certain prejudices." Once these
mere prejudices were removed, then space and time could be seen in
all their mathematical, immaterial purity.

The Cartesians, the very foundation of whose philosophy is being
dismissed, are not so much as named, let alone called philosophers.
They are, from Newton's height, indistinguishable from the vulgar
common folk who, mired in their daily cares, are unable to think
abstractly.

There is a sense in which this scholium is the conclusion to the
central argument of the definitions, considered as a whole. These
definitions constituted an argument for the inclusion of centripetal
force ((née attraction) as a mathematical principle of natural philsophy.
In the scholium, centripetal forces are used to demonstrate the
existence both of absolute motion, and, a fortiori, of absolute space
and time.

> It is indeed a matter of great difficulty to discover, and effectually
> to distinguish, the True motions of particular bodies from the Appar-
> ent: because the parts of that immoveable space, in which those motions
> are perform'd, do by no means come under the observations of our
> senses. Yet the thing is not altogether desparate; for we have some
> arguments to guide us, partly from apparent motions, which are
> differences of true motions; partly from the forces which are the causes
> and effects of true motions. For instance, if two globes, kept at a

given distance one from the other by means of a cord that connects them, were revolved about their common centre of gravity, we might, from the tension of the cord, discover the endeavour of the globes to recede from the axis of their motion and from thence we might compute the quantity of their circular motions.

This example of the two globes shows how Newton tried to use forces to prove the existence of absolutes. The globes, due to their inert material nature, endeavored to recede from their circular orbit; but they could not because this inertia was balanced by a centripetal force, namely the cohesion of the cord. That the globes were really moving, and not just moving relative to their surroundings, was demonstrated by the tension of the cord. Although an observer might himself be revolving identically as the globes and hence see the globes as motionless, he could still detect the tension in the cord and thereby be certain that, despite appearances, the globes (and himself) were really moving.

Newton sought to demonstrate this point with a somewhat more complicated experiment.

If a vessel, hung by a long cord, is so often turned about that the cord is strongly twisted, then filled with water, and held at rest together with the water; then by the sudden action of another force, it is whirl'd about the contrary way, and while the cord is untwisting itself, the vessel continues for some time in this motion. The surface of the water will at first be plain as before the vessel began to move, but the vessel, by gradually communicating its motion to the water, will make it begin sensibly to revolve, and recede by little and little from the middle, and ascend to the sides of the vessel, forming itself into a concave figure (as I have experienced), and the swifter the motion becomes, the higher will the water rise, till at last, performing its revolutions in the same times with the vessel, it becomes relatively at rest in it. This ascent of the water shows its endeavour to recede from the axis of its motion and the true and absolute circular motion of the water, which is here directly contrary to the relative, reveals itself, and may be measured by this endeavour.

This was supposed to be a mortal blow to the Cartesian materialization of space, and Newton assured his readers that he had experienced what he described. First neither the pail nor the water were in motion; then just the pail; then both the pail and the water; then just the water. Newton wished to prove that four different states of motion existed during the course of the experiment. The Cartesian would allow only two—first the pail and water were in relative rest, then in relative motion, then in relative rest, then once again in relative motion. It might appear to us that there were four, but how are we to prove that our vantage point is superior?

Newton's reply was that we did not have to prove that our vantage point was superior. There was a proof of the four states which needed no allusion to mere appearances. When the water was moving, it rose up the sides of the pail. When it was at rest, it did not. When the pail and water were relatively at rest, and the water was up the side of the pail, they were both moving. When it was not, they were at rest. It was as simple as that.

Newton, albeit in a scholium, had proven the existence of absolutes, of an absolute space and time which existed in and of themselves, independent of anything material. He had saved philosophy from those who "confound real quantities with their relations and sensible measures" and thereby "defile the purity of mathematical and philosophical truths." He had purified the ground.[2]

The ground may have been purified, but the defilers were still in Isaac Newton's audience. They were still there looking for an opportunity to justify their materialism. They were still there, for example, in Book one, section two. The whole of Book one was on "The Motion of Bodies." After getting over the preliminary mathematics in section one, Newton turned immediately to centripetal forces.

He placed in the midst of section two a scholium addressed to those who still wished to dismiss centripetal forces as irrational. He had just demonstrated the proposition, "Every body, that by a radius drawn to the centre of another body, howsoever moved, describes areas about that centre proportional to the times, is urged by a force compounded of the centripetal force tending to that other body, and of all the accelerative force by which that other body is impelled." A body moving under the influence of a centripetal force will describe in a given time an area proportional to that time—this was a particularly important proposition since planets did in fact describe in a given time an area proportional to that time, as his informed readers would have well known. An important step had been taken toward establishing the centripetal character of the planetary force.

Newton, having geometrically demonstrated this proposition and drawn a few corollaries from it, then added his scholium. It was for those readers who saw each of his propositions as leading closer and closer to making the geometrical center toward which the body in question tended, the physical source of the force, readers who saw this and in their wickedness resisted it.

> Because the equable description of areas indicate that there is a centre to which tends that force with which the body is most affected, and by which it is drawn back from its rectilinear motion, and retained in its orbit; why may we not be allowed, in the following discourse, to use the equable description of areas as an indication of a centre, about which all circular motion is performed in free spaces?

The tone is agreeable; no mention of defilements. Here is a reasonable man asking his readers to be reasonable. Why would anyone not allow him, just for the sake of the following discourse, what will permit him, as a mathematician, to do what he has to do?

The Cartesians could only reply that, if Newton was just doing what he said he was doing, then perhaps there would be no reasonable objection. However, who could help suspecting he was not? The Cartesians were being asked to grant a number of assumptions, ostensibly just for the sake of mathematics, but assumptions which, once granted, made it very difficult to consider the Cartesian system physically real.

Now we were to concede that mathematically forces appear to act toward a center. If we object that this is physically impossible, Newton replies he does not mean it physically. And if we ask why then does he speak of one body being drawn to the center of another body, rather than saying that it was just drawn to a center (bodies being decidedly physical objects), Newton replies that he is using his language "promiscuously," and we are not to pay any attention to it. How could the Cartesians help but suspect that even Newton's promiscuity had its purpose? They could not help suspect that; however, they could not yet prove it. They would only be able to prove it too late, when the case had already been decided aginst them.

Time and again throughout the first book, the Cartesians would think Newton was finally about to drop his veil, only to see him clasp it to himself once again. In Book one, section eleven, he had at last begun to talk about "The Motions of Bodies tending to each Other with Centripetal Forces." Up to this section, Newton had tried to speak only of bodies being drawn toward mathematical points. And now, the Cartesians might have thought, he will be forced into the open. He will have to speak of bodies mutually attracting one another.

In Newton's introduction to this section, there were ample grounds for hope.

> I have hitherto been treating of the attractions of bodies towards an immovable centre; though very probably there is no such thing existent in nature. For attractions and attracting are always reciprocal and equal .... And if there be more bodies, which either are attracted by a single one, which is attracted by them again, or which all attract each other mutually, these bodies will be so moved among themselves, as that their common centre of gravity will either be at rest, or move uniformly forwards in a right line.

This was as straightforward a statement as Newton would make. But by this time his readers must have known that, having made such a plain statement, he would then immediately retract its most obvious meaning. The above passage continued:

> I shall therefore at present go on to treat of the motions of bodies attracting each other; considering the centripetal forces as attractions; though perhaps in a physical strictness they may more truly be called impulses. But these propositions are to be considered as purely mathematical; and therefore, laying aside all physical considerations, I make use of a familiar way of speaking, to make myself more easily understood by a mathematical reader.

Was Newton speaking in a familiar way, the way which he had earlier said defiled philosophical truths? And would he do so to help his mathematical reader, precisely the reader who presumably has no need for such misleading common sense?

How are the poor Cartesians to respond? Here they had been expecting finally to be able to ask their question—How can attractions physically take place, if not through some impulse communicated by an invisible fluid?—and what did Newton do? After having spoken in a way that left no doubt he believed attractions to be physical, he turned to the Cartesians to say that while he will go on to consider "the centripetal forces as attractions . . . in a physical strictness they may truly be called impulses." He conceded that the Cartesians were right—or at least he appeared to.

The Cartesians, however, could scarcely feel that anything whatsoever had been conceded when Newton could then try to prove propositions which began with conditions such as "If two bodies S and P, attracting each other with forces inversely proportional to the square of their distance . . . ," and which were obviously intended to cover the actual system of the world. Here was Newton proving that "Bodies, whose forces decrease as the square of their distances from their centers may move among themselves in ellipses; and by radii drawn to the foci may describe areas very nearly proportional to the times." Where the laws of planetary motion were being deduced from the assumption of an attraction, could the rejection of Cartesian whirlpools be far removed?

Yet Newton was patient. He only gradually accumulated his case. By the end of the first book he had shown how the planetary motions could be explained by a centripetal force mathematically identical with gravity. It was only in the second book that he eliminated its main competitor, the Cartesian whirlpool or vortex. Even in the second book, Newton saved the *coup de grâce* until the very end.

The second book was entitled "The Motion of Bodies in resisting mediums." The last section was "The Circular Motion of Fluids." After he derived these motions, Newton added his final scholium of the first two books. It was fitting that the final bad news was given to the Cartesians in the final aside.

The motions of bodies carried around by vortices are not those observed of the planets; in particular, the planets are observed to accelerate and decelerate in ways that would be impossible for a vortex. "Hence it is manifest that the Planets are not carried round in corporeal vortices. . . . The hypothesis of vortices is utterly irreconcilable with astronomical phenomena, and rather serves to perplex than explain heavenly motions."

The Cartesians had been vanquished with their own objections still unasked. And Newton's basic principle had already been accepted. In the last sentence of Book two, Newton admitted his system of the world was implicit in his first book—"How these heavenly motions are performed in free spaces without vortices, may be understood by the first Book." It was a system of the world governed by a gravitational attraction. And Newton promised, "I shall now more fully treat of it in the following book of the system of the World."

Newton's remaining readers, now presumably Newtonian or at least anti-Cartesian, might well have expected to find in this book a Newton more at ease with them. If they did expect such a Newton, they had underestimated his wariness. In fact, Book three of the *Principia* like the concluding part of *The True Intellectual System of the World*, almost remained unpublished.[3]

In 1686, Newton wrote to Halley that he was almost finished with all three books of the *Principia*. Halley, upon reading this, might have begun to congratulate himself on having been such a sly Odysseus; but then Newton added, as if an afterthought, "The third I now design to suppress. Philosophy is such an impertinently litigous lady, that a man had as good be engaged in lawsuits, as have to do with her. I found it so formerly, and now I am no sooner come near her agin, but she gives me a warning."

The warning Newton heard was the rumor that Hooke, on the basis of their 1680 correspondence, was preparing to contest priority on some central parts of the system. Newton, who would yield all priority to the ancients, would yield none to his living rival. Moreover, he would no more dispute direclty with Hooke than he would with the Cartesians.

Hooke and who knows how many others of the wicked were preparing to draw Newton into vain disputes. Newton would not give them the chance. He would never describe his system directly, even after having vanquished the Cartesians. Those who wished to know the penetralia of the world's system could piece it together for themselves from Book one. In this way, the wise could know the system, while the designs of the wicked would be thwarted.

Halley replied quickly. He appealed to Newton's duty to mankind, to philosophy herself, to the whole learned world which so depended upon Newton to reveal the long concealed truths of his system. In this last appeal, there was the suggestion (did Newton need anything more than a suggestion?) that everyone was so dependent upon Newton that if he did not reveal his truths, then his rivals would appear victorious.

> I am heartily sorry, that in this matter, wherein all mankind ought to acknowledge their obligations to you, you should meet with any thing that should give you disquiet; or that any disgust should make you think of desisting in your pretensions to a Lady, whose favours you have so much reason to boast of. 'Tis not she, but your rivals, envying your happiness, that endeavour to disturb your quiet enjoyment; which when you consider, I hope you will see cause to alter your resolution of suppressing your third book, there being nothing which you can have compiled therein, which the learned world will not be concerned to have concealed.

Newton yielded. Nonetheless, Halley was not completely successful. In form, the third book was not as originally intended. At the close of his letter to Newton, Halley had added one final argument, one too many. "Sir, I must now again beg you, not to let your resentments run so high, as to deprive us of your third book wherein the application of your mathematical doctrine to the theory of comets and several curious experiments, which, as I guess by what you write, ought to compose it, will undoubtedly render it acceptable to those, who call themselves Philosophers without Mathematics."

Halley did finally get a Book three from Newton. But it was one designed to exclude those who call themselves Philosophers without Mathematics. This, and much else, Newton made plain in the published preface to the third book.

> In the preceding books I have laid down the principles of philosophy; principles not philosophical but mathematical: such, to wit, as we may build our reasonings upon in philosophical inquiries. These principles are the laws and conditions of certain motions, and powers of forces, which chiefly have respect to philosophy; but, lest they should have appeared of themselves dry and barren, I have illustrated them here and there with some philosophical scholiums, giving an account of such things as are of more general nature, and which philosophy seems chiefly to be founded on .... It remains that, from the same principles, I now demonstrate the frame of the System of the World. Upon this subject, I had, indeed, compos'd the third book in a popular method, that it might be read by many. But afterwards, considering that such as had not sufficiently entered into the principles could not easily discern the strength of the consequences, nor lay aside the prejudices to which they had been many years accustomed, therefore, to prevent the disputes which might be raised upon such accounts, I chose to reduce the substance of that book into the form of propositions (in the mathematical way), which should be read by those only who had made themselves masters of the principles establish'd in the preceding books. Not that I would advise anyone to the previous study of every Proposition of those books, For they abound with such as might cost too much time, even to readers of good mathematical learning. It is enough if one carefully reads the definitions, the laws of motion, and the first three sections of the first book. He may then pass on to this book of the System of the World, and consult such of the remaining propositions of the first two books, as the references in this, and his occasions, shall require.

Here Newton appeared at his most solicitous, at least at first glance. He was, in fact, displaying how solicitous he was about his readers. He explained how the scholia had been placed throughout the first two books precisely to help the less philosophically astute. He explained why he was forced to make the lamentable choice to treat the system of the world in a mathematical way. His own natural instinct was to make it popular; he first wrote it in that manner. With what reluctance must he have realized that the whole third book had to be completely rewritten in a different form? And what stronger evidence of his concern to ease his readers' burden than his suggestion that they skip over eleven of the fourteen sections of Book one, and the whole of Book two, lest working through take "too much time"? Such from the author himself.

This final, conclusive bit of display, nevertheless, had its disturbing aspect, disturbing enough to give a quite different perspective to this self-portrait. The advice about how to read the first two books does not come in the preface to the *Principia*, where it might be expected, but rather in the preface to the third book, presumably just after diligent readers had finished working through the last of the sections which could have been skipped. Or did Newton presume all his readers to be diligent?

In this preface to the third book Newton explained the function of the scholia in the first two books, and suggested how those books might be read, as if to someone as unfamiliar with the contents of the first two books as he was with the third. Did Newton really presume his readers to be diligent? Or did he rather suspect that some of his readers, perhaps after finishing the scholium to the definitions, would immediately jump to "Book Three: System of the World," there expecting to find Newton's conclusion presented in an accessible form, there expecting to find an opportunity to exercise those pre-judices to which they had been many years accustomed, and there intending to dispute with one Isaac Newton if he dared challenge any of those prejudices?

If any readers did jump to the third book with such base intentions, they found the same Isaac Newton in wait for them, in wait to tell them he did not wish to dispute with the ignorant, with the common people who defile philosophy by entering into her unprepared. This he told them, and his words were kind but his meanings unyielding. Then he turned them away from the book of the system of the world. And he dictated to them what they must do if they were ever to "pass on to this book." And he warned them that even with such a preparation they sometimes would still have to return to the first books until they had mastered the principles therein.

So spoke Newton at the entrance to the system of the world. The readers who from the preface might have had their suspicions about him now knew that he had his suspicions about them also. The final version of Book three was, needless to say, a guarded affair.

Following strict mathematical form, Newton demonstrated that, in fact, all the planets and, all the known moons of those planets, are held in their orbits by the force of gravity. He then proceeded to demonstrate at length how the gravitational attractions—"attraction" could be used now—of the moon and sun for the water on earth caused the tides. He also demonstrated that the comets moved in highly eccentric orbits which could be explained by gravity as effectively as had been the orbits of the planets.

No mention of the original philosophy was made. (The earlier version of Book three was to have begun, "It was the ancient opinion of not a few in the earliest ages of philosophy. . . .") The Lord of Creation was found just in occasional allusions.

Newton only lapsed into the essay form originally intended for Book three in his treatment of comets. When discussing the composition of the tails of comets, he even allowed himself to speculate on the purpose of comets in the plan of creation.

> And it is not unlikely but that the vapor [given off in the tails of comets], thus perpetually rarify'd and dilated, may be at last dissipated and scatter'd through the whole heavens, and by little and little be attracted towards the Planets by its gravity, and mixed with their atmosphere. For as the seas are absolutely necessary to the constitution of our Earth, that from them, the Sun, by its heat, may exhale a sufficient quantity of vapours, which, being gathered together into clouds, may drop down in rain, for watering of the earth, and for the production and nourishment of vegetables; or being condens'd with cold on the tops of mountains (as some philosophers with reason judge), may run down in springs and rivers; so for the conservation of the seas, and fluids of the Planets, Comets seem to be requir'd, that, from their exhalations and vapors condens'd, the wastes of the Planetary fluids spent upon vegetation and putrefaction, and converted into dry earth, may be continually supplied and made up. For all vegetables entirely derive their growths from fluids, and afterwards in great measure are turn'd unto dry earth by putrefaction; and a sort of slime is always found to settle at the bottom of putrefied fluids. And hence it is that the bulk of the solid earth is continually increased. and the fluids, if they are not supplied from without, must be in continual decrease, and quite fail at last. I suspect, moreover, that 'tis chiefly from the Comets that spirit comes, which is indeed the smallest but the most subtle and useful part of our air, and so much required to sustain life of all things with us.

Such a discursive, suggestive Newton was almost as untypical of Book three as he was of the *Principia* as a whole. More typical was his proof of what was perhaps the central proposition of Book three, if not the *Principia* as a whole, *"That there is a power of gravity pertaining to all bodies, proportional to several quantities of matter which they contain."*

That all the Planets gravitate one towards another, we have proved before, as well as that the force of gravity towards every one of them, consider'd apart, is inversely as the square of the distances of places from the center of the planet. And thence (by prop. 69, Book 1, and its corollaries) it follows that the gravity tending towards all the Planets is proportional to the matter which they contain.

Moreover, since all the parts of any planet A gravitate towards any other planet B; and the gravity of every part is to the gravity of the whole as the matter of the part to the matter of the whole; and (by law 3) to every action corresponds an equal reaction; therefore the planet B will, on the other hand, gravitate towards all the parts of the planet A; and its gravity towards any one part will be to the gravity towards the whole as the matter of the part to the matter of the whole. Q.E.D.[4]

CHAPTER FOUR

ISAAC NEWTON AND THE NEWTONIANS
(1687-1727)

The *Principia* was reviewed for the *Philosophical Transactions* by Edmund Halley. The first sentence conveys the tone. "This incomparable Author having at length been prevailed upon to appear in publick, has in this Treatise given a most notable instance of the extent of the powers of the Mind; and has at once shewn what are the Principles of Natural Philosophy, and so far derived from them their consequences, that he seems to have exhausted his Argument, and left little to be done by those that shall succeed him."

For Halley it is *the* principles of natural philosophy that Newton has shown, not just the mathematical principles. The Cartesians were, in contrast, more inclined to take Newton at his word. The chief Cartesian review of the *Principia*, which appeared in the *Journal des Scavans*, gave Newton carefully measured praise.

> Monsieur Newton's work is the most perfect Mechanics one can imagine . . . . But it must be confessed that these demonstrations may be regarded as only mechanical, since the author himself acknowledges at the bottom of the fourth page and in the beginning of the fifth that it is not as a Physicist that he has considered their principles, but as a simple Geometer. He confesses the same thing in the beginning of the third book in which he endeavors nevertheless to explain the system of the world . . . . To create a work as perfect as it is possible to be, Monsieur Newton has only to give us a Physics as accurate as his Mechanics.

Much the same reception was accorded the *Principia* by the most famous Cartesian natural philosopher, Christiaan Huygens. Huygens professed great admiration for Newton's work, and he conceded that Newton had rendered Descartes' vortices untenable. However, this did not incline Huygens toward accepting Newton's principle of gravity. As Huygens wrote in a letter to a Newtonian supporter, "I do not mind that he is not a Cartesian provided that he does not offer us suppositions like that of attraction." All Newton had proven was that Descartes had postulated the wrong kind of vortices. In 1690 Huygens published *Discourse on the Cause of Weight* in which he described the right kind.

The Newtonian supporter to whom Huygens had written the letter was Fatio de Duillier, a young Swiss aristocrat who by 1690 seems to have supplanted Halley as Newton's favorite. When in the early 1690's Newton began to make plans for a second edition of the *Principia*, Fatio was his chief assistant. In this capacity, Fatio wrote to Huygens to inform him of an important argument for Newton's system which had not been included in the first edition. Newton had discovered clear proof that "the Ancients such as Pythagoras, Plato, etc. had all the demonstrations which he gives in the true System of the World, and which are founded on a gravity which diminishes reciprocally as the square of distance." Huygens replied that Newton was doing the Pythagoreans a great honor believing them to be such good geometers.

Huygens' tepid response does not seem to have dissuaded Newton. A year after this letter, Newton confided his plans for a new edition to David Gregory, another newly found admirer. According to Gregory, Newton in his new edition was planning to demonstrate the "agreement of this philosophy with that of the ancients, and principally with that of Thales." The drafts of the historical sections, to be included as scholia, had reached galley proofs when Newton postponed the new edition.

One reason for the postponement might have been the mental breakdown Newton suffered in the summer of 1693. Some of Newton's friends, with his initial encouragement, were in the midst of trying to get him government preferment, with apparent unsuccess, when he began to turn on them. To one he wrote, "I am extremely troubled at the embroilment I am in, and have neither ate nor slept well this twelve month, nor have my former consistency of mind. I never designed to get anything by your interest . . . but am now sensible that I must withdraw from your acquaintance, and see neither you nor the rest of my friends any more, if I may but leave them quietly." Another he accused of having "endeavoured to embroil me with women and by other means." This latter friend he had thought "twere better if you were dead."

This breakdown did not last long, despite persistent rumors of its continuance. Soon Newton did get preferment. In 1696, he moved to London to accept a position at the Mint. In 1703, he became President of the Royal Society. In 1704, he was knighted.[1]

As he rose to his eminence as Britain's only philosopher-knight, Newton used his influence to assist his followers. Edmund Halley, for instance, gained a position with a government mint, became secretary of the Royal Society, and eventually was appointed Astronomer Royal.

Fatio de Duillier got no comparable appointments. He had been converted to an enthusiastic sect of French prophets who, when they were not speaking in tongues, were predicting in lurid terms the imminent conflagration of the world. When they were arrested, Fatio was arrested with them; and Newton did nothing more to help him. (Nonetheless, rumor had it that Newton himself had wanted to go to one of the meetings of these prophets, and was only dissuaded by friends who feared that he, too, might be converted.)

Fatio was no longer needed. Although Newtonian philosophy was making but little progress on the continent, in Britain there seemed an ever increasing number of willing vassals, eager to do Sir Isaac's bidding.

There was David Gregory, the admirer to whom Newton had divulged his proof that Thales was a Newtonian precursor. With Newton's help, Gregory had become Professor of Astronomy at Oxford. In his *Philosophical and Geometrical Elements of Astronomy*, Gregory gave a systematic presentation of the Newtonian philosophy, both mathematical and physical, and made public for the first time the claim that this philosophy was "both known and diligently cultivated by the most ancient Philosophers."

At Oxford, there was also John Keill, himself a protegé of Gregory. Keill served with Halley as Secretary of the Royal Society; he eventually succeeded to Gregory's chair at Oxford. In his *Introduction to the True Physics*, Keill ridiculed the Cartesian vortices as "contrary to almost all the Laws of Nature" and praised Isaac Newton "whose prodigious Genius had laid open more and abstruser Mysteries of Nature than men could ever have hoped for." In his *Introduction to the True Astronomy*, Keill went further, calling "ISAAC NEWTON" (as the name was printed) a "genius of divine Nature."

Cambridge University was not surpassed by Oxford in the ardor of its Newtonians. By 1700, the most powerful of the Cambridge Newtonians was Richard Bentley, newly appointed master of Trinity College. Bentley's identification with the Newtonian cause came from a series of lectures he had given in 1692. These lectures were intended to confute atheism with the evidence of natural philosophy. Before delivering them, Bentley had written to Newton asking for a list of contemporary works that would prepare him for reading the *Principia*.

Newton immediately sent such a list. After he had delivered his lectures, and while he was preparing them for publication, Bentley wrote to Newton once again, this time sending him questions on natural philosophy which were still troubling him. On these natural philosophical topics, Newton wrote Bentley four letters.

In general, Newton reacted to Bentley's efforts with the same uncharacteristic enthusiasm he had earlier expressed concerning More's attempts to unravel biblical prophecies. He was especially pleased with Bentley's intended use of the *Principia* as a confutation of atheism. "When I wrote my Treatise about our System I had an Eye upon such Principles as might work with considering Men, for the Belief of a Diety, and nothing can rejoice me more than to find it useful for that Purpose."

Newton carefully enumerated those parts of the system of the world which, in Newton's words, "I do not think explicable by mere natural Causes, but am forced to ascribe it to the Counsel and Contrivance of a voluntary Agent." Bentley, however, had made one mistake. He had treated gravity as a material power. Newton wrote, "Pray do not ascribe that Notion to me; for the Cause of Gravity is what I do not pretend to know, and therefore would take more Time to consider of it." In a later letter, Newton explained his position.

> That Gravity should be innate, inherent and essential to Matter, so that one Body may act upon another at a Distance thro' a Vacuum, without the Mediation of any thing else, by and through which their Action and Force may be conveyed one to another, is to me so great an Absurdity, that I believe no Man who has in philosophical Matters a competent Faculty of thinking, can ever fall into it. Gravity must be caused by an Agent acting constantly according to certain Laws; but whether this Agent be material or immaterial, I have left to the Consideration of my Readers.

Bentley did have a competent enough faculty to consider the ultimate cause of gravity as spiritual. After all, the potential material cause of gravity, the vortex, had been cleared from the heavens by Newton. So in the published version of his lectures, *The Confutation of Atheism from the Origin and Frame of the World*, Bentley led his readers to the same inference to which he thought Newton had led him.

First Bentley proved that "a Power of mutual Gravitation, without contact or impulse, can in no-wise be attributed to mere Matter."

(Such an attribution was derided as "repugnant to Common Sense and Reason . . . utterly inconceivable.") Then Bentley inquired as to the significance if gravity really existed. "What if it be made appear, that there is really such a Power of Gravity perpetually acting in the constitution of the present System? This would be a new and invincible Argument for the Being of God: being a direct and positive proof, that an immaterial living Mind doth inform and actuate the dead Matter, and support the frame of the World." Then, like his Master, he backed away from defending this as a thesis. "I will lay before you certain Phaenomena of Nature; and leave it to your consideration from what Principle they can proceed." The phenomena were Newton's, those he used to establish the principle of gravity as that which maintained the frame of the world; the phenomena were Newton's, and so was the decision to leave the final inference to the consideration of the readers.

Bentley, of course, was not the only prominent Newtonian at Cambridge. Newton himself had nominated William Whiston as the successor to his professorship at Cambridge. Whiston a few years earlier had applied Newtonian philosophy to the explication of *Genesis*. In his *A New Theory of the Earth*, a work he submitted in manuscript to both Newton and Bentley, Whiston showed how Newton's philosophy accounted for the literal words of the Bible. For instance, he demonstrated how the Deluge must have been caused by a comet passing close to the earth. (He also described gravity as depending "entirely on the constant and efficacious, and, if you will, the supernatural and miraculous Influence of Almighty God.")

The most impressive instance of Newtonian patronage at Cambridge occurred not in the case of Whiston, but in that of Roger Cotes. Cotes, who had replaced Fatio as Newton's new assistant in the preparation of the long delayed second edition of the *Principia*, was only twenty five when in 1706 Newton, with the help of Bentley and Whiston, gained for him the newly created Pulmian Professorship of Astronomy and Natural Astronomy.

Cambridge was also the scene of perhaps the cleverest instance of Newtonian proselytizing. The Newtonian Samuel Clarke had been given the task of providing a new Latin translation for Jacques Rohault's *Traité du Physiéue*, the standard natural philosophy textbook at Cambridge and a thoroughly Cartesian work. Clarke's first edition of his translation was straightforward. The second edition, however, that of 1702, bore the subtitle *"illustrated with Dr. Samuel Clarke's Notes taken mostly out of Sir Isaac Newton's Philosophy"*; at crucial points in Rohault's argument the notes attempt to refute him. When Rohault wrote that "Attraction, Sympathy, and Antipathy . . . ought not to be allowed at all, by reason of their Obscurity," Clarke added the exception of the "universal Gravitation of Matter"—"all such Attraction is by all means to be allowed, as it is not the Action of Matter at a Distance, but the action of some immaterial Cause which perpetually moves and governs Matter by certain Laws." When Rohault defended the vortices, Clarke noted that they were "mere Fictions and contrary to the Phaenomena of Nature," and then recounted Newton's arguments against the vortices, Clarke adding that it was Newton, not Descartes, who had "established the true system of the world beyond all controversy," Newton who had achieved what was "almost beyond the genius of man."

This is not to say that all was entirely amicable among the Newtonians, competing as they were for their master's favor, with this competition sometimes being reinforced by older institutional rivalries. For instance, Whiston's *New Theory of the Earth* was attacked from Oxford by John Keill. A controversy of increasing bitterness ensued. Keill contended that comets are, by Newtonian theory, of such slight mass they could not possibly exert such great gravitational attraction to cause the Flood. In the end, Newton appears to have sided with Keill.

Whiston, however, was anything but bashful about prosecuting his own claims. Moreover, he had views on the prophets which did not entirely agree with Newton's. And he insisted upon publically defending views about the early church doctrine with which Newton agreed, but thought better left unpublished. In short, Whiston lacked the discretion that marked a true philosopher. He might have had the knowledge of a Newtonian, but he had the instincts of the common herd. And so he fell from favor.

When Whiston was proposed for membership in the Royal Society, Newton blocked his election. When Whiston was about to lose his professorship at Cambridge because of his published views on early Christian doctrine, Newton, then at the height of his power, did nothing to save him.

Whiston, as none who knew him even slightly would have thought unusual, did get the last word. In his memoirs, published after Newton's death, he explained his fall from favor in general, and

Newton's denial of him at the Royal Society in particular, in plain terms.

> Now if the Reader desires to know the Reason of Sir Isaac Newton's Unwillingness to have me a Member, he must take Notice, that as his making me first his Deputy, and giving me the full Profit of the Place, brought me to be a Candidate, as his Recommendation of me to the Heads of Colleges in Cambridge, made me his Successor; for did I enjoy a large Portion of his Favour of twenty Years together. But he then perceiving that I could not do as his other darling Friends did, that is, learn of him, without contradicting him, when I differed in Opinion from him, he could not, in his old Age, bear such Contradiction; and so he was afraid of me the last thirteen years of his life.

This description of Newton is in keeping with the general portrait of him contained in the memoirs. Newton was described by Whiston as "of the most fearful, cautious, and suspicious Temper, that I ever knew."

Neither this view of Newton's temperament, nor Whiston's own fall from favor, lessened his estimate of the Newtonian philosophy. In his memoirs Whiston described it as "the wonderful Newtonian Philosophy: Which indeed I look upon in an higher Light than others, and as an eminent Prelude and Preparation to those happy 'Times of the Restitution of all Things, which God has spoken of by the Mouth of all his holy Prophets since the World began,' *Acts* iii, 21." Whiston only hoped that "my own most important discoveries concerning True Religion and Primitive Christianity, may succeed in the second place to his surprising Discoveries." He hoped that his and Newton's discoveries together might constitute the knowledge men were supposed to have before the end of time. He hoped that these discoveries "may together have such a Divine Blessing upon them, that the 'Kingdoms of this World,' as I firmly expect they will, may soon 'become Kingdoms of our Lord, and of his Christ, and he may reign for ever and ever! Amen. Amen.' "

And if his fall from favor did not lessen Whiston's estimate of the Newtonian philosophy, neither did it, at least in Whiston's account, lessen his concern for the personal well being of the aging Newton. In fact, Whiston claimed that just such a concern led him to withhold from publication a book of his own which contradicted Newton. "I knew his Temper so well that I should have expected it would have killed him."[2]

> Some I know disapprove this conclusion [universal gravitation] and mutter something about occult qualities. They are continually

cavilling with us that gravity is an occult property, and occult causes are to be quite banished from philosophy. But to this the answer is easy: that those are indeed occult causes whose existence is occult, and imagined but not proved; but not those whose real existence is clearly demonstrated by observations. Therefore gravity can by no means be called an occult cause of the celestial motions, because it is plain from the phenomena that such a power really does exist. Those rather have recourse to occult causes who set imaginary vortices, of a matter entirely fictitious and imperceptible by our sense, to direct these motions.

This is from Roger Cotes' polemical preface to the long awaited second edition of the *Principia*, published only in 1713. According to that preface, the hypothesis of vortices is "ridiculous and unworthy of a philosopher, since it is altogether without foundation and does not in the least serve to explain the nature of things." Moreover, the hypothesis was a falsehood of the worst kind, one that endangered the foundations of true religion. Cotes assured his readers that the Cartesian philosopher, if consistent, "will inevitably sink into the mire of that infamous herd who dream that all things are governed by Fate and not by Providence, and that matter exists by necessity of its nature always and everywhere being infinite and eternal."

The Newtonian system, in contrast, "will be the safest protection against the attacks of atheists, and nowhere more surely than from this quiver can one draw forth missiles against the band of godless men." Cotes did not expand on this claim. He had only to refer readers to the "General Scholium" which Newton had added as a conclusion to the *Principia*. This was for those who saw the whole *Principia* as a thing dry and barren. Newton had added it lest there be any doubt that, in his own words, this "most beautiful system of sun, planets, and comets could only procede from the counsel and dominion of an intelligent and powerful Being."

This Being governs all things, not as the soul of the world, but as Lord over all; and on account of his dominion he is wont to be called *Lord God* . . . It is the dominion of a spiritual being which constitutes a God: a true, supreme, or imaginary dominion makes a true, supreme, or imaginary God. And from his true dominion it follows that the true God is a Living, Intelligent, and Powerful Being. And, from his other perfections, that he is Supreme, or most Perfect. He is Eternal and Infinite, Omnipotent and Omniscient; that is, his duration reaches from Eternity to Eternity; his presence from Infinity to Infinity; he governs all things, and knows all things that are or can be done. He is not Eternity and Infinity, but Eternal and Infinite; he is not Dura-

tion or Space, but he endures and is present. He endures forever, and
is everywhere present; and, by existing always and everywhere, he
constitutes Duration and Space. Since every particle of Space is
always, and every indivisible moment of Duration is *everywhere*, certainly the Maker and Lord of all things cannot be *never* and *nowhere* . . . .
God is the same God, always and everywhere. He is omnipresent not
virtually only, but also *substantially*; for virtue cannot subsist without
substance. In him are all things contained and moved; yet neither
affects the other; God suffers nothing from the motion of bodies;
bodies find no resistance from the omnipresence of God.

To this last assertion, which seemed to relate God to space itself,
Newton affixed an historical footnote to document that this was also
"the opinion of the ancients." Among the ancients whom Newton
believed to hold this opinion were Thales, Pythagoras, and Moses.

The General Scholium was not the only addition made by Newton
to the second edition of the *Principia*. Among other things, Newton
added more precise experiments in his treatment of the resistance of
fluids and more accurate observations to his theory of comets; he
completely re-worked his lunar theory and improved his calculations
of centripetal forces. To such humble, though not humiliating tasks
Newton had reduced natural philosophers, even himself. Natural
philosophy, now that Newton had uncovered the basic frame of the
world, was reduced to a series of additions or emendations to the
Principia.[3]

Of all the additions that still remained to be made to the system
of the *Principia*, one was far more important than any other. Newton
had mentioned it in his preface to the first edition.

> I wish we could derive the rest of the phenomena of Nature by
> the same kind of reasoning from mechanical principles, for I am
> induced by many reasons to suspect that they may all depend upon
> certain forces by which the particles of bodies, by some cause hitherto
> unknown, are either mutually impelled towards one another, and
> cohere in regular figures, or are repelled and recede from one another.
> These forces being unknown, philosophers have hitherto attempted
> the search of Nature in vain; but I hope the principles here laid
> down will afford some light either to this or some truer method of
> philosophy.

All the phenomena of nature could not be explained by the force of
gravity, but all perhaps could be by forces like gravity. So important
was this study of non-gravitational forces, now once the existence of
gravity itself had been established, that Newton almost added to the

end of the first edition of the *Principia* a "Conclusion" which, in effect, exhorted his readers to the search for these forces. A surviving draft of this Conclusion begins:

> Hitherto I have explained the System of this visible world, as far as concerns the greater motions which can easily be detected. There are however innumerable other local motions which on account of the minuteness of the moving particles cannot be detected, such as the motions of the particles in hot bodies, in fermenting bodies, in putrescent bodies, in growing bodies, in the organs of sensations, and so forth. If any one shall have the good fortune to discover all these, I might almost say that he will have laid bare the whole nature of bodies so far as the mechanical causes are concerned. I have least of all undertaken the improvement of this part of philosophy. I may say briefly, however, that nature is exceedingly simple and conformable to herself. Whatever reasoning holds for greater motions, should hold for lesser ones as well. The former depend upon the greater attractive forces of larger bodies, and I suspect that the latter depend upon the lesser forces, as yet unobserved, of insensible particles.

Newton's own experiments in optics were an important part of his search for those forces which would complete his system of nature. Suppose, as Newton tended to do in his early optical papers, that light was composed of minute particles. A ray of light, therefore, would be a stream of minute projectiles. These projectiles, like their larger counterparts, would continue to move in a straight line until acted upon by a deflecting force. These projectiles were so minute, they could go exceptionally close to other bodies. (They could actually go between the particles of glass.) Hence they were ideal to detect the existence of lesser forces than gravity, forces which only act effectively across minute distances.

Newton had a book length treatise on optics prepared for publication well before he finished the *Principia*. Nonetheless, he held it back. Presumably he did not wish to engage in any further disputes on this subject with the ignorant. So Newton waited. One by one the critics of his earlier optical work died. In 1703, the most hated of his critics, Robert Hooke, finally died. In 1704, Newton permitted his *Opticks* to be published. Even so, how the study of light could be used to complete Newton's system was not apparent from the main body of his work. Rather it was suggested in a series of "Queries" affixed to the end of the work, as if afterthoughts. Moreover, just as the General Scholium did not appear in the first edition of the *Principia*, so the most important query did not first appear in the 1704 edition of the *Opticks*; rather it was tucked away in the Latin translation of 1706, without any indication it had been added.

The first of Newton's queries asked, "Do not Bodies act upon Light at a distance, and by their action bend its Rays; and is not this action (*Caeteris Paribus*) strongest at the least distance?" The last and greatest query, the one added only in the 1706 edition, asked, "Have not the small particles of bodies certain powers, virtues or forces by which they act at a distance not only upon rays of light for reflecting, refracting, and inflecting them, but also upon one another for producing a great part of the phenomena of nature?"

The first query Newton could present as if it were a rhetorical question, so strongly did the phenomena of light argue for an affirmative answer. The last, the use of the phenomena of light as a basis on which to explain the greater part of natural phenomena not already explained in the *Principia*, needed long and careful argument, which Newton did not hestitate to give, once he had made it clear that this was only a query.

That he did, in the end, expose himself on so unsettled a matter was not the only indication of how important he regarded it for the completion of his system as a whole. Into this last query Newton incorporated a revision of the conclusion he had earlier intended for the *Principia*.

However, it was not included as the conclusion of the last query, as the final words of the *Opticks* itself. Newton did wish to exhort philosophers of futute generations to complete his work, but he wished his last words to intimate what they would achieve if they finished that work. Their achievement would reach far beyond the narrow confines of natural philosophy. A finished natural philosophy could retrieve for man the pristine innocence that once was his, and that he had lost when he corrupted himself. This was what Newton wished to intimate with his last words.

> I have only begun the analysis of what remains to be discovered about light and its effect upon the frame of Nature, hinting several things about it, and leaving the hints to be examined and improved by further experiments and observations of such as are inquisitive. And if natural philosophy in all its parts, by pursuing this method, shall at length be perfected, the bounds of moral philosophy will be also enlarged. For so far as we can know by natural philosophy what is the First Cause, what power He has over us, and what benefits we receive from Him, so far our duty towards Him, as well as that towards one another, will appear to us by the light of Nature. And no doubt,

if the worship of false gods hat not blinded the heathen, their moral philosophy would have gone farther than to the four cardinal virtues; and instead of teaching the transmigration of souls, and to worship the Sun and Moon, and dead heroes, they would have taught us to worship our true Author and Benefactor, as their ancestors did under the government of Noah and his sons before they corrupted themselves.

He wished to intimate that to retrieve the true philosophy would be to redeem our true selves.[4]

CHAPTER FIVE

THE NEWTONIANS
(1727-44)

The British Newtonians, not surprisingly, appear to have agreed with Isaac Newton that the microcosm presented the most important task remaining for natural philosophy, although most of their own energies seem to have been spent popularizing Newton's philosophy and defending him from the slanders of envious continental philophasters. Newton had virtually exhausted the macrocosm, but the microcosm was yet to be set in order. The number and relationships of atomic forces were yet to be determined with the certainty of a *Principia*.

Nevertheless, it was inconceivable that the resolution of this problem would not come soon. All that might be needed was one break—perhaps a new phenomenon, perhaps an old one viewed in a new way—and then the foundations of natural philosophy would be finished, forever.

For Newton's own most complete sketch of a theory that might accomplish this they had only to turn to the last query of the *Opticks*, "Have not the small particles of bodies certain powers, virtues or forces by which they act at a distance not only upon rays of light for reflecting, refracting, and inflecting them, but also upon one another for producing a great part of the phenomena of nature?" Newton argued there as follows.

The refraction of light evidences an attractive force between corpuscles of light and those of transparent bodies, one that effectively acts only across minute distances. Might not such a short-ranged attractive force act between other corpuscles? And could it not even be as universal as gravitation? Such an attractive force acting between the particles of a body could account for the cohesion of the body.

A similar atomic-level attractive force, this one between the respective corpuscles of substances of two different kinds, could account for many of what Newton called "chemical operations," such as the dissolving of salt in water. (The salt, specifically heavier than the water, would not rise up into the water unless there was an attractive force acting between the two, a force strong enough to offset this difference in density.)

5

Newton also argued for the existence of a repulsive atomic force. He recognized that such a force was more problematic than the attractive, since it lacked any direct correlative in the astronomical realm. Of course, in the *Principia* Newton had used the notion of a "centrifugal force." This was the opposite of the centripetal force; it was the force by which a body resisted being held in an orbit. However, that force was obviously derivable from the passive nature of matter, its inertia. A repulsion between the small particles of a body (an atomic or corpuscular repulsion as it was alternately called) was as active a force as gravity itself. Yet, paradoxically, it was a negative activity.

Newton tried to overcome what he anticipated would be the inherent prejudice against this paradoxical force. He pointed out that just as there are negative numbers in arithmetic, so should there be negative forces in nature. He explained, in greater detail than he had used with the attractive, how a repulsive force was implied by some phenomena of light—by the reflection and inflection of light, and perhaps by its emission as well.

Actually Newton in the *Principia* had already suggested such a force, albeit briefly. In a section of Book two, he had demonstrated that the postulation of a repulsive force between air particles would explain some of its observed behavior. In the last of his *Opticks* the behavior of air was central to the theory of the microcosm being developed.

A crucial question for that theory, as Newton knew, concerned the relationship between the two active forces which were supposed to rule the microscopic realm. Could all bodies possess in some sense both attraction and repulsion or were there basically two kinds of matter in nature, one that was attractive and another that was repulsive?

In the last query, Newton himself appeared to opt in favor of a scheme in which all corpuscles in some sense can be said to exhibit both attractive and repulsive forces. This he exposited in his treatment of fermentation, the name given by Newton to chemical operations in which air is produced. In these operations, air particles which had been attractive components of a solid body were agitated until they were thrown into a repulsive state—that is, until they became normal elastic air. That this process is possible for all kinds of matter and is one which is reversible, was crucial to Newton's unified vision of the corpuscular world as he developed it in the last query.

All corpuscles are fundamentally the same; considered together they simply form a spectrum. At one end of the spectrum are the very small and weak-forced particles. They are volatile—that is, they resist very little the change from being mutually attractive to being mutually repulsive and back again. When they are mutually attractive, they form a liquid; when they are mutually repulsive, they form, to use Newton's phrase for water vapor, a "kind of air." Due to the small size of their particles, these substances never have more than a tenuous hold upon their state.

At the other end of the spectrum are the particles of great size and force. When attracting one another, they cohere so strongly and are so resistant to change that they can be properly termed "fix'd." When in an analogously strong state of repulsion, these particles become equally stable components of the atmosphere; they become the particles of "true, permanent air." (Both descriptive phrases are Newton's.) While the transition between the repulsive and attractive states for these larger particles must of necessity be more difficult to effect in the laboratory and less frequent in occurrence in nature than for their more volatile counterparts, Newton was certain that this transition is still common. So air and solids, rather than being composed of different kinds of corpuscles, were now simply the different states of the same corpuscles.

Attractive or repulsive—each corpuscle at any particular time was one or the other, and each could be either. When this was assumed, when a repulsive force was allowed to complement the attractive at the microscopic level, then this world too could be seen as an ordered whole.[1]

Despite their abject relationship to Sir Isaac, British Newtonians do seem to have disagreed with some of his suggestions about how a natural philosophy of the microscopic world—a corpuscular philosophy, as it was called—might be developed. Specific portions of his queries they found unconvincing. In particular, they found unconvincing Newton's speculations on repulsive force.

Not that, on such subjects of disagreement, the younger men disputed with Newton openly. They knew better than to do that. Rather they just quietly omitted from their writings on natural philsosophy any detailed discussion, or perhaps any discussion at all, of those points in Newton's corpuscular philosophy which they apparently found distasteful. The best that the polemical Roger Cotes, for instance, could say on behalf of corpuscular repulsion was that it was "not advanced without reason."

The reluctance of early Newtonians to accept Newton's arguments for repulsive force might be attributed to an understandable desire to preserve at least one place where the great man's word was not final. Newton had said the last word on so many things, might not this one be left for Newtonians to give? If this was a factor, it does not seem to have been the only one. In the case of repulsion, in particular, there was a persuasive argument against its existence.

This argument, of course, is not to be found in the writings of those who simply chose not to write of repulsion at all. Rather it is found in one of the few works sympathetic to repulsion written in England during Newton's lifetime, Benjamin Woorster's *Compendious Account of Natural Philosophy*, first published in London in 1722. What is interesting about this obscure work is not what its equally obscure author wrote in favor of corpuscular repulsion, but what he admitted against it.

In his last query Newton had asserted categorically that air particles do become components of solid bodies, that the change of air from a repulsive to an attractive state is commonly observed in chemical operations. Woorster freely admitted in 1722 that this crucial experimental support of the last query was yet to be found. As Woorster put it, "The repulsive virtue of the particles of air is not to be overcome and changed into attraction by any force whatever." Why bend to Newton's authority on repulsive force, why admit yet another fundamental principle into nature when the crucial phenomenon it predicts does not appear?

Shortly before Newton's death in 1727, this phenomenon was made to appear. The man who did make it appear, Stephen Hales, was not himself a member of the Newtonian circle. Hales had been educated at Cambridge after the publication of the *Principia*, when Newton's influence there had become particularly strong. Although Hales was generally interested in natural philosophy, his central concern within it was physiology. While still an undergraduate Hales devised original experiments to measure blood pressure in animals. Nevertheless, for some reason he did not choose a university career. In 1709 he became the pastor of a small parish outside of London, for which position he owed no philosopher. There he eventually found time to continue his physiological experiments. By 1713 he had resumed his experiments on the mechanics of circulation. And by the seventeen twenties he had begun to examine the movement of fluids in plants, especially trees, and slowly developed his own views on the natural economy of the plant. His experiments on plants were, in his own judgment, sufficiently novel that he read them before the Royal Society, with Newton presumably in the chair as president. The experiments were admired, and Hales found himself pressed to allow the Society to publish them as a separate book, much as it earlier had published the *Principia*. For a time, Hales demurred. Already he was off on a new set of inquiries.

In his study of the natural economy of the plant, Hales had been impressed by the role of air, and had performed many experiments to measure the amount of air a plant used in its natural processes. He found that the plant absorbed much more air than it expired, and the difference was far too great to be attributed to the dissolving of air in the sap. An alternative explanation was that the air had become a constituent part of the plant, exactly what Newton had earlier claimed happened to air in matter generally. So Hales turned to the more general study of air, to look for evidence that air particles sometimes become incorporated in inorganic solid bodies as well as organic. The written result was what Hales entitled "A Specimen of an Attempt to Analyze the Air, By a Great Variety of Chymio-Statical Experiments."

Hales had, by his own account, attempted to demonstrate that air could be "changed from a strongly repelling to as strongly an attracting state and back again." To do this Hales first showed that air, true permanent air and not just weakly repelling vapors, could be produced from bodies either by heating ("distillation") or mixing ("fermentation"), produced in such large quantities that air particles must have been cohering constituents of the original substances. Moreover, comparably large quantities of air could be absorbed by other substances through the same process of heating or mixing. For instance, he found that two grains of phosphorus when distilled would break into flame and absorb as much as twenty-eight cubic inches of air.

Hence Hales had experiments to support some of the moot points of the last query. This, however, was not enough. What was also needed was a coherent explanation of these experimental results in terms of Newtonian forces. Hales essayed to supply this also.

For the production of air he stayed close to Newton. During the process of distillation or fermentation the constituent air particles of some substances become so agitated that they are driven back into a repulsive state and are hence emitted from the body as elastic air.

The absorption of air was more difficult to explain. Newton had not himself explained very clearly why some substances needed to be distilled or fermented in order to exert their attraction for air particles effectively, nor had he explained why fire seemed so intimately associated with the fixing of air. This consequently was Hales' main philosophical task. His own theory of combustion was carefully exposited through the case of the absorption of air by sulphur.

While under normal circumstances solid or powdered sulphur will not absorb air, it will, when sufficiently heated, readily fix large quantities. The process of heating, therefore, must, in some way, increase the effectiveness of the attractive force of the sulphur for the air. What happens is that heating agitates the sulphur corpuscles and eventually break them apart, throwing them up into the air as a vapor or fume. The sulphur is, quite simply, boiled. This sulphur vapor then so thoroughly intermixes with the air that the sulphur can exert its short-range attraction for air.

The burning of fire is caused by the repulsive force of the air. The air particles being in a repulsive state repel all other corpuscles including the sulphur. Hence in the intermingling of the sulphur and the air a violent battle occurs between the sulphur attempting to fix the air and the air resisting its advances.

Hales reported his new experiments to the Royal Society in 1726. Isaac Newton might not have been surprised at this first dramatic confirmation of the speculations of his last query. However, this could not be said for the members generally. Their reaction was perhaps indicated by a word used by the Secretary to describe Hales' conclusion in the Society's Record Book—Hales, according to the Secretary, had "transmuted" air into the form of solid bodies.[2]

In 1727, Stephen Hales at last consented to have his work, the work on plants together with that on air, published; it appeared as *Vegetable Staticks ... Also a Specimen of An Attempt to Analyse Air*. To this work, Isaac Newton, in his capacity as president of the Royal Society, affixed his *Imprimatur*, dated February 1727. By the end of March, he was himself dead. He died, his doctors said, from a stone stuck in his bladder. Otherwise, he had been, they said, in excellent health. But he just could not quite pass the stone, and no known medicine could dissolve it.

Soon Stephen Hales had become the most famous living British natural philosopher. That he should be so after the death of Newton was fitting, for his work typified the development of Newtonian natural philosophy in the eighteenth century.

It typified what happened to that philosophy as a support for religion. Newton, for all his conviction that air could be a cohering part of solid bodies, had still maintained that a periodical replenishing of "the most subtle and useful part of air" was necessary to preserve life on this planet. He had, thereby, discovered one reason the comets, with their unharmonious orbits, had been included in the Divine Architect's plan. In the long term, they were as necessary for life as the clouds which bring rain. Or so Newton thought. Stephen Hales, in his very effort to prop up a weakness in the Newtonian philosophy, had demonstrated that ordinary air could maintain life without cosmic help.

This was not a great defeat for the Divine Architect. It was almost imperceptible, like the drying of water from a great tree. But it was a defeat that would recur again and again, almost continuously throughout the eighteenth century. So His Providence slowly shriveled, and the very life gradually, but irretrievably, withered out of Him. And, in the end, the Newtonian philosophy became sustenance for the very philosophical atheism Newton intended it to kill. The same Laplace who thought there could be only one Newton said, when asked of the God's place in his philosophy, "I have no need of that hypothesis." Laplace the natural philosopher needed but one Newton, and no God.

Stephen Hales' work was typical of what happened to the Newtonian philosophy in yet another way. He had resolved a fundamental difficulty in the Newtonian system, only in the process to discover a more fundamental one.

Quotations from Newton's queries to the *Opticks* occupied a prominent position in Hales' "Specimen." One was used to give authoritative support for the whole project of producing air from solid bodies; another for the theory of fire; and another to buttress his explanation of fermentation. But Newton was not the only person to whom Hales deferred as an authority on air. He also cited "Dr. Freind" who had given "a very ingenious Rationale of the chief operations in Chymistry."

John Freind was another of the Oxford Newtonians. He had delivered a series of lectures on chemistry in which he tried to use Newtonian attraction to account for as varied reactions as fermentation and combustion. These lectures were duly published first in England in 1709, and then on the continent in 1710. The continental edition was itself attacked in a journal generally hostile to Newtonian principles. Freind replied, on the pages of the *Philosophical Transactions*, that he was but following the example of Newton, assuredly the man who had discovered the true method for philosophizing. The next year Freind was elected a Fellow of the Royal Society.

Nonetheless, the specifics of Freind's lectures were not always consistent with Newton's theories as developed in his last query. This was particularly true of Freind's treatment of air. For Freind, elasticity was an essential property of the air particles. For Newton, of course, it was not; elasticity was merely an effect of the mutual repulsion of the air particles, a repulsion which could be changed into attraction through chemical manipulations. On this issue, Hales was obviously on Newton's side; he had demonstrated, as he put it, that "elasticity is no immutable property of air."

There was, however, a more fundamental issue separating Newton and Freind. Freind had assumed that air was a special type of substance, qualitatively different from all others; its particles were elastic, those of other substances were not. In contrast, for Newton in his last query, air differed only quantitatively from other matter—its associated forces of attraction and repulsion were just larger than those of ordinary matter. For Newton, the particles of ordinary matter can be elastic like air; it is just that, as vapors, their repulsive force is much weaker than that of permanent air. Freind rather implied that vapors (and solids) appear elastic only because they have air trapped in their pores.

On this fundamental issue, Hales disagreed with Newton. Hales had just changed the unique property of air. Now air was special no longer because it was elastic; now it was special because it could be elastic. Ordinary matter can exert just attractive force; air can exert either attractive or repulsive force. Air alone, to use Hales' phrase, is "amphibious."

> There is diffused thro' all natural, mutually attracting bodies, a large proportion of particles, which as the first great Author of this important discovery, Sir Isaac Newton observes, are capable of being thrown off from the dense bodies by heat or fermentation into a vigorously elastick and permanently repelling state; And also of returning by fermentation, and sometimes without it, into dense bodies: *It is by this amphibious property of the air, that the main and principle operations of Nature are carried on.*

Hales had found not just a single spectrum of matter as Newton had; he rather had found two—one for attractive bodies, one for attractive-repulsive. The physical world contained two fundamentally different kinds of matter, elastic and inelastic—or, more precisely, possibly elastic corpuscles and permanently inelastic ones.

Hales' experiments on the production of air did show that a sizable proportion of many solid bodies could be changed into the elastic fluid air. Of course, there was always a larger proportion of the bodies in question which could not be so transformed. Hence the basic experience of Hales in these experiments was of two fundamentally different kinds of bodies—that which could be changed into air and that which could not. What he had done in these experiments was simply separate them.

Obviously, this part of Hales' work did not, in the last analysis, present a serious difficulty to a defender of the last query. The fact that most matter could not be changed into air by Hales might just indicate the inadequacy of available methods. As experimental techniques improved, perhaps the proportion of "permanently inelastic" matter would get smaller and smaller. Or so it could have been argued with respect to Hales' experiments on the production of air. There was, however, no comparable argument to explain away his experiments on the fixing of air.

In the explanation of these experiments a fundamental dichotomy between elastic and inelastic matter, between air and sulphur, was virtually unavoidable. There was the substance which is fixed and there was the substance which does the fixing. It was no good to say that the sulphur could in principle, if not yet perhaps in practice, be changed into a repulsive vapor. In Hales' theory the sulphur particles were first raised up into the air as a vapor—the sulphur *is boiled*. But even when the sulphur is a vapor, it and air still are fundamentally different. The air is repulsive, it repels the sulphur particles; the sulphur is attractive, it attracts the air particles: precisely this difference between air and sulphur is what causes fire.

So there were two aspects of the work of Stephen Hales on air. On the one hand, Hales rescued the last query from one difficulty. He had demonstrated that air changed from an elastic to an inelastic state and back again, as Newton had predicted. This virtually established, among British Newtonians at least, Newton's theory of air as exposited in the last query; *a fortiori* it established the existence of repulsive force. Now that the attraction-repulsion theory of matter had been firmly established for air, the next natural step would be to attempt to extend it to all matter. But it was precisely at this step that Hales

had found for Newtonian natural philosophy a new problem, one
perhaps even more difficult than the first.

The last query seemed to require that vapors were vapors insofar
as they were repulsive, insofar as their constituent particles repelled
one another. Hales' work on combustion, on the other hand, seemed
to show that the constituent particles of sulphur vapor attract very
strongly the particles of air, strongly enough in fact to change the
air particles from a repulsive to an attractive state. These two different
theories can, it would seem, be reconciled only if it is admitted that
the particles of sulphur vapor are repelling each other while simultaneously attracting the air particles. To admit this, however, would
be to undermine the dichotomy between the attractive and the
repulsive states, the very dichotomy upon which both these theories
were built.

This was a pattern that would recur again and again throughout
the eighteenth century with those who tried to finish Newton's
philosophy. One weakness overcome, yet another one found. This
one, like the last, had to be resolved, or it might threaten the very life
of the whole philosophy. And so the Newtonians would begin again.

Hales' work was typical of this. But his own reaction to it was
not typical of Newtonians. He did not begin again. The cure of this
newly discovered weakness might perhaps finish the system of the
microscopic world as surely as the *Principia* had virtually finished the
system of the macroscopic. Yet Hales did not begin again.

Hales lived for thirty years after the publication of his work on
air, and these were active years for him. He continued his work as a
pastor. He eventually completed his experiments on animal circulation.
He tried to use his new found prominence to effect simple reforms—
for instance, he campaigned to have improved ventilation in ships,
hospitals, jails, or anywhere else where large numbers of people were
confined. He even tried to discover a cure for the disease that killed
Newton; he failed in that, but he did later unmask someone who
falsely claimed to have found such a cure.

He did all this and more, yet he never attempted to strengthen
the foundations of natural philosophy. Having found a weakness there
a second time, he simply turned away and left it. The reason for this
decision might have been implicit in the preface to his book on animal
circulation, which was published in 1733.

In this preface he justified his interest in natural philosophy by
alluding to the Divine Architect. Hales wrote that he was studying

the animal economy "in which there is so just a Symmetry of Parts, such innumerable Beauties and Harmony in the uniform Frame and Texture of so vast a Variety of solid and fluid Parts, as must ever afford Room for farther Discoveries to the diligent Enquirer; and thereby yield fresh Instances to illustrate the Wisdom of the divine Architect."

Hales had expressed a similar conviction at the beginning of his *Vegetable Staticks*: "The searching into the works of Nature, while it delights and inlarges the mind, and strikes us with the strongest assurance of the wisdom and power of the divine Architect, in framing for us so beautiful and well regulated a world, it does at the same time convince us of His constant benevolence and goodness towards us."

The 1733 preface, nonetheless, had a slightly different emphasis. It emphasized how inexhaustible the wisdom of the Architect was. We are to look to the innumerable beauties, and thereby realize the unending task of natural philosophy. Such an attitude might have offended those who would see this as somehow denying the time of the end. To them Hales replied that, given our present state of knowledge, obviously the time of the end has not yet come, nor will it in the foreseeable future.

> We must be content in this our infant State of Knowledge, while we know in part only, to imitate Children, who for want of better Skill and Abilities, and of more proper Materials, amuse themselves with slight Buildings. The farthest Advances we make in the Knowledge of Nature, the more probable and the nearer to Truth will our Conjectures approach: so that succeeding Generations, who shall have Benefit and Advantage both of their own Observations, and those of preceding Generations, may then make considerable Advances, when *many shall run to and fro, and Knowledge shall be increased*, Dan. xii. 4. In the meantime, it would but ill become us in this our State of Uncertainty, to treat the Errors and Mistakes of others with Scorn and Contempt, when we cannot but be conscious, that we ourselves see Things *but as thro' a Glass darkly*, and are very far from any Pretensions to Infallibility.

Hales, having reached the foundations of Newtonian natural philosophy, was convinced that he, for one, was living in the meantime. And he was going to behave accordingly. He was not going to engage in the construction of any great buildings with their propylaea and penetralia. Perhaps in many generations after Newton, such could be done. In the meantime, men must learn to live with one another in the darkness.[3]

Patience with the darkness was not typical of Newtonian philosophers. Scarcely a year after the publication of the *Vegetable Staticks*, another Newtonian had tried to use it as the basis for a complete system of the microscopic world. This Newtonian was John Theophilus Desaguliers.

Desaguliers was himself a member of the Newtonian circle. When Keill discontinued his lectures on natural philosophy at Oxford to move to London, Desaguliers, who had been his assistant, took them up. Eventually, he too moved to London, becoming a popular lecturer. Newton used him as a paid experimenter at the Royal Society. When some of Newton's optical work was attacked in France in 1715, Desaguliers gave the experimental reply in the *Philosophical Transactions*. Isaac Newton was godfather to one of Desaguliers' children.

Desaguliers, like Newton, was interested in the recovery of the pristine philosophy. He was a prominent member of a group that believed this philosophy was to be found in the secret traditions of the Masonic Guilds. Desaguliers wrote the dedication to the first publication of this group, *The Constitution, History, Laws, Charges, Orders, Regulations and Usages, of the Right Worshipful Fraternity of ACCEPTED FREE MASONS collected from Their General Records, and the faithful Traditions of many Ages*. And some said he had written most of the rest. The official history of the freemasons, which was to be read "at the admission of a New Brother," began:

> Adam, our first parent, created after the image of God, the great Architect of the Universe, must have had the Liberal sciences, particularly Geometry, written on his heart; for ever since the fall we find the principles of it in the hearts of his offspring, and which, in the process of time, have been drawn forth into a convenient method of propositions, by observing the Laws of Proportion, taken from Mechanism; so that, as Mechanical Arts gave occasion to the learned to reduce the elements of Geometry into method, this noble science, thus reduced, is the foundation of all those arts, (particularly of Masonry and Architecture) and the rule by which they are conducted and performed.

Architecture, the Mechanical Arts, and ultimately Geometry—all this contained within it the pristine philosophy. This was the God-like knowledge, for, as God had built the universe, so man could build, and in building manifest the divine image within himself.

While the principles of masonry had apparently been written on the hearts of men, in fact most of it had been passed down through history. The freemasons' history of their fraternity traced their lineage from Adam to Noah to "Grand Master Moses" to Solomon, and from the Jews to Greece and Pythagoras and eventually down to seventeenth-century Britain.

Among the many materials included in the first publication of the freemasons' constitution were a series of songs celebrating the secret knowlege which the masonic lodges still possessed. The master's song had a chorus:

> Who can unfold the Royal Art?
> Or sings its Secrets in a Song?
> They're safely kept in Mason's Heart
> And to the ancient Lodge belong.

The first two verses of the Fellow-Craft's Song were even more exuberant:

I

> Hail, Masonry! thou Craft divine
> Glory of Earth, from Heav'n reveal'd;
> Which dost with Jewels precious shine,
> From all but Masons' Eyes conceal'd.

II

> As Men from Brutes distinguisht are,
> A Mason other Men excels;
> For what's in Knowledge choice and rare
> But in his Breast securely.

The tunes to which these songs were to be sung were not included, presumably to be known to initiates only.

The God of the masons was far from the God of the General Scholium. There Newton had said explicitly that to speak of God building was to speak imperfectly, and only by way of allegory. The masonic idea of God is remarkably similar to that Barrow mocked as making Him seem "like some carpenter or mechanic repeating and displaying *ad nauseum* his one marionettish feat." Nonetheless, this was the Architect God, the shrivelling God of the eighteenth century, the dying god of those who envisioned Newton as the dispeller of whirlpools, the quieter of whirlwinds.

In 1728 Desaguliers wrote an extensive review of *Vegetable Staticks* for *Philosophical Transactions*. In this he praised Hales as a true Newtonian who had demonstrated beyond question "several truths" Sir Isaac had asserted in his queries. In this review, Desaguliers also chided the philosophers of little faith who had "called in question" those several truths. These men had now been shown for what they were, philosophers "of an inferior class who were not acquainted with those Facts and Experiments upon which Sir Isaac Newton had built his Queries." (In that same year, Desaguliers wrote a poem celebrating the ascension of a new British monarch, George II; it was entitled, *The Newtonian System of the World, the best model of Government: an Allegorical Poem.*)

The year after he reviewed Hales' book, Desaguliers published a paper in which he seems to claim that Desaguliers, if not Hales, was going to use Hales' discoveries to complete Newtonian philosophy. The paper (unlike the poem) was titled modestly enough—"An attempt to solve the Phenomenon of the Rise of Vapours, Formation of Clouds, and Descent of Rain." Nonetheless, any Newtonian would know that this subject was at the heart of the problem presented by Hales for the Newtonian philosophy.

Is air a unique substance? Is only it amphibious? For those followers of the last query, like Desaguliers, who wished to answer in the negative, the most obvious example of another substance which is equally amphibious is water. The rise of vapors, formation of clouds, and descent of rain demonstrate just such an amphibious nature. This at least is what Desaguliers tried to argue in his paper. And in the process he developed an elaborate theory of matter based on that of the last query.

The paper, however, failed to persuade his British contemporaries. Rather it simply focused attention on rain as a phenomenon which defied Newtonian explanation. As Benjamin Martin, a natural philosophy lecturer second in popularity only to Desaguliers, put it, " 'Tis no small disparagement to the Atomical or Newtonian Philosophy to suggest its insufficiency to account for the formation, rise and resolution of vapours into rain." This was from someone who had also written "Sir Isaac was *infallible* in everything that he proved and *demonstrated*, that is to say, in all his philosophy."

By the time Desaguliers died in 1744 he had made one further step toward finally resolving the problems of rain and combustion. By that time he thought he could explain them as the effects of electrical forces.

From the second decade of the eighteenth century, electrical phenomena had been of increasing importance to British natural philosophers. For instance, it was some electrical experiments performed at the Royal Society which led Newton, late in his life, long after the death of Huygens, to speculate that perhaps a subtle fluid extended throughout space really caused gravity after all.

Desaguliers' use of electrical forces, however promising, led him to a further complication. He could not explain how these forces were related to the atomic forces by which he had earlier tried to explain evaporation; and he could not reduce these atomic forces to the electrical ones. So electricity remained for him "a surprising paradox of nature." The old paradox had been explained by a new one.

Desaguliers, nonetheless, remained undaunted. In his last years he could still write, "Attraction and Repulsion seem to be settled by the Great Creator as First Principles in Nature. . . . We are not solicitous about their Causes, and think it enough to deduce other Things from them." And he could still write contemptuously of those who "pester'd the Learned World with Philosophical Romances such as the Cartesian System, contriv'd for the Diversion of the lazy and talkative."

His happy childhood had never ended.[4]

PART II

UTILITY

CHAPTER SIX

JEREMY BENTHAM
(to 1808)

Jeremy Bentham first formulated the principle of utility in 1769. Decades later Bentham could still recollect his pleasure of discovery; he could even recollect the measure he had placed on it. "When I had sketched a few vague notions on the subject, I looked delighted at my work. I remember asking myself—Would I take £500 for that sheet of paper? Poor as I was, I answered myself—No! that I would not."

This recollection, like Newton's of the apple, was recorded in the famed man's old age by a doting admirer. Bentham, in this recollection, did not claim to be the father of his principle, at least in the sense of having been its originator. Bentham had discoverd the principle of utility in the writings of other men. This he freely admitted, and his praise for those from whom he had learned this great truth was generous, even effusive.

Yet this praise did know bounds. Utility had been born in the minds of other men, but it would only come to maturity in Bentham's. Utility was a first principle of moral science, the philosophy of man, just as gravity was a first principle of physical science, the philosophy of nature. Before Newton many philosophers had considered, and a few had espoused, the principle of gravity; but only Newton had proven that it ruled the physical realm. Before Bentham many philosophers had considered, and a few had espoused, the principle of utility; but moral science still lacked its Newton. Jeremy Bentham intended to be that Newton himself. And, by the time of Bentham's death, at least one of his followers, Southwood Smith, believed Bentham had achieved no less.

> The discovery and application of the true physical law at the foundation of all physical phenomena, has produced a total revolution in the philosophy of physics. The discovery and application of the true psychological law, equally at the foundation of all mental phenomena, is destined to produce a like revolution in the philosophy of morals. Before the principle announced by Newton, as affording the true exposition of the constitution and motion of all physical bodies, has already fallen every other theory, how remote soever the antiquity in which it took its origin, how plausible soever the solution it gave of apparent but deceptive phenomena, how great soever the

ability with which it had been defended, and the authority by which
it had been sanctioned: before the principle announced by Bentham,
as affording the only true theory, and directing to the only right and
proper object and end of morals, legislation, and government, is
destined to fall every INSTITUTION, however ancient, how much
soever eulogised, how deeply soever venerated, by whomsoever
pronounced to be the perfection of human reason, which is not really
conducive to human happiness; every LAW, constitutional, civil,
and penal, with whatever danger to partial and sinister interests its
abrogation may be pregnant, which is not conducive to security,
to liberty, and to justice; every MODE OF PROCEDURE in the
administration of law which does not render justice accessible, speedy,
and cheap—which does not minimize delay, vexation, and expense;
every RULE OF CONDUCT, whether relating to public or to private
life, the observance of which does not tend to educe, from the source
of pleasure it is intended to regulate and control, the largest obtainable
amount of felicity, and to exclude in the completest degree, the corresponding pain with which almost every pleasure is but too apt to
be linked; every SANCTION, physical, judicial, moral and religious,
which does not secure at the smallest cost of suffering, the most
perfect and uniform conformity of the general will and action to the
appointed rule.

Bentham in his humbler moods did not consider himself Newton's
equal. He would have agreed with Laplace that there could only be
one Newton. Newton had demonstrated the rationality of the universe,
a universe of which man was but a part. The true philosophy of man
could be but a part of the true philosophy of nature. Benthamism
could be but a part of Newtonianism.

Newton's position in the history of philosophy's pursuit of first
principles was unique. This Bentham had, on occasion, admitted.
Indeed, in one of his effusive moments Bentham expressed his keen
sense of loss that Newton's apple had not somehow been preserved
so that it might be reverenced as a relic. "The apple let it be from
which Newton derived the first hint of the attraction of gravitation;
the ever memorable apple which, as an object of worship to the
latest posterity, ought to have been preserved from corruption in a
hermetically sealed glass-case; ought to have been transmitted as an
object of worship to the latest inheritors of this our globe."

Newton had demonstrated the rationality of the universe, a universe
of which man was but a part. But was man really just a part of this
rational universe? Might he not be, when compared to the world he
inhabits, a being not ruled by the kind of principles which rule
everything else, a quirk of nature, the exception?

If he was so, then the significance of Newton's discovery would be stunted. The philosophy of man, after all, is not just another sort of philosophy to the philosopher, since he in describing man is describing himself. The Cambridge platonists themselves had insisted that man's accurate understanding of who he was and what he should be was the ultimate end of all man's search for knowledge, for this was a knowledge which would transform the life of him who possessed it. As one of them had put it, "When the Tree of Knowledge is not planted by the Tree of Life, and sucks not up sap from thence, it may be as well fruitful with evil as with good and bring forth bitter fruit as well as sweet."

The tree of knowledge bears its most important fruit in the lives of men. Bentham, whatever his mood, would have eagerly agreed with this assessment; it meant that, while Newton's discovery was philosophically more fundamental, Bentham's was humanly more significant. As Bentham once put it, "What Newton did, was to throw light on one branch of science—But I have planted the tree of Utility —I have planted it deep and spread it wide." Newton could only describe the laws of nature, but Bentham could give laws to mankind. This was the greater responsibility.

A lawgiver could make rational laws, or irrational ones. A lawgiver could make laws in conformance with the principles of human nature, or in spite of them. A lawgiver could make people happy or he could make them miserable. Jeremy Bentham would be the first truly philosophical legislator. He would make rational laws in conformance with human nature. He would make mankind happy.

Bentham recognized this to be an ambitious task, but he never completely despaired of it. And once he became so exuberant at the prospect of his inevitable triumph that he spoke, only half-jokingly, of a future life in which his philosophical ancestors, daily kneeling before the thrones of himself and his followers, would make offerings of incense.

Whatever honor these ancestors would give Bentham in a future life, Bentham was scrupulous in his offerings to them in this one. Francis Bacon, John Locke, David Hume, David Hartley, Joseph Priestley, Adam Smith—the list of just British philosophers duly acknowledged and honored was long. While most of the acknowledged forerunners of Bentham were philosophers of the eighteenth or, at the earliest, the seventeenth centuries, occasionally the list would be stretched to include such ancient philosophers as Lucretius

and Epicurus. The earliest lawgiver Bentham could find who understood the principle of utility was Moses himself; this understanding,
however, was completely corrupted as the Mosaic Law was transmitted through time. Nonetheless, the principle had been gradually
recovered throughout the seventeenth and eighteenth centuries,
sufficiently that Bentham could confidently expect to achieve in the
moral realm what Newton had achieved in the physical. Jeremy
Bentham was going to write a human *Principia*.[1]

> Nature has placed mankind under the governance of two sovereign
> masters, *pain* and *pleasure*. It is for them alone to point out what we
> ought to do, as well as to determine what we shall do. On the one
> hand the standard of right and wrong, on the other the chain of causes
> and effects, are fastened to their throne. They govern us in all we do,
> in all we say, in all we think: every effort we can make to throw off
> our subjection, will serve but to demonstrate and confirm it. In words
> a man may pretend to abjure their empire: but in reality he will re-
> main subject to it all the while. The *principle of utility* recognizes this
> subjection, and assumes it for the foundation of that system, the
> object of which is to rear the fabric of felicity by the hands of reason
> and of law. Systems which attempt to question it, deal in sounds
> instead of senses, in caprice instead of reason, in darkness instead
> of light. But enough of metaphor and declamation: it is not by such
> means that moral science is to be improved.

So began Jeremy Bentham's *Introduction to the Principles of Morals
and Legislation*. If Bentham could demonstrate the principle of utility
to be sensible, rational, enlightening, and if he could also demonstrate
all contrary moral principles to be nothing but dark capricious sounds,
then truly a science of morals and legislation would begin.

Confident as he was he could fulfill this promise, Bentham at the
very beginning of his *Introduction* saw his effort as beset by an
apparently insuperable paradox. The principle of utility is the principle
against which everything else should be judged; because of this
exalted status, the principle apparently could never be demonstrated
with certainty. Apparently it could only be stated with the utmost
clarity. This Bentham did, before he tried to explain the paradox.
"By the principle of utility is meant that principle which approves
or disapproves of every action whatsoever, according to the tendency
which it appears to have to augment or diminish the happiness of the
party whose interest is in question: or, what is the same thing in
other words, to promote or oppose happiness." From this definition a
number of corollaries could be drawn; Bentham could, for example,

explain how "ought," "ought not," "right," and "wrong" are to be understood: "Of an action that is comfortable to the principle of utility one may always say either that it is one that ought to be done, or at least that it is not one that ought not to be done. One may say also, that it is right it should be done: that it is a right action; at least that it is not a wrong action." The definitions flowed smoothly one from another; but a paradox remained.

How was Bentham to prove that his readers *ought* to follow the principle of utility, to prove this without, by definition, assuming what was supposed to be proved? Actually Bentham had not quite claimed to be able to prove his first principle. "Proof" was not among the words of his first paragraph. All Bentham had said he was going to do was to "improve moral science" by placing the "fabric of felicity" into the hands of "reason and law." He had never said he was going to prove his principle; he was rather going to show his to be based in reason, other principles in caprice.

This became a crucial distinction as he raised this paradox and admitted that it could not be resolved. "Is it [the principle of utility] susceptible of any direct proof? It should seem not: for that which is used to prove everything else, cannot itself be proved: a chain of proofs must have their commencement somewhere. To give such proof is as impossible as it is needless."

It was needless because Bentham's readers were men who, no less than the rest of humanity, were ruled by pleasure and pain. Intelligent and honest men would recognize this indubitable fact; and, in recognizing it, they would be recognized their instinctive adherence to that principle of morals and legislation which also recognizes this subjection, the principle of utility. Bentham, for himself, was certain that never has existed a "human creature breathing, however stupid or perverse, who has not on many or perhaps on most occasions of his life deferred to it."

"It" was, of course, the principle of utility, Bentham adding for emphasis "by the natural constitution of the human frame, on most occasions of his life deferred to it." Bentham was speaking to those of his readers who were not so stupid or perverse as to deny this, those who were in their lives, if not in their philosophies, already followers of the principle of utility.

Having thereby established agreement that the principle of utility was the true one, Bentham could disprove the other principles of morality by definition. Such principles of morality were either the principle of utility in disguise, or they were some other principle; insofar as they were the principle of utility in disguise, they were superfluous; insofar as they were not the principle of utility, they were pernicious. As Bentham summarized his method of definitional refutation, "To prove any other principle, therefore, to be a wrong one, there needs no more than just show it to be what it is, a principle of which the dictates are in some point or other different from those of the principle of utility: to state it is to confute it."

When other principles were stated properly—that is, stated in terms of the principle of utility—it was found there were really but two principles other than utility, the principle which always disagreed with utility and the principle which only sometimes disagreed. The first of these Bentham called the principle of asceticism; it urges men to approve of an action insofar as it diminishes total human happiness, and to disapprove of it insofar as it increases human happiness. To state this principle is, of course, to confute it. The monks who have appeared to follow the principle of asceticism have largely done so to "ingratiate themselves with the Deity," and thereby to increase their pleasure in a future life. Those pagan philosophers who appear to recommend a principle of asceticism are also espousing the principle of utility in disguise; they, it seems, have disguised it to themselves by hasty speculation.

> The principle of asceticism seems originally to have been the reverie of certain hasty speculators, who having perceived, or fancied that certain pleasures, when reaped in certain circumstances, have, at the long run, been attended with pains more than equivalent to them, took occasion to quarrel with everything that offered itself under the name of pleasure. Having then got thus far, and having forgot the point which they set out from, they pushed on, and went so much further as to think it meretricious to fall in love with pain. Even this, we see, is at the bottom but the principle of utility misapplied.

Whatever its origins, to state the principle of asceticism is to confute it, because to state it is to realize that it can never be consistently applied. Even those few saints who appear to have come closest to applying it consistently to their own lives have not believed it "a merit, much less a duty, to make others miserable: although it should seem, that if a certain quantity of misery were a thing so desirable, it would not matter much whether it were brought by each man upon himself, or by one man upon another." So utility is to be preferred to asceticism, since it, unlike asceticism, could be consistently applied and thereby generate a completely rational system of morals.

But what if an agent decides that he will act sometimes in accordance with the one principle, sometimes the other, depending how he felt? His decisions, therefore, would be ultimately dictated by his feelings, and not by utility or asceticism. Such an approach Bentham first called the principle of sympathy and antipathy, and then later renamed it the principle of caprice.

> By the principle of sympathy and antipathy, I mean that principle which approves or disapproves of certain actions, not on account of their tending to augment the happiness, nor yet on account of their tending to diminish the happiness of the party whose interest is in question, but merely because a man finds himself disposed to approve or disapprove of them: holding up that approbation as a sufficient reason for itself; and disclaiming the necessity of looking out for any extrinsic ground.

To state this principle is to confute it, for to state it is to realize that it is not a principle at all. The principle of sympathy or antipathy is rather an excuse for unprincipled action. It denies the existence of an external standard against which all actions should be judged. It denies that the human realm is ultimately rational. It denies that moral science can be improved, just as physical science has been. The readers could now see what happens when one tries to deviate from the principle of utility. You are left with, instead of light, darkness—with, instead of reason, caprice.

Armed with this analysis, the readers, with Bentham's help, could unmask covert appeals to this "principle" of caprice. Appeals to moral sense, commonsense, the fitness of things, the law of nature, the law of reason, right reason, natural justice, natural equity, good order were all usually appeals to the principle of caprice. There was only one sort of appeal to caprice which Bentham respected—this he called the "fairest and openest of them all."

> The fairest and openest of them all is that sort of man who speaks out and says, I am of the number of the Elect: now God himself takes care to inform the Elect what is right: and that with so good effect, that let them strive ever so, they cannot help not knowing it but practicing it. If therefore a man wants to know what is right and what is wrong, he had nothing to do but come to me.

Such a man would be making no claims to reason whatsoever. Of course, as Bentham realized, the advocate of caprice need not go so far to find a defense for his position. In fact, he might even reply that he was not, in principle, against the application of reason to human affairs. It was just that, in practice, such certainty was never obtainable. One could never measure the net happiness that would be produced by two different acts; nor could one any more assess with precision the effectiveness or ineffectiveness of a given law in producing the general happiness of the populace. Men were not astronomical bodies; so in dealing with men one could never aspire to certainty, only likelihood.

Bentham was prepared for this objection; indeed the rest of his *Introduction* was designed to answer it. He was going to show that, if enough care was taken, such certainty was possible. He was going to show how pleasures and pains, the forces which attract men to and repel them from certain actions, could be treated with the same kind of precision as are the physical forces which attract and repel matter.

Bentham enumerated in detail the pleasures and pains of man. He found no less than fourteen categories of pleasure and no less than twelve of pain. Even within these categories he made further discriminations; for example, he counted nine different sensual pleasures, the last of which was the pleasure "derived from the gratification of the appetite of curiosity, by the application of new objects to any of the senses." (This last sensual pleasure is carefully distinguished from pleasure "of novelty, excited by appearances of new ideas"; the latter is a pleasure of the imagination, not of the senses, and belongs in that category.) The reader, even the resisting reader, would be hard pressed to find a pain of his own that could not be categorized as either a pain of privation, or a pain of the senses, or a pain of awkwardness, or of enmity, or of ill-name, of piety ("the pains that accompany the belief of a man's being obnoxious to the displeasure of the Supreme Being"), of benevolence ("the pains resulting from the view of any pains supposed to be endured by other beings"), or malevolence, or memory, or imagination, or expectation, or association. If a savage felt sorry about the pain he imagined a tree felt when he cut it down, this would be a pain of benevolence because it was a pain supposed by the savage, albeit mistakenly, to be endured by the tree. It would be difficult to find a pain that could not be classified under one of these headings; but, if a reader did, that would in no way hurt Bentham's system. The reader would simply have improved the system; and that was just what Bentham was trying to do, to provide a basis on which moral science could be improved.

The enumeration of pleasures and pains only preluded a more complicated enumeration. Bentham had to enumerate those circumstances which affected an individual's susceptibility to a given pain or pleasure. This was crucial because obviously pleasures and pains were not uniformly proportional to their causes. Age, sex, occupation, lineage, class, religion, physical health, mental health—Bentham found no less than thirty-two circumstances, which, "all or many of them, will need to be attended to as often as upon any occasion any account is taken of any quantity of pain or pleasure, as resulting from any cause."

In enumerating not only all the pleasures and all the pains, but also all the circumstances which could affect their strength, Bentham had, in principle at least, exhausted all possible motives for human actions. Men are governed by pleasure and pain; such are the forces which attract and repel human beings. Any effective human motive is analysable back to these forces, much as Newton analysed the motion of the planets back to inertia and gravity. As Bentham put it, "A motive is substantially nothing more than pleasure or pain, operating in a certain manner." To gain or increase a pleasure, to avoid or ease a pain, these are the only effective motives.

The example of a cruel or malicious man proved no exception to this rule. The cruel man still has, Bentham observed, "a kind of pleasure that is his motive: the pleasure he takes at the thought of the pain which he sees, or expects to see, his adversary undergo." We might, of course, judge that the pleasure of the cruel man is insufficient justification for the infliction of pain on another human being; in this case one man's suffering of pain outweighs the second's enjoying of pleasure. Here we can begin to see the implications of the principle of utility for a law giver.

We cannot expect a man to act against his own interest, his own net pleasure. We cannot, therefore, expect the cruel man to abstain from an act just because this act will cause another man pain. We can only expect him to refrain from any act if he associates with it sufficient pain, his own pain, to outweigh any pleasure he might gain. To formulate laws which will make this so, laws which will make it in everyone's selfish interest to act for the greatest good of the greatest number, is the vocation of the legislator, a vocation which can now be seen to be the most important vocation a man can have.

Before such legislation could be written in practice, many things needed to be distinguished in principle. Considered in itself, a punishment is just as bad an act as an offence, for both inflict pain. Just as the types and degrees of offences needed to be carefully distinguished, so did the types and degrees of punishments. And great care had to be given to determine, by indubitable rules, how to make a punishment proportional to an offence. Bentham laid down these rules, rules such as "The value of punishment must not be less in any case than what is sufficient to outweigh that of the profit of the offence." Having asserted these rules, Bentham concluded his *Introduction* by discussing those cases in which an offender, even though he had acted against the common good, ought to be allowed to go unpunished because punishment would do more harm than good. The philosophically astute legislator could make mankind happy, but he could not make mankind perfectly happy.[2]

Although the *Introduction* was finished, and printed, by 1780, Bentham did not want it to appear apart from that which he intended it to introduce—a finished system of penal laws, which would show that the distinctions made in principle in the *Introduction* would bear fruit in practice.

This system of law was particularly important in light of a polemic Bentham had written a few years before completing his *Introduction*, a polemic against the chief contemporary apologist for the legal *status quo*, William Blackstone. In his anonymously published *A Fragment on Government*, Bentham had begun by reminding his readers that they were living during an age in which "knowledge is rapidly advancing towards perfection." That this was such an age Bentham took to be obvious from the great advances which had been made in natural philosophy. Bentham also thought it obvious that "correspondent to discovery and improvement in the natural world is reformation in the moral." This was the context in which Blackstone was attacked for what was termed his "antipathy to reformation." Blackstone was content with the English practice of allowing historical precedent to be the chief basis for legal decision, as if the irrational past should be allowed to determine the potentially rational future, as if a code could not be written which would raise law above the caprice of individual judges. Readers who had agreed with the attack of *Fragment on Government* could have had little doubt that its author, whoever he was, might just be the person to lead the necessary reformation. Nonetheless, the author himself chose to conclude on a note of modesty. He had only tried to show that Blackstone was not "*he that should come*, but that we may be still *looking for another*." The author himself abjured any ambition to be "he that should come." "My mission is at end, when I have *prepared the way before him*."

Bentham's *Introduction* had further prepared the way. It equipped his readers to unmask all false moral prophets, not just Blackstone. Then alone would his readers be capable of recognizing "he that should come." And when they were finally capable of this recognition, Bentham wished them to turn the page to find his penal code.

This penal code, unfortunately, proved more resistant to reason than had man's ultimate motives. When in 1789 Bentham had still not finished the code (he never finished it), he released the *Introduction*. The *Introduction* was almost completely ignored in his own country. One of the few disciples it did attract was the Swiss Etienne Dumont. Himself indignant at the lack of recognition his master had received, Dumont eventually persuaded Bentham to allow him to prepare a French edition which would contain not only the *Introduction*, but also some of his previously unpublished manuscripts on legislation.

Dumont was a true disciple. In later years, his highest praise for any other philosophy was, "It is convincing, it is truth itself, it is almost Benthamic." This unrestrained enthusiasm for Bentham's philosophy was evident in Dumont's preface to his edition of Bentham. Dumont claimed that this philosophy represented the beginning of a new enlightened age of legislation. Politics and morality had at last been made scientific. In particular, Dumont judged the *Introduction to the Principles of Morals and Legislation* worthy of high praise; that work, "though not hitherto distinguished by any great share of popular applause, is already considered in that light by the small number of competents by whom its merits have been appreciated."

This edition of the *Introduction* with Dumont's preface finally gained the attention of the *Edinburgh Review*, the organ of the Whigs, the more liberal of the two major British political parties and hence the more likely to be sympathetic to Bentham's proposals—it gained attention, but no honor. Concerning Dumont's preface, the reviewer observed, "These pretensions, it cannot be denied, are sufficiently magnificent; and the confidence with which they are announced naturally leads us to inquire into the facts by which they are supported." Then the reviewer followed with a long précis of the *Introduction*; and this précis itself was followed by a short evaluation. "If there is little that is false or pernicious in this system, there is little that is either new or important." Bentham had stated in complicated language, with many ingenious, yet impractical distinctions, what is a platitude: laws should be made for the common good. As to what the common good is in any particular case we are no better off than when we started; in short, Bentham "has left the science of morality in the same imperfect condition in which it was left by his predecessors." Faced with a moral decision, an individual still must rely on his own sense of right and wrong, with all its attendant uncertainty. Any decision so based, of course, cannot be considered a scientific decision. "Certainly no man was ever so arrogant or so foolish as to insist upon establishing his own individual persuasion as an infallible test of duty and wisdom to all the rest of the world." As for Bentham himself, the reviewer praised him for "the sagacity and independence which distinguishes all his speculations."

Bentham did not want such praise for his speculations. He wanted them accepted as a test of duty and wisdom. Argument alone apparently would not do this. He had shown how practical his principle was. If in one small area he could demonstrate the practicality of his principles, then arguments like that of the *Edinburgh Review* would be infallibly refuted. A whole penal code was perhaps too large an ambition for this first step; that was suitable only as a long term goal. By 1789 he had settled on a more immediate, limited one.[3]

"Morals reformed—health preserved—industry invigorated—instruction diffused—public burdens lightened—Economy seated as it were, upon a rock—the gordian knot of the Poor-Laws not cut, but untied—all by a simple idea in Architecture." The simple, most useful idea is embodied in Bentham's plans for the "Panopticon or The Inspection House." This idea would be useful for "punishing the incorrigible, guarding the insane, reforming the vicious, confining the suspected, employing the idle, maintaining the helpless, curing the sick, instructing the willing in any branch of industry, or training a rising race in the path of education." This idea could and should be used in "perpetual prisons in the room of death, or prisons for confinement before trial, or penitentiary-houses, or houses of correction, or work-houses, or manufactories, or mad houses, or hospitals, or schools."

All these diverse institutions have one thing in common: they all use inspection; they all have people committed to them who must be periodically inspected if the institution is to achieve its end. From this generalization Bentham deduced that the more constantly the inmates are inspected, the better the institutions will be. Constant surveillance was the ideal, but, of course, that was impractical. Bentham, however, believed he had found a way that this ideal might be approached. Let the inmate never be sure that he is not being watched, and let him have reason to believe that he is being watched; if this is achieved, it rationally follows that he will conceive himself to be under perpetual surveillance. He will, therefore, act as if he were being continually watched—that is, as his watchers want him to act. He would do so because he would perceive it to be in his self-interest.

This is reasoning of a piece with that of the *Introduction to the Principles of Morals and Legislation*. This time, however, Bentham was prepared to show how these principles could be put into practice. Bentham's "simple idea in Architecture" could make the inferences from his principles come true. Bentham had worked out all the details for building a prison, a philosophically sound prison. (Presumably its extension to schools, hospitals, and the like would come later.) He named his prison after the perpetual surveillance under which the prisoners would feel themselves to be living, the Panopticon.

The Panopticon penitentiary would be a circular building; the cells of the prisoners would be on the circumference, the inspector's lodge in the center. The inspector's lodge would be connected to the cells by individual windows shuttered in such a way—Bentham describes exactly how—that the inspector could peep in without himself being observed. To this simple plan Bentham added many ingenious touches: a sewerage system extending to each cell for the sake of cleanliness and security; a lighting system so that inspection could be extended through the night; and even a communication system between lodge and the cells. ("To save the troublesome exertion of voice that might otherwise be necessary, and to prevent one prisoner from knowing that the inspector was occupied by another prisoner at a distance, a small *tin tube* might reach from each cell to the inspector's lodge. By means of this implement, the slightest whisper of the one might be heard by the other, especially if he had proper notice to apply his ear to the tube.")

Such a building would achieve "the *apparent omnipresence* of the inspector (if divines will allow me the expression), combined with the extreme facility of his real presence." The relationship of the prisoner to his inspector Bentham found aptly expressed in the Psalm one hundred thirty-nine.

Thou art about my path, and about my bed:
   and spiest out all my ways.
If I say, peradventure the darkness shall cover me,
   then shall my night be turned into day.
Even there also shall the hand lead me; and
   thy right hand shall hold me.

Actually the Psalm was apt only as Bentham excerpted it. In the
original, after the first verse of Bentham's version, there comes:

For there is not a word in my tongue, but lo,
   O Lord, thou knowest it altogether.
Thou hast beset me behind and before, and laid
   thine hand upon me.
Such knowledge is too wonderful for me; it is high,
   I cannot attain into it.

There was no knowledge too god-like for Bentham's gaoler. Of
course, when attained, this knowledge also gave the opportunity for
misuse. Bentham, nonetheless, believed that such misuse could be
prevented by placing a head inspector over the lesser inspectors.
His duty would be to conduct surveillance on the inspectors.

While the efficient operation of the Panopticon was obviously in
the interest of society as a whole, it also had to be in the selfish
interest of the head inspector. Bentham was certain it could be made
so. All the inmates would be required to work at suitable trades;
they should be given a small wage sufficient to motivate them to
work hard and well. They would, for example, be able to use this
money to buy special food. (Bentham suggested that the ordinary
food be kept bland to make the earned food more attractive.) The
products of prisoners' labor would be sold to pay for the running of
the penitentiary. Any money left over, any profit, would be the
head inspector's. To insure the honesty of the inspector, to make his
honesty in his own selfinterest, Bentham would require him to
publish his accounts.

Bentham first sketched his plan in a series of letters; he subsequently
elaborated it in great detail in a postscript added to the collected
letters when they were published in 1791. Bentham, it appeared, had
thought of everything. Everything concerning the prison itself:
the roof of the building should be made of plaster. Everything
concerning the management of the prisoners: a prisoner was to have
$7\frac{1}{2}$ hours of sleep on working days, and he was not to be allowed to
blow his nose except in a handkerchief. Bentham's plan, it seemed,

had anticipated everything, everything except how he would ever get any government to implement it.

Bentham tried to get his Panopticon plans accepted not only in England, but also in France and Ireland. He wrote to a member of the French assembly, offering to come to France to build a Panopticon, and then to become the head inspector himself, free of charge. The National Assembly was impressed enough to give him an "honorable mention" in their minutes for his "most ardent love of humanity," but not enough to accept the offer.

In Ireland Bentham did not even get an honorable mention for his efforts. There his plan was approved all the way to the Lord Lieutenant, needing only his assent for final acceptance; but the Lord Lieutenant dismissed the Panopticon with the remark, "They will all get out." Bentham surmised that "the laconicalness of the observation, in conjunction with the tone and deportment which accompanied it, were such as sufficed to show that attempts at explanation would have been fruitless."

So too, it turned out, were attempts at explanation in England itself, but only after Bentham had spent years trying to explain. Bentham energetically lobbied for his plan, and attacked alternatives. But whenever he seemed close to satisfying his desire, "the business," as Bentham put it, "lingered." By 1792 he had gotten his plan before the First Lord of the Treasury. Two full years later, the members of Parliament finally passed a bill approving Bentham's plan, but they neglected to provide the necessary financing. When in 1797 Parliament finally seemed ready to act through a Parliamentary Commission, the lord on whose estate the prison was to be built withdrew his offer of land. (He did not, he finally decided, want a prison on his estate, even a philosophically sound one.) Then Bentham found, after much effort, another suitable site,. Then, a new bill, a competitor which would replace the Panopticon, was proposed to the Parliamentary Commission. Bentham refuted the competing bill. He was given reason to believe that his refutation had been accepted. And then, the competing bill was passed.

In retrospect, Bentham compared his efforts on behalf of the Panopticon to the search that young Telemachus was supposed to have made for his father Ulysses. "When rambling in quest of his father Ulysses: as often as he thought himself on the point of receiving the paternal embrace, consigned by some delusion or other to final disappointment—how opposite in my case to what is called poetical justice." In the end, Bentham decided that it was the king himself, George III, who had blocked the Panopticon. "But for him all the paupers in the country, as well as all the prisoners in the country, would have been in my hands." [4]

Bentham's failure to get his Panopticon built consigned him, by his own account, "if not to the bottom of the abyss of despair, at any rate but a little distance from it." And, by any account, Bentham had ample cause for despair. He was now approaching sixty years of age, his major attempt at practical reform a failure, his code of penal law neither finished nor likely to be, his principle of utility either completely ignored or dismissed as a truism.

Nonetheless, Bentham, while he came very close to what he termed "absolute destruction," soon regained his composure. There was as he turned sixty a special reason for hope, for confidence in the future. Bentham, the bachelor, had finally found a true son, a man of whom he could later say, "I was the spiritual father." The man was James Mill.

CHAPTER SEVEN

JAMES MILL AND THE BENTHAMITES
(1808-32)

Since 1802, when he was only twenty-one, James Mill had been earning his living as a journalist. He first wrote for the *Anti-Jacobin Review and Magazine*, the writers of which were supposed to be "the declared champions of religion, morality, and social order, as supported by the existing establishments, ecclesiastical and civil, of this country." They would champion both the monarchy—"the only legitimate form of government"—and the Church of England against the "malignant genius of JACOBISM."

> We know the spirit of Jacobism too well to be deceived by any appearances which it may assume that are foreign from its nature; we know its purpose to be fixed and determined; though vanquished in one shape, it will rise up in another; and nothing short of its annihilation can justify confidence, or produce security. We shall, therefore, continue to watch its motions, with anxious solicitude, and incessant attention; we have traced it from the root, through all its various ramifications, to the very summit, and our efforts will not cease until we have not only lopped off every noxious branch, but felled the hideous trunk itself to the ground.

If he ever shared this attitude, the young Mill soon outgrew it. When he became editor of his own magazine, *The Literary Journal or Universal Review of Literature Domestic and Foreign*, he included in its first issue an article, perhaps by his own hand, explaining the extremes of the French Revolution in less threatening terms. The French, it was well known, had "a certain volatitlity and lightness of disposition" which resulted both in "an extreme susceptibility of all impressions" and in "excessive vanity." This lightness of disposition contributed to the beginning of the atrocities of the revolution; these atrocities in turn destroyed what little control moral principles ever did exercise over the French mind.

> With respect to sentiments of morality, the principles of nature will always have considerable force. But it is certain that the sight of the crimes, and the habitual fears in which every man has lived, must have had a very unfavorable effect upon the minds of the people. They have been compelled to foster self-love, and malignant rather

> than benevolent sentiments towards others; respect for virtue has
> been lost; and it is little now considered either as a ground of self-
> estimation or of dignity in the eyes of others; indeed it is the prin-
> ciple, even of their philosophers, that utility only constitutes duty.

The unspoken implication was clear. Jacobism was a disease, but
it was a peculiarly French disease. Who could imagine such a typical
product of the volatile, vain French mind taking root in the serious,
modest British mind? Who, for example, could imagine a British
philosopher mistaking selfishness for virtue, utility for duty?

By the time James Mill first met Bentham in 1808, Mill's fortunes
had taken a turn for the worse. The *Literary Journal* had folded in 1806,
and Mill was finding it difficult to support his newly begun family
through his journalism alone.

Although no account of the first meeting has survived, their relationship seems to have developed quickly. Within a year Mill was
regularly taking his dinner with Bentham; and he was writing that
"everything which comes from the pen or from the mind of Bentham
is entitled to profound regard." In 1809 Bentham bought a country
residence at which Bentham and Mill (and Mill's family) could spend
the summer together. And in 1809 Mill was writing that Bentham
"had done more to elucidate the true grounds of legislative inference
than all the jurists who had gone before him."

Despite the summers and dinners, Bentham still wished his spiritual
son closer to him. Mill moved his family into an old house on the
grounds of Bentham's city estate. The house, however, was so
old—Milton, it was said, had written *Paradise Lost* there—that Mill
thought it unhealthy. Mill moved his family back to their former
lodgings. But Bentham still thought this too far away. Finally he
leased a suitable house nearby his—this one not so old—and sub-
leased it to Mill at half-price. (Much later, Bentham wrote concerning
Mill: "He was one of the earliest and most influential of my disciples.
The house he lives in looks into my garden.")

James Mill clearly profitted materially from his relationship with
Bentham, at a time when he desperately needed such a profitable
relationship. Nevertheless, no one has ever suggested that self-
interest was a motive for Mill in becoming close to Bentham, no one
even among the many who came to dislike Mill. And those who
disliked Mill were not above questioning his motives. One who
disliked him very much, John Bowring, attributed to Bentham the
assessment of Mill: "His creed of politics result less from the love

for the many than from the hatred for the few. It is too much under the influence of selfish and dissocial affection."

If Bentham really did have any such reservations about Mill—and he is supposed to have described him as being "as proud as Lucifer" —Mill himself was capable of reminding the old man of his good fortune. It was, the younger man once pointed out to the elder, "a very fortunate occurence, that any man with views and propensities of such rare occurrence as mine, should happen to come in toward the close of your career to carry on the work without any intermission." This boast Mill did much to make good.

In 1809, for instance, Mill reviewed a posthumously published historical work by the recent government minister, Charles James Fox. Fox had attempted in this work to portray the reign of Charles II as one of good laws and bad government. "The best moment of the best constitution that ever human wisdom framed" was also, because of the character of the men in power, a time of oppression and misery. Seeing this, Fox could not help but exclaim: "How vain then, how idle, how presumptuous, is the opinion, that laws can do everything! and how weak and pernicious the maxims founded upon it, that measures, not men, are to be attended to!"

Such an attitude, exalting as it did politicians at the expense of political philosophers, was scarcely compatible with Bentham's philosophy. And James Mill carefully pointed out deficiencies in the minister's reasoning, deficiencies which were "but too decisive proof how little progress the philosophy of Mr. Fox has made in the analysis of the principles of government, and the discovery of those fundamental conditions, on which alone the security of social happiness can rest." A sound constitution is, by definition, one that provides a remedy for potential maladministration. Good laws are, by definition, those which make action for the common good in everyone's self interest. What else could be meant by the phrases "good laws" and "sound constitution"? Therefore, Mill could only conclude that "if the good laws of Charles the Second's time were inadequate to secure liberty, they were not good enough." Such laws could be improved, of course, only by those who know the principles of government, by those who had discovered the fundamental conditions of social happiness; and, the implication was clear, Charles James Fox was not one of these.

We must look to the men more than the measures—Mill could not have expected in so short a review to refute so pervasive a view of politics so completely that no reply was possible. Yet this view of politics did need such a decisive refutation, or politics and law would be forever consigned to the darkness, or at best to the twilight. Great government would always be dependent upon the unpredictable, the occurrence of that freak of nature, that caprice of history, the genius, the great leader, the hero. And man's society would never quite be part of the Newtonian universe in which it lived, and breathed, and had its being. Bentham himself had long been aware of the need for such a decisive refutation.[1]

How could one avoid the implication that there was an irreducibly irrational element within government, an element which could never be taken into account by a law-giver, no matter how philosophically astute? Newton had rationalized the physical world by proving that it was located within an absolute space and time, absolutely homogeneous. Was human space and time equally homogeneous? Could principles of legislation laid down by one man in one place at one time make all men in all places at all times happy?

Jeremy Bentham naturally was most interested in this question in a more specific form. Could Jeremy Bentham's principle be successfully applied to all countries at all times? If they could not, then he would not deserve to sit at the right hand of Newton.

Bentham had himself explored this very issue in a short essay included in the original Dumont collection of his works, "The Influence of Time and Place on Legislation." There he carefully catalogued the various circumstances that could affect legislation; he catalogued them so carefully with so many examples that his readers could scarcely avoid concluding that he was truly sensitive to the variety of circumstances—sensitive to this variety and annoyed with those reformers who were not. "Hot-headed innovators, full of their own notions," he had called them.

Nonetheless, upon analysis, Bentham discovered that of all the great variety of circumstances only climate and geography would necessarily entail a variation in laws. (What might, for example, be a mild punishment in a mild climate might be a severe punishment in a severe climate.) And these variations due to geography or climate would, moreover, be of little significance since, according to Bentham's observations, "the whole of history proves that there is no circumstance connected with climate and texture of earth incompatible with happiness."

Men, no matter what the climate or the geography of the land in which they live, can be made reasonably happy, if only they have the correct laws governing their actions. The legislator cannot change climate or geography, but all else is, in principle, within his power to change. Government, religion, education, custom—each of these, or all of them, could be changed by legislators, and should be, if the principle of utility predicted that the change would increase the net sum of happiness. The legislator, again in principle, would be as capable of deciding this for a foreign country as for his own. "Legislators who, having freed themselves from the shackles of authority, have learnt to soar above the mists of prejudice, know as well how to make laws for one country as for another: all they need is all the relevant facts; they need to be informed of the local geography, the climate, the bodily constitution of the inhabitants, their manners, legal customs, religion. These are the data they require: possessed of these, all places are alike."

Possessed of these, the legislator could, if he wished, give to a people all the happiness possible—not perfect happiness perhaps, but a greater happiness than previous generations would have deemed possible for mere men. "We shall never make this world the abode of perfect happiness: when we shall have accomplished all that can be done, this paradise will yet be, according to the Asiatic idea, only a garden; but this garden will be a most delightful abode, compared with the savage forest in which men have so long wandered."

Bentham nonetheless made, in effect, a major admission in this essay. He admitted that he had not so much resolved the difficulties presented by the apparent variations in time and place, as he had rather expressed his confidence that they could be resolved. He had answered in theory what was, most fundamentally, a problem of practice, a problem which could be solved only by a philosopher actually soaring above the mists of prejudice to legislate effectively for a society radically different from his own. This would be a fundamental test of Bentham's philosophy—of its universality, and, therefore, of its worth—and Bentham knew just the country on which it should be made. "To a lawgiver, who having been bred up with English notions shall have learnt how to accomodate his laws to the circumstances of Bengal, no other part of the globe can present difficulty."

There were practical advantages to this choice also. India had already been under British influence for a considerable lenght of time.

Moreover, the relationship between these two lands had undergone near the end of the eighteenth century a fundamental transformation. Rather than leaving Indian laws as they were, the British governors of India, due to the administrative reforms of Lord Cornwallis, had begun to impose British legal procedures upon Indian society.

By 1802 Bentham knew the country on which this test should be tried. By 1810 he also knew the man who should perform the test. This would be the first major assignment for his new found son, James Mill.

Bentham could not bequeath to Mill the power over the Indian subcontinent necessary to perform the test. Nonetheless, Mill could do for Indian society what Bentham had done for European. He could perform the experiment in his thoughts. He could judge Indian traditions by utilitarian standards. And Mill could also perform an additional task, in keeping with the central concern of "The Influence of Time and Place on Legislation"; Mill could judge the British attempt to reform Indian administration by its conformance to both utilitarian ideals and Indian realities.[2]

This was an assignment for which Mill was more prepared than perhaps Bentham could reasonably have hoped. For years before he met Bentham, James Mill had, in fact, been working on a large-scale history of British rule in India. He had been working at it in the hope that its eventual publication would make his literary reputation and in the process gain for himself and his family some financial security.

However much this coincidence of interest might have helped establish Mill and Bentham's close association, the coincidence itself is not quite as remarkable as it might at first appear. British rule in India was a subject of widespread interest in England in the early nineteenth century, and particularly controversial was the imposition of English institutions upon the Indian society.

As long as we get what we want out of India, why not leave the Indians to their own ways? This was the question asked by many in the East India Company which was charged with getting out of India what was wanted. Sir Thomas Munro, Governor of Madras, was of the opinion the Indians could take care of their own affairs—"the natives of this country have enough of their own to answer every useful object of internal administration." The problem he thought was with the English—"Englishmen are as great fanatics in politics as Mohammedans in religion. They suppose that no country can be saved without English institutions."

Many of those in favor of British institutions for India were concerned not so much about saving the country as saving the souls of its inhabitants. What undeniable evidence of original sin and of the need of natural man for divine grace did this benighted people provide! A whole race of men, as one observer described them, "degenerate and base . . . obstinate in their disregard of what they know to be right, governed by malevolent and licentious passions . . . sunk in misery by their vices." What evidence of original sin they provided! And what evidence of divine providence that they have finally been put in our hands! So spoke Christian evangelicals in the early nineteenth century of the Indians. (So they spoke in the nineteenth century much as, in the seventeenth, the more extreme puritans had for a time spoken of high church Anglicans.) And these Evangelicals were heard all the way into Parliament, where in 1814 one of their leaders exhorted, "Let us endeavor to strike out roots into the soil by the gradual introduction and establishment of our own principles and opinions; of our laws, institutions, and manners; above all, as the sources of every other improvement, of our religion, and consequently of our morals."

Such enthusiasm left many of the experienced administrators of India exasperated. Sir Thomas Munro, for instance, was not just speaking for himself when in annoyance at the reformers who wished to reduce the world "to such a state of dull uniform repose," he exclaimed, "Give me a thousand times in preference the world as it now stands, with all its beautiful variety of knowledge and ignorance —of knowledge—of manners, customs—religions and superstitions —of cultivated fields and wide extended deserts—of war and peace." As for the relative merits of Indian and European culture, Munro wrote, "If civilization is to become an article of trade between the two countries, I am convinced that this country [Britain] will gain by the import cargo."

In support of this opinion, Munro could cite the leading British orientalist of the day, Sir William Jones. Jones insisted that the Indian people had produced a civilization of considerable intrinsic value, although it admittedly differed in many ways from the European. Jones was even prepared to suggest that the Indians had, independently of the West, made that greatest of cultural achievements, the discovery of gravity, Jones quickly adding that this in no way diminished

Newton. When James Mill's massive three volume *History of British India* finally did appear in 1817, most of the first volume was spent assessing Jones' high estimate of Indian civilization.

Mill, as he was careful to point out in the preface to his work, had one particular advantage over other recent writers on India. Mill had never been to India. He was, therefore, able to maintain a judicious distance from his subject. He was less likely than someone who has traveled through parts of the vast subcontinent, to mistake those parts for the whole. And he was less likely to become so involved with the Indian people that he would adopt it as his business to eulogize them, as had Sir William Jones.

Mill's account was no eulogy. The character of the Indian people he found disgusting, so disgusting as to be comparable even to that most uncivilized race, the Chinese.

> Both nations are too nearly in equal degree tainted with the vices of insincerity; dissembling, treacherous, mendacious, to an excess which surpasses even the usual measure of uncultivated society. Both are disposed to excessive exaggeration with regard to everything relating to themselves. Both are cowardly and unfeeling. Both are in the highest degree conceited in themselves, and full of affected contempt for others. Both are, in the physical sense, disgustingly unclean in their persons and their houses.

This is not the kind of people who could produce a Newton—indeed, their view of nature was, if possible, even more disgusting than themselves.

> No people, how rude and ignorant soever, who have been so far advanced as to leave us memorials of their thoughts in writing, have ever drawn a more gross and disgusting picture of the Universe than what is presented in the writings of the Hindus. In the conception of it no coherence, wisdom, or beauty, ever appears: all is disorder, caprice, passion, contest, portents, prodigies, violence, and deformity.

Upon examining in English translation the Hindu poetry highly praised by Jones, Mill found it to be filled with inflation, ridiculous metaphors, obscurity, tautology, repetition, verbosity, confusion, and incoherence; in short, it is "trifling and childish to a degree which those acquainted with only European poetry can hardly conceive."

Moreover, the Hindu love of drama cannot be taken, as it was by Jones, as indicative of a civilized sensibility. After all, the Chinese also love drama, and "our British ambassador and his retinue found their dramatic representations very rude and dull entertainments."

In addition, according to Mill literature is not the best measure of civilization. A more accurate measure would be provided by efforts more demanding of reason and objectivity, such as the writing of history. An objective recording of the facts of the past is practiced only when "reason begins to have considerable influence in the direction of human affairs." The Hindus, of course, have not produced any history worthy of name; even the best among them has "not yet reached that point of intellectual maturity."

Mill did not think Jones a malicious man. Jones, like most men, simply had a confused idea of what constituted civilization. And, like most men, he tried to magnify the importance of his own favorite pursuit. He might even have had a benevolent motive for his eulogies, thinking that if he "exalted the Hindus in the eyes of their European masters" he would somehow improve their lot. If he did think this, he understood the nature of government even less than he understood the nature of civilization. Mill, who confidently understood both, had put the Indians back in their proper place.

Yet he had done so without directly employing the idea of civilization he had criticized Jones for only partly understanding. Mill's judgments of the Hindus were usually relative, not absolute. He would, in practice, not judge them uncivilized, but rather less civilized than the Europeans, than the British. This practice seems to reflect more his perception of his readers than his perception of his subject. In the beginning, he only expected his readers to be capable of making relative judgments of value; only by the end of his history did he hope to have educated them to make absolute ones. Only by the end did he hope to have made his readers see Hindus and Europeans not just relative to one another, but both relative to an absolute standard of civilization. Just as Newton had made men envision the natural world in an absolute space and thereby made them see the indubitable principle of gravity, so Bentham, with the help of Mill, would make men envision the human world in an absolute space and thereby make men see the indubitable principle of utility.

Nevertheless, Mill had begun to prepare for this movement from the relative to the absolute even in his treatment of Indian civilization. He had, for example, occasionally praised the Indians at the expense of the British: even so primitive a society as this had written codes of law. On occasion, then, the readers got a glimpse of an absolute standard against which their society, too, could be measured.

This was the standard by which all human societies could be judged. The standard was, of course, the principle of utility.

During his discussion of Indian civilization, Mill was at ease with his readers. He was expressing his misgivings about Indian culture, but they were misgivings which were as complimentary to his British readers as they were to himself. A whole race of people without a single person as mature as ourselves. This left the readers enjoying their relatively civilized outlook, while Mill recounted at length the events leading to the complete subjection of India to British rule, a subjection which now seemed as inevitable as it was potentially laudable, the mature father-nation lending a civilizing hand to its immature son. This process Mill carefully described up to and including the reforms of Cornwallis. Then Mill stopped his narration, and began to evaluate British rule. Now the relationship with his reader was not so comfortable, for now the relative judging Mill had allowed his readers in the earlier section was allowed no longer. Now those who were being judged, and found wanting, were the British themselves.

Earlier Mill had used his readers' pride in themselves, encouraged it even. Now he condemned it. "Under the influence of a vulgar infirmity, that *Self* must be excellent, and everything which affects the pride of *Self* must have surpassing excellence, English institutions, and English practices, have been generally set up as a standard, by conformity or disconformity with which, the excellence or defect of everything in the world was to be determined." The British, in an exercise in self-flattery, had assumed that since their institutions were better than the Indians', they must be the best. The British consequently had imposed those institutions upon Indian society through the reforms of Cornwallis. The result Mill recounts at length. The result was disaster. Crime was rapidly increasing, and Indian society was drifting toward chaos. Why should better institutions have had such a negative effect?

This question gave Mill the opportunity to deliver his utilitarian message. The British legal system may well be better than the Indian; it is, however, by the absolute standard, quite flawed. The imperfections in the legal system make its success dependent upon men, not upon the laws themselves. When such an imperfect system is applied to a civilized society, the negative effects of the imperfections are softened by the civilized character of the men involved. However, when applied to an uncivilized nation, one whose members lack any sense of personal character, the same imperfections cause the whole system to collapse. This is what happened in India. Mill made the point as follows.

> A system of law, marked by so many infirmities, may, in a country like England, where crimes are easily suppressed, and where the sentiments and manners of the people accomplish more than the law, afford an appearance of efficacy, and get the credit of much of that order which it does not produce; but in a country like India, where a crime is difficult to repress, and where the law receives little aid from the sentiments and the manners of the people a far more perfect system is required.

Mill then sketched the reforms which would be needed if the system of laws was to operate independently of the character of the people ruled—the reforms were those Bentham had been advocating for years, everything from written legal codes to panopticon prisons. But these reforms alone, Mill admitted, would not be enough for India.

In order for India to become more civilized, her people had to develop more character, had to become more like the British, had to be educated. A massive colonization by British settlers would provide Indian society with the strong paternal hand it needed. Living among the Indian people, these settlers would come to understand the quirks of the Indians, and could then supply the particular information necessary for drawing up a comprehensive code of laws for India. Most importantly, these settlers, these civilized men diffused throughout India, would serve as an example to the Indians themselves. This example, almost as much as a rational legal code, would give the Indians a sense of character.

So, in the end, Mill returned to flattery. The source of British problems in India had been the egotistical self-congratulation to which, Bentham had proved, all men were prone. Mill hoped to gain his readers' assent to his analysis of the problem by praising them. If there were only more like you out there, things would be much better.

However, there was an edge to all this flattery, for you would be of no help out there if you continued to view your own institutions as perfect. You could be of help only if you could judge your own institutions and customs, as well as the Indians', against the objective standard of civilization itself. You could be of help only if you were a little more like the author of *The History of British India*.[3]

James Mill, perhaps because of this edge of criticism, doubted that his British readers would find his history sufficiently pleasurable to make it a popular success. He wrote a friend shortly before publication, "I am pleased with the quantity of instruction it will convey, though I am more than doubtful as to the entertaining qualities, by which alone reputation is acquired."

Whatever apprehension Mill had about the public reception of the *History*, he was sufficiently pleased with its intrinsic achievement that he now planned to give the world what Bentham had so long promised but had never quite delivered. Bentham had been publishing pieces suggesting reform of now this, now that part of law. History gave Mill the perspective to complete a whole system. He wrote to another friend, at about the time his history was published, concerning his future plans as follows.

> The next work which I meditate is a History of English Law, in which I mean to trace, as far as possible, the expedients of the several ages to the state of the human mind, and the circumstances of society in those ages to show their concord or discord with the standard of perfection; and I am not without hopes of making a book readable by all, and if so, a book capable of teaching law to all. And after this, I will do what I can to exhibit in full a system of Jurisprudence.

Mill wrote neither of these works, largely as a result of the success of his *History*. His readers apparently found his flattery pleasurable enough to make his reputation. Mill had now a reputation as a writer, and as an authority on the affairs of India. As such, he was appointed to a powerful post in the London office of the British East India Company. The post, although taking so much time as to prevent his ever doing the research requisite for his proposed history of English law, was nonetheless a source of considerable satisfaction for him. Three years after he was appointed his enthusiasm was undiminished. He wrote in a letter: "I must glory a little in my own virtue, for though I might procure a leave of absence for the asking, there are so many dispatches to answer and the happiness and misery of so many millions are affected by what I write, that I cannot find in my heart to abstract a day from the labours of this place." Bentham was, if anything, even more delighted: "I shall be the dead legislator of India, Mill the living."

While he was still working on his history, Mill had published an essay summarizing what he thought had to be done in India. Now, at India House, London, the very center of British Government of India,

Mill was setting about to do what he had earlier recommended to others as "now fit to Hindustan"—"a simple form of arbitrary government, tempered by European honour and European intelligence," a government in the true interest of the India people, a government "mild and paternal." However, one of his central contentions he never again mentioned, his contention that only a government centered in India itself could act effectively in its people's interest.

Even with his new duties, Mill did find enough time to finish some essays for a supplement to the *Encyclopedia Britannica*. These were all published by 1824, and were apparently well enough received to merit a separate printing by themselves in 1825 and again in 1828. Of all the essays, that entitled "Government" caused the most comment. (This one was even serialized in a newspaper.) In it Mill tried to deduce from utilitarian premises the ideal form of government.

Assuming that the happiness of an individual is determined by his pleasures and pains; assuming also that the end of government is to increase the collective happiness of men, "to increase to the utmost the pleasures, and to diminish to the utmost the pains which men derive from one another"; assuming also that governments are necessary because actions which contribute to individual happiness do not always add to the total happiness of the group—assuming all this, what form should government always take?

First a prior question: What forms of government are there? Mill agreed with the traditional answer that there are basically but three forms of government. The power to protect the group against the selfishness of the individual can be retained by the group, in which case we have a democracy, a rule by all. Or it can be delegated to one man, in which case we have a monarchy, a rule by one. Or it can be delegated to more than one man, in which case we have an aristocracy or oligarchy, a rule by a few. Assuming these are the three alternative forms of government, which form is the most rational, given the assumptions already made about the nature of man and the end of government?

In a pure democracy, the community as a whole must be assembled for the government to perform its operations. However, assembling the community "as often as the business of government requires performance almost precludes the existence of labor, hence that of property, hence the existence of the community itself." If a community was governed by democracy, soon the community would no longer possess anything worth protecting, hence government would no longer be necessary. A pure democracy, therefore, could not, from the very nature of the case, be an effective government, for it would tend to destroy rather than to protect the goods of the community.

Neither can an aristocracy or a monarchy be an effective government. The interests of a government, if it was monarchic or aristocratic, would not always be identical with those of the community as a whole. Members of a government, as we know from the principles of human nature, will always act in their own self-interest. (After all, if individuals and small groups were able to act consistently for the good of the community, then governments would not be necessary.) The governing group would, therefore, simply impose its caprice upon the people as a whole.

At this point Mill anticipated that his readers would want to glory a bit in their own virtue. He anticipated them saying that such knavery might be true of the common run of men, but there are some men who are above such things, who would act out of a sense of duty, who would act for the common good simply because it was their sacred public trust to do so. He anticipated them speaking generally of exceptional men, while they thought particularly of themselves. And so Mill spoke to his readers in a language he was sure they would understand, the language of flattery.

Obviously no men are farther advanced in human excellence than the English gentleman. This was a statement Mill's readers could accept, at least for the sake of argument, without supporting evidence. The English gentleman, therefore, may be taken as a "favorable specimen of civilization, of knowledge, of humanity, of all the qualities, in short, that make human nature estimable." What English gentleman could deny such a modest assumption?

However, as usual in Mill, flattery is the prelude to an unpleasant point. If the English gentleman possesses all that is estimable in human nature, then he becomes a test whether human nature, stripped of legal restraints, should be esteemed at all. If, when given absolute power, the English gentleman behaves selfishly, then so will all other men.

English gentlemen, when they did gain such power over their fellow man in the West Indies, behaved very selfishly indeed. These gentlemen, these epitomes of civilization, found themselves willing "not only to deprive their slaves of property, and to make property of their fellow creatures, but to treat them with a degree of cruelty, the very description of which froze the blood of their countrymen, who were placed in less unfavorable circumstances." If you, my readers, were placed in the unfavorable circumstances of running a West Indian plantation, you, Mill need not add, would do things even descriptions of which now would freeze your blood. With this little scholium on English gentlemen in the West Indies Mill's "closest deduction from the acknowledged laws of human nature" was confirmed by "direct and decisive experiments." No doubt remained that a monarchy or aristocracy, if unchecked, will reduce the rest of the community "at least to the condition of negroes in the West Indies."

If one tried to balance the monarchic and aristocratic elements within a single government, the result, Mill claimed returning to deduction, would eventually be the same. Sooner or later, one of the elements would get the upper hand, and "the moment one of the parties is superior, it begins to profit by its superiority, and the inequality is daily increased." Eventually, the superior part of the government would be able to treat the inferior part in just the way it treats the rest of society—namely, in the same way English gentlemen of the West Indies treat their slaves.

At this point, Mill had brought his readers to the central problem of the philosophy of government. Democratic government is desirable but impractical; aristocratic, or monarchic, government is practical but undesirable.

This problem is quite similar to that Bentham had faced long ago in his Panopticon plans. How can the inspector be made to act for the common good when it conflicted with his self-interest? He cannot, for men only act for their self-interest. Bentham revised the question. How can the common good and the inspector's self-interest be made identical? Make his continuance in the profitable position of inspector depend upon his acting for the common good; make him periodically stand for public review.

Mill in his essay "Government" does not mention Bentham's Panopticon, but his solution to the problem of good government is similar to Benthm's solution to the problem of good prisons.

Government had to be monarchic or aristocratic. However, the one or the few who rule must have the continuance of their rule dependent upon their acting for the common good. They must, therefore, submit to periodic democratic review.

> In the grand discovery of modern times, the system of representation, the solution of all the difficulties, both speculative and practical,

will perhaps be found. If it cannot, we seem to be forced upon the extraordinary conclusion, that good Government is impossible. For as there is no individual, or combination of individuals, except the community itself, who would not have an interest in bad Government, if entrusted with its powers; and as the community itself is incapable of exercising those powers, and must entrust them to some individual or combination of individuals, the conclusion is obvious: The Community itself must check those individuals, else they will follow their interest, and produce bad Government.

Having established that good government is possible only if the government is made to stand for periodic democratic elections, Mill concluded the essay by giving his judgments on a number of practical questions—most fundamentally, the question of what qualifications could be required of all voters without hurting the quality of government. If, for example, voting privileges were to be restricted to males over forty, would this lead to the reduction of those under forty to a state of slavery? To this particular question, Mill, himself now in his forties, answered in the negative, pointing out that most men over forty have at least one son under forty whose interests they have at heart—that is, whose interests they cannot distinguish from their own self-interest.

There remained one final delicate question for Mill to settle: how far down the social scale should suffrage be extended? Mill knew that his middle class readers would be little inclined to extend suffrage beneath themselves—after all, it was not in their interest to do so. Faced with this difficulty, Mill, as usual, resorted to flattery. The middle class, Mill reminded his middle class readers, "is universally described as both the most wise and the most virtuous part of the community."

> Another proposition may be stated, with a perfect confidence of the concurrence of all those men who have attentively considered the formation of opinions in the great body of society, or, indeed, the principle of human nature in general. It is, that the opinions of that class of the people, who are below the middle rank, are formed, and their minds are directed by that intelligent and virtuous rank, who come the most immediately in contact with them, to whom they fly for advice and assistance in all their numerous difficulties, upon whom they feel an immediate and daily dependence, in health and in sickness, in infancy and old age; to whom their children look up as models for their imitation, whose opinions they hear daily repeated, account it their honour to adopt.

(Presumably they had not heard of what happened to slaves in the West Indies.)

Continuing the flattery, Mill drew the implication. The lower classes, if enfranchised, would certainly vote for people of whom the middle class approved. And that would mean more votes for the candidates representing middle class interests. "There can be no doubt that the middle rank, which gives to science, to art, to legislation itself, their most distinguished ornaments, the chief source of all that has exalted and refined human nature, is that portion of the community of which, if the basis of Representation were ever so far extended, the opinion would ultimately decide. Of the people beneath them, a vast majority would be sure to be guided by their advice and example."

Mill admitted that lower class people in the city do sometimes riot—"the occasional turbulence of a manufacturing district," Mill called it. This, however, was only because in manufacturing districts, like in Bengal, not enough members of the middle class have settled there; and hence many a working man has "no virtuous family of the middle rank to sympathize" with his "afflictions." Mill, in conclusion, insisted the gentlepeople of the middle rank recognize that this urban deprivation of the working class would have no general effect on elections under universal suffrage.

> It is altogether futile with regard to the foundation of good government to say that this or the other portion of the people, may at this, or the other time depart from the wisdom of the middle rank. It is enough that the great majority of the people never cease to be guided by that rank; and we may, with some confidence, challenge the adversaries of the people to produce a single instance to the contrary in the history of the world.[4]

When Mill's essays for the encyclopedia supplement were reprinted in 1828, his essay "Government" was singled out for attack on the pages of the *Edinburgh Review* by Thomas Babington Macaulay, a writer whose own repution as a historian was soon to dwarf that of Mill. Little in Mill's deductive proof of the possibility of good government Macaulay found compelling.

Some of the deductions, according to Macaulay, did not seem to follow; in fact, Macaulay thought that sometimes one could as easily deduce from Mill's premises the opposite conclusion from that which he deduced. Perhaps one can deduce from the premise that all men act out of self-interest the conclusion that absolute rulers will not act in the interest of the people; but one could just as easily deduce the opposite conclusion.

> No rulers will do that which produces pain to themselves. But the unfavorable sentiments of the people will give pain to them. Therefore, no rulers will do anything which may excite the unfavorable sentiments of the people. But the unfavorable sentiments of the people are excited by everything which hurts them. Therefore no rulers will do anything which may hurt the people. Which was the thing to be proved.

And if Mill's deductions did not satisfy Macaulay, neither did the premises from which he deduced them. Mill, for instance, deduced that successful balanced governments were impossible from the premise that different parts of a government cannot be kept long at the same strength. But one can no more answer simply a question about what part of a government is stronger than one can answer simply whether England or France is the stronger country.

> For some purposes France is stronger than England. For some purposes England is stronger than France. For some neither has any power at all. France has the greater population, England the greater capital: France has the greater army, England the greater fleet. For an expedition to Rio Janeiro or the Philippines, England has the greater power. For a war on the Po or the Danube, France has the greater power. But neither has power sufficient to keep the other in quiet subjection for a month. Invasion would be very perilous; the idea of complete conquest on either side utterly ridiculous.

Mill was trying to answer in generalities questions which do not even make sense unless one speaks in specifics. This, according to Macaulay, was Mill's fundamental mistake. He used a method of arguing which was inappropriate to his subject. To be sure, geometers can reason effectively by deduction, but they are doing so from defined principles. Mill was not. Even granting that all men act out of what they take to be their self-interest, different men see their self-interest differently. We can only know what a man takes his self-interest to be through his actions, after the fact, if then. Once this is realized, the utilitarian principle becomes a mere truism. And a science of politics cannot be founded on a truism. A truism does not enable us to get behind the irreducible variety of men; it just pretends to. Truism or not, we must still admit that "man differs from man; generation from generation; nation from nation. Education, station, sex, age, accidental associations, produce infinite shades of variety." Or so Macaulay argued.

Macaulay was careful not to deny that a science of man is a possibility of the distant future; but, if there is to be such a science, it will have to be gotten through methods of inquiry in complete contrast to the *a priori* syllogizing of James Mill. As Macaulay put it, "We may hope to form a system as far inferior in pretension to that which we have been examining, and as far superior to it in real utility, as the prescriptions of a great physician, varying with every stage of every malady and with the constitution of every patient, to the pill of the advertising quack which is to cure all human beings, in all climates, of all diseases."

James Mill for himself dismissed Macaulay's attack upon his essay as an instance of a man who, finding reason to be against some cherished beliefs, turned upon reason itself. He refused to reply, at least directly. And, in a sense, he did not need to. By 1829 he and Bentham had begun to attract a significant following.[5]

Many of the new Benthamites, though not all, had been introduced to Bentham by James Mill. There was Francis Place, self-educated tailor and experienced labor agitator; George Grote, a banker and aspiring historian; David Ricardo, gentleman and political economist; John and Charles Austin, both lawyers. And these were not all. Among the rest was the new Benthamite James Mill liked the least, John Bowring—who, now that Mill was so independently busy at India House, had virtually supplanted Mill as Bentham's favorite.

George Grote, in his activities, was typical of the Benthamite inner circle. Grote, like the rest, actively worked in support of Benthamite reforms; he, in particular, led the group in their fight for the establishment of a university in London, and, when it was established, he worked to get professors as sympathetic as possible to the true philosophy appointed. (John Austin, for example, whose delicate health made an active legal practice impossible, soon became Professor of Law.) Grote, like the rest, wrote in support of specific Benthamite reforms; his "The Essentials of Parliamentary Reform" summarized the group's position on this issue. And, like the rest, he helped prepare some of the master's manuscripts for publication; Grote prepared *An Analysis of the Influence of Natural Religion on the Temporal Happiness of Mankind.* (When this was published in 1822, it appeared under a pseudonym, Philip Beauchamp, because Grote feared that his conclusion—the influence was bad—might open him to prosecution.*)

---

* And lest anyone think that it was only natural religion, religion ostensibly based upon reason, that contributed to the unhappiness of mankind, Francis Place edited Bentham's attack on Christianity, *Not Paul but Jesus*, which also

Grote did all these things. But most of all he shared the confidence of Bentham and the rest that they possessed the first principles which, if acted upon, could make mankind happy. As he put it, he believed that a society would be happy "if only one were permitted to assume, what the vehement imagination of Plato ventures to claim in his *Republic*, the coincidence of philosophy and power in the same hands." That happiness would result from such a coincidence, Grote knew with "infallible certainty."

To provide a forum for this growing number of supporters, Bentham established in 1824 the *Westminster Review*, a radical review which could counteract the influence of the conservative *Quarterly Review* and the moderate *Edinburgh*. In the *Westminster Review*, readers could find articles presenting the utilitarian point of view on a wide variety of subjects—they could find an article by John Austin attacking the law of primogeniture on the grounds that it was in conflict with the principle of utility ("the test to which it must be submitted is utility"); or one by James Mill stripping off the civilized facade of the *Quarterly* or *Edinburgh Review* to show the self-interest behind it; or they could find George Grote explaining the glory that was Greece, and explaning, by implication, the source of all cultural achievements ("What is the grand motive which produces that intense and exclusive devotion of mental powers to one end, without which excellence in no department is attainable? In this there is little difficulty. The motive, almost uniformily and without exception is, a strong desire for public applause."); or they could find Grote's wife Harriet arguing that the French nobility, and almost all others by implication, are a "most selfish, ignorant, and frivolous race"; or they could find the editor himself, John Bowring, describing Jeremy Bentham as possessing "the most acute and vigorous mind of the present age—that mind which has perhaps never been rivalled in any age in powers of logical deduction and comprehensive analysis."

Naturally it was on the pages of the *Westminster Review* that Mill's essay on "Government" received its defense. The exact authorship of the reply was not clear. At first Bentham himself was thought to have written it; Bentham, however, later insisted he had only provided memoranda for the defense, and had nothing to do with the actual

---

appeared under a pseudonym—this one with an elaborate first name, and a simple surname, Gamaliel Smith. In Bentham's opinion, Paul not Christ had founded Christianity, and had in the process perverted Christ's essentially utilitarian message.

writing. Like so much of his later writing, this one was presented to the world by the hand of a disciple.

The defense admitted the existence of "partial exceptions to the rule that all men use power as badly as they dare." These exceptions, however, do not in any significant way cast doubt upon the truth of the general rule; these men, after all, are really, in the defense's phrase, "freaks of nature." Morover, the defender did not understand how Macaulay could seriously suggest that a theory of government should not be deduced from the almost universal principles of human nature. "In the name of Sir Richard Birnie and all the saints, from what else should it be deduced?" Having defended Mill with such argument, the defender could conclude his essay with a celebration of the discovery of utility.

> Throughout the whole horizon of morals and politics the consequences were glorious and vast. It might be said, without danger of exaggeration, that they who sat in darkness had seen a great light. The mists in which mankind had jousted against each other were swept away, as when the sun of astronomical science arose in the full development of the principle of gravitation. . . . All the sublime obscurities which had haunted the mind of man from the first formation of society—the phantoms whose steps had been on earth, and their heads among the clouds—marshalled themselves at the sound of this new principle of connection and of union, and stood a regulated band where all was order, symmetry, and force. What men had struggled for and bled, while they saw it but as through a glass darkly, was made the object of substantial knowledge and lively apprehension. The bones of sages and of patriots stirred within their tombs, that what they dimly saw and followed had become the world's common heritage. And the great result was wrought by no supernatural means, nor produced by any unparalleled concatenation of events. It was foretold by no oracles, and ushered by no portents, but was brought about by the quiet and reiterated exercise of God's first gift of common sense.

However well this might have expressed the Benthamites' view of themselves, such writing could not be intended to impress readers who were not yet confident that utility had stirred the bones of sages and patriots within their tombs. Macaulay, for one, remained unpersuaded.

> The humble mechanic who discovers some slight improvement in the construction of safety-lamps of steam vessels does more for the happiness of mankind than the 'magnificent principle' . . . will do in ten thousand years. The mechanic teaches us how we may in a small degree be better off than we were. The utilitarian advises us with great pomp to be as well off as we can.

Macaulay, thinking that Bentham had written the unsigned defense, remarked, "Mr. Bentham seems to us to act much as Sir Isaac Newton would have done if he had gone about boasting that he was the first person who taught bricklayers not to jump off scaffoldings and break their legs." And when Bentham disavowed complete authorship of the piece, claiming to have just given a disciple some notes from which the final version was written, this gave Macaulay the opportunity to importune him to "endeavor to find better editors for his compositions."[6]

Despite his ridicule of the Benthamites' conviction that they had penetrated to first principles, Thomas Macaulay like other Whigs could and did agree with them on specifics. Macaulay agreed with many of Bentham's specific criticisms of the legal system. He also agreed with Mill that suffrage should be broadened. In the late twenties there was growing sentiment for a reform in the electoral system. Within Parliament the movement was in fact led by members of Macaulay's party, the Whigs. Outside Parliament, agitation was led, at least some of the time, by avowed Benthamites.

The problem was the conservative block in Parliament, especially in the House of Lords. The Benthamite analysis of the situation was straightforward. The reform was not in the self-interest of the members of Parliament, especially the Lords, since it would in effect require them to vote more often for the common good, and less often for their own selfish ends. These conservative members of Parliament must be made to perceive this reform to be in their self-interest. They must be made to perceive their situation if the reform is passed to be more pleasurable than if it is not. In short, they must be threatened.

As one of the leading Benthamite agitators, Francis Place, is supposed to have said, "*We must frighten them*. . . . No reality we can create will be sufficient for our purpose. We must work on Lord Grey's imagination. We must pretend to be frightened ourselves. We must send him a parcel of London shopkeepers—men who are, many of them, really frightened—who will tell him they cannot answer for the safety of the city if the just demands of the people are trifled with." As one of the other Benthamites put it in retrospect, "Much was said that no one really believed." And just in case some of the Benthamites were a little squeamish about consciously misrepresenting the situation, James Mill in 1830 published in the

Westminster Review an essay arguing with great philosophical force that prevarication for the common good, since it was simply withholding information from those who did not deserve it, was "meretricious." (James Mill, like Bentham, occasionally confused "meretricious" with "meritorious.")

The Reform Bill was finally passed in 1832. On the strength of their identification with it, the Benthamites elected a significant number of sympathizers to the House of Commons, at least fifty. There were great hopes that the Benthamites, with a few more elections, would soon challenge the strength of the Whigs and the Tories. According to one plan, the Whigs would eventually be forced to decide whether they would align themselves with the Benthamites or with the Tories.

Actually, however, it was the Benthamites who were faced with the difficult choices. They, in practice, could gain strength only at the expense of the Whigs; yet opposing the Whigs meant opposing the best legislation they could, in practice, hope to get passed. This choice split the Benthamites. They found electoral politics a less suitable environment than Mill had found the oligarchic bureaucracy.

In less than a decade the Benthamites had ceased to be a significant factor in Parliamentary politics. By 1838, few of the Benthamites were left in Parliament, and one of the few who was, George Grote, wrote a friend, "Our contemporary politics are in a state of profound slumber, from which I fear they are not likely to awake, except to cause us disgust and discouragement. There is nothing in them fit to occupy the attention of a commonplace but sincere patriot, much less of a philosopher." (When this term of office expired, Grote refused to stand for reelection.) The triumph of the reform bill, and the succeeding election, were in fact the beginning of the decline of the Benthamite movement.

Jeremy Bentham himself did not live to see this decline. In fact, he did not even live to see the triumph. Bentham died the day before the Reform Bill was finally made law.

On his death bed Bentham seemed concerned that his own life might be interpreted as having contradicted his first principles. He offered a rebuttal. "I am a selfish man, as selfish as any man can be. But in me, somehow or other, so it happens, selfishness has taken the shape of benevolence."

Bentham would probably have not been surprised to discover that the *Edinburgh Review* would not accept this final self-assessment.

When his dying words became public, a writer for the *Review* suggested that the truth of the matter was almost the opposite. Bentham should have said, "I am a benevolent man; but in me, somehow or other, benevolence has taken the shape of vanity."

Almost immediately after the death of Bentham, John Bowring, with the assistance of another Benthamite John Hill Burton, began work on an edition of Bentham's writings. Bentham's analysis of his own benevolence was reported in a lengthy memoir Bowring wrote for the edition. Burton supplied an introduction in which he tried to assess his master's achievement. (Burton thought this introduction important enough that he had it reprinted at the end of a one volume selection from Bentham's writings he edited, *Benthamiana.*)

Burton, of course, did not fail to mention Bentham's many practical reforms. In the style of the master himself, he carefully enumerated twenty-nine measures which Bentham had advocated and were subsequently adopted by the Parliament. He listed, moreover, another ten proposals of Bentham which, while not yet adopted, had gained what Burton called " a considerable and respectable class of supporters."

Nevertheless, these achievements were listed by the way. Burton's introduction was entitled "Introduction to the Study of Bentham's Works." His readers were those future generations who would turn to Bentham for the principle which would guide them in the continuing transformation of the human jungle into a garden. These readers he wished to convince that it was not Bentham's successful reforms which constituted his enduring achievement, rather it was his use of the principle of utility, the principle of the greatest good for the greatest number.

> It was not the principle itself, that constituted his discovery, but his rigid adherence to it in all his expositions—his never losing sight of it, in what he did himself or called upon others to do. He did not say that the world had hitherto been ignorant of such a principle. . . . He found, indeed, that it was at the root of all systems of religion and morality; that all codes of law were more or less founded upon it; and that it was, in all places and at all times, an unseen and unacknowledged guide to human action. But he was the first to bring forth this guide, to prove to the world that it should be followed implicitly, and to show that hitherto, from not keeping their guide in view, men had often wandered from the right path.

Burton's plea to his readers was not to wander from the right path. It was a plea Burton felt he had to make. He had to make it because Bentham, for all his wide success in practical reforms, had not been widely successful in making people see clearly the principle which he saw. "His general principle has received few adherents, in comparison with the number who have adopted his detailed applications of it. There is no project of change, or plan of legislative reform, in which it has been adapted; there are many who accede to his practical measures, while repudiate his general principle."

Burton was not here criticising Bentham for spending too much time attending to practical reforms. He was rather criticising men of little reason, the capricious men who refused to base their decisions on philosophical first principles. And he was doing so in 1838, when such men had just destroyed the Benthamites as an effective political party.

Bentham died at a happier time. When he wrote his will he did not doubt that he would be revered by an ever widening circle of followers, revered as the man who had put mankind permanently on the right path. Everything about the treatment of his remains should be consistent with his principle of utility. He left specific instructions to assure that as much use as possible was made of his corpse. First it was to be dissected for medicine; and, then, what was left was to be put to a more specialized use. Newton's apple had not been preserved as an object of worship. Future Benthamites would have no such regrets. Bentham's body was to be preserved and reverenced like a relic or mummy; it was to be what Bentham termed his "auto-icon."

His disciples carried out his instructions. His auto-icon was made as he directed. Then it was donated to the University of London, which they had helped found, to be displayed in a glass case, much as Bentham had wished Newton's apple could have been.

Into the twentieth century, Jeremy Bentham was still there, sitting on a chair, perched as if waiting, his dissected remains covered by his favorite suit, his right hand propped by his favorite cane, his eyes shaded by his favorite hat, unblinking eyes, blank to the world he had favored with his own vision.[7]

CHAPTER EIGHT

JAMES MILL AND JOHN STUART MILL
(1808-40)

After the publication of his *History*, James Mill was to write, apart from a textbook on economics, but one more influential book before his death in 1836. Moreover, this one, written during his vacations from India Office, was substantially finished by the time of Macaulay's attack on his essay on government. The ideas of the book were largely derived from earlier thinkers, especially John Locke, David Hume, and David Hartley, all of whom Bentham had cited as forerunners of Benthamism. The book was not, however, a further application of the principle of utility. Rather it was an attempt to derive utility itself from even more fundamental principles of human nature. It was to derive utility by, as Mill entitled the work, *An Analysis of the Phenomena of the Human Mind*. He had long wished to write such a work; he had long wished, as he put it to Francis Place, "to make the human mind as plain as the road from Charing Cross to St. Paul's."

Mill began his analysis with a quotation from John Locke: "I shall inquire into the original of those ideas, notions, or whatever else you please to call them, which a man observes and is conscious to himself he has in his mind; and the way the understanding comes to be furnished with them." Here was a piece of empirical research that did not need the time required of the historical. The experience was supplied not by historical research, but rather by personal introspection. Mill was going to make an analysis of "that which a man observes and is conscious to himself he has in his mind." As a researcher, Mill would only have to analyze what he had observed and was conscious to himself he had in his mind. As a writer, Mill would then assist his readers in analyzing what they individually could observe in their own minds.

This put Mill in a, for him, unusual relationship with his readers. Mill could not present to his readers any direct evidence of how their own minds worked, for Mill could not directly observe his readers' minds. Only his readers, individually, could do that. So Mill could only argue indirectly. He could describe what he finds in his own mind, and hope that his readers would find the same within their own. If a reader objected that his mind did not work like that, all that Mill could do was urge him to look again. It behooved Mill, therefore, to proceed slowly, almost painfully, and to be continually solicitous of his readers' progress.

This care is found even in words Mill chose to express his decision to begin the analysis with the sensations, "the most simple, at least the most familiar, of mental phenomena." Mill, the maker of unqualified denunciations of Indian civilization, was more careful here, careful not to offend a reader who was not quite sure that sensations are the simplest phenomena he finds in his own mind.

That sensations are, in fact, the simplest of all mental phenomena was a central thesis of Mill's *Analysis*. Mill's first step in proving this to his readers—or "learners" as he consistently called them—was to have them develop the habit of perceiving their sensations as a class of feelings. Mill promised that once this was learned, then his learners would be prepared to analyze "more mysterious phenomena" and to make these phenomean mysterious no more.

The habit could be learned only through repetition. So Mill slowly guided his readers through every general type of sensation, helping them perceive distinctly sensations of Smell, Hearing, Sight, Taste, and Touch. (The general categories seem to have been capitalized to make an impression, although not as great an impression as the more general category "SENSATION.") The five senses were not the only kinds of sensations that Mill included in his enumeration; his readers were also invited to recollect Sensations of Disorganization (the pains of cuts, burns and the like), Muscular Sensations (the pleasures of exercise, the pains of muscular fatigue), Sensations of the Alimentary Canal (the pains of hunger, the pleasure of a full stomach, the pains of indigestion). The inclusion of these final three categories of sensation show the disciple of Bentham at work carefully enumerating, and through this enumeration managing to include more pains and pleasures among the ultimate simples of the mental world.

The readers, having learned to see sensations as a distinct class of mental phenomena, having learned it so thoroughly that it was now a habit of mind, were now prepared to analyze more mysterious mental phenomena. The key to this analysis Mill could fit in a single sentence. "It is a known part of our constitution, that when our sensations cease, by the absence of their objects, something remains." After the sun has set, I can still think of it, and I can distinguish my thinking of the sun from my seeing it. Such a mental entity, such a copy, image, or trace of my sensation of the sun Mill named an "IDEA." And having so named it, he paused to make certain no reader had been left behind. "It is of great importance, before the learner proceeds any farther, that he should not only have an accurate conception of this part of his constitution; but should acquire, by repetition, by complete familiarity, a ready habit of marking those immediate copies of his sensations, and of distinguishing them from every other phenomenon of his mind."

In order to assist the readers to form fully this second desired habit of mind, Mill slowly worked through ideas copied from each of the eight kinds of sensation. Mill showed the readers, or rather invited the reader to show himself, that the idea was indeed different from the sensation of which it was the remains. He showed this for all eight, from those of the sensations of sight—"We can think of those colors in the dark"—to those based on occurrences in the alimentary canal—"Indigestion is the name of the idea, in which the feelings of the intestinal canal are mainly concerned." At the end of this habituating process, Mill paused to praise his readers, albeit tentatively, on the progress he hoped they had made. "If the illustrations I have employed have enabled my reader to familiarize himself with this part of his constitution, he has made great progress towards the solution of all that appears intricate in the phenomena of the human mind."

What Mill meant by "the solution of all that appears intricate" is the demonstration that mental phenomena which seem to transcend the world of the senses, really do not. Ideas which seem to transcend the world of the senses are really only residues of sensations. These sensations tie the mental world to the physical world, a physical world which, thanks to Newton, is now known to be ordered. If the life of the mental world could be reduced to sensation, then the mental world would be reduced to the physical, and man would be as completely exhaustible by rational principles as the planets are.

Ideas make the human mind appear more "intricate" than the physical world. Both Henry More and René Descartes were convinced that because man actively thinks he must be spiritual. Now Mill's readers had made sufficient progress in solving the phenomena of the mind to begin to question Descartes, More, and those like them. Man thinks ideas, but ideas are originally caused by sensations. Of course, merely showing that ideas originated in sesnsation was not quite to solve all the intricacy associated with them. However ideas originate, once we have them we seem frequently able to use them as we please, we can think them in almost any order or combination we wish—moreover, these orders and combinations themselves appear so intricate, so diverse that they might be taken to transcend the material. They, if not the ideas themselves, might not be causally tied to the Newtonian universe.

This intricacy Mill perceived as the last major impediment to a complete foundation for the philosophy of mind, an impediment his readers, with his help, would remove once they understood the great principle of the association of ideas. This was the principle which, according to Mill, gave to utility its ultimate psychological basis. This was the principle which contained the principle of utility as but a special case.

> Thought succeeds thought, idea follows idea, incessantly. If our senses are awake, we are continually receiving sensations, of the eye, the ear, the touch, and so forth; but not sensations alone. After sensations, ideas are perpetually excited of sensations formerly received; after those ideas other ideas; and during the whole of our lives, a series of those two states of consciousness, called sensations, and ideas, is constantly going on. I see a horse: that is a sensation. Immediately I think of his master: that is an idea. The idea of his master makes me think of his office; he is a minister of state: that is another idea. The idea of a minister of state makes me think of public affairs; and I am led into a train of political ideas.

A series of sensations is obviously related to a series of causes in the physical world. And this series, however intricate in appearance, is reducible to physical laws. But can a series of ideas also be tied to similar causes? According to Mill, it can be by what he calls the "General law of the 'Association of Ideas' ": "Our ideas spring up, or exist in the order in which the sensations existed, of which they are the copies." In other words, the order of our ideas is, in fact, determined by the order of our sensations. For instance, ideas which usually occur successively are found, upon analysis, to be the residues of sensations which usually occur successively. Likewise, ideas which occur simultaneously are the residues of sensations which occur simultaneously. In this way, Mill enumerated twelve such specific instances of the general law or principle of the association of ideas and thereby hoped to dispel virtually all the mysteriousness of the human mind.

Once this was done, Bentham's own philosophy could be deduced quite easily. The readers could not deny, could they, that all sensations were not equally desirable? Nor could they object, could they, when Mill named the desirable, "Pleasure," the undesirable, "Pain"? Then Mill had only to invoke the association of ideas to derive Bentham's own analysis of human motivation. "When the idea of the Pleasure is associated with an action of our own as its cause; that is, contemplated as the consequent of an action of ours, and incapable of otherwise existing; or when the cause of a Pleasure is contemplated as the consequent of an action of ours, and not capable of otherwise existing; a peculiar state of mind is generated which as it is a tendency to action, is properly denominated MOTIVE."

A man, to use Mill's own example, is tempted to commit adultery with the wife of a friend. "The composition of the motive is obvious." However, the man also associates with the idea of the adultery a variety of pains, the hurt he would do the friend, his own pains of guilt later on. Does he choose to commit the adultery? That will depend entirely upon which motive is stronger, whether the pleasure associated with the adultery is greater than the pain associated with the aftermath.

Mill had reached the same point as Bentham, but here the psychological foundation given Bentham's reasoning, the foundation in association, enabled Mill to take a step omitted by Bentham. Bentham, faced with the fact that some men do indeed commit adultery could only assess the advisability of adding a law against adultery to the list of pains the potential adulterer would have to contemplate. Mill, however, could suggest a more fundamental remedy. The fact that some men do commit adultery was, for Mill, simply "a case of bad Education; and one highly unfortunate for the value of the pleasures in question is infinitely outweighted by the value of the pains. The business of a good education is to make the associations and the values correspond." Education, the creation of the proper set of associations (much as Mill had tried to do for the reader of his *Analysis*), was another means for the amelioration of the human race.

Just as a legislator could mold society, so an educator could mold the invidual. Moreover, in this molding process the educator has a significant advantage over the legislator. The legislator can hope only to control men's actions from without, by imposing laws upon them; the educator, in contrast, could hope to control men's actions from within, by permanently affecting their character. The subjects of the legislator would always see themselves as distinct from his laws; remove the laws and they will revert to their earlier behavior. In contrast, the subjects of the educator, if he has gotten complete enough control over them early enough, will be unable to distinguish themselves from the character he had molded them into. The subjects would be what the educator wanted long after the educator no longer had any direct control over them, *if* the educator had complete enough control, early enough.[1]

James Mill appears to have seen this implication of Bentham's philosophy long before he described it in print. In fact, within a year after he met Bentham he had begun to act upon it. Within a year he had set about making the character of his three-year-old son, John Stuart.*

Bentham, needless to say, took at the time an active interest in the process. One reason Bentham is supposed to have arranged for the Mills to live with him during the summers was so to allow him personally to observe young John's progress. And when in 1812 James Mill was taken seriously ill, Bentham quickly wrote to Mrs. Mill offering, if the worst happened, to take charge of John Stuart Mill's education. After it became clear that the worst was not likely to happen, James Mill himself responded to Bentham's offer.

> If I were to die any time before this poor boy is a man, one of the things that would pinch me most sorely, would be, the being obliged to leave his mind unmade to the degree of excellence, of which I hope to make it . . . . [T]he only prospect which would lessen that pain, would be the leaving him in your hands . . . . [T]hen we may perhaps leave him a successor worthy of both of us.

While John Stuart Mill was a potential successor worthy of both of them, he was also more to them than that. He was, in his very person, a test of the older men's philosophy. Could human beings be shaped to pre-conceived ends by a careful controlled environment? This was the test that was John Stuart Mill, the kind of test Macaulay had implied Benthamism would never survive.

That John Stuart was to be such a test was apparently common knowledge among those close to the Benthamites. One of these, Francis Place, reported to James Mill his exchange with a mutual acquaintance who was unsympathetic to the Benthamite philosophy:

> Wakefield is a believer in innate propensities . . . and so fully is he satisfied of the truth of his theory, that he expects to see your

---

* John Stuart Mill was named after Sir John Stuart, a conservative member of Parliament who was James Mill's patron at the time. The second son, born in 1814, was named James Bentham Mill.

John's innate propensities break out presently and form his character...
The position I take against him is that the generality of children are
organised so nearly alike that they may by proper management be
made pretty nearly equally wise and virtuous.

Like Place, Bentham and James Mill were not worried. As soon as
John's education began to progress, his father placed the young boy
in charge of the instruction of Mill's other children. He made it in
John's interest to teach the other children well by making the boy as
culpable for their mistakes as he was for his own.

The situation was reminiscent of the Panopticon. Bentham had,
after all, suggested that the inspection principle would be useful in
schools as well as prisons. In 1815, partly at least inspired by the
progress of John Stuart, Bentham published his *Chrestomathia*, which
adapted the Panopticon to the use of schools. Now the school master
occupied the position of inspector. He was supposed to sit at the
center of nine circles of desks, those desks being divided into groups
just as the prison had been divided into cells. The master was to sit in a
special swivel chair which would enable him to turn in an instant to
inspect any section of the school. What was to be taught was a chrestomathia, a collection of all that was useful for human beings to know
for the sake of the greatest happiness. This collection, Bentham
thought, could be organized into a large table, or tree of knowledge
as he once called it.

The school was to be built in the garden of Bentham's city house.
Francis Place was put in charge of the practical arrangements. However, from the first, James Mill, applying Benthamite psychology to
the master himself, had warned Place, "Bentham may, and will
probably, work round to finding it a nuisance in his garden." By 1817,
when Place had raised half the money necessary for building the
school, Mill was still warning him that "there are a multitude of
disagreeables connected with it [the building of the school in the
garden] which he [Bentham] will not at present allow himself to
think, but which will swell into great objections hereafter." Trees
would have to be taken down, the whole garden disrupted. Still
Place persevered with his fund raising, and by 1820 was ready to
start the building. Then Bentham withdrew the offer of his garden;
and, Place being unable to raise the additional money to buy a
suitable site, the project was dropped.

The Chrestomathia school never became more than a figment of
Benthamite imagination. John Stuart Mill was more than that. He had

been carefully guided through the classics, mathematics, science (theories, he later complained, but no experiments), logic, political economy, history, law. He had even studied literature, and tried his hand at poetry. (His father believed that since poetry is so commonly overvalued, it is useful to be able to write it.)

By 1821, at the age of fifteen, John Stuart Mill still had not read Bentham. He had, however, for years been carefully prepared for the moment he first would. And when he finally did read Bentham, his reaction, at least as he recollected it in his autobiography, was all that his father and Bentham could have hoped it to be.

> My previous education had been, in a certain sense, already a course of Benthamism. The Benthamic standard of "greatest happiness' was that which I had always been taught to apply . . . . Yet in the first pages of Bentham it burst upon me with all the force of novelty. What thus impressed me was the chapter in which Bentham passed judgment on the common modes of reasoning in morals and legislation . . . deduced from phrases like "law of nature," "right reason", "the moral sense," "natural rectitude," and the like, and characterized them as dogmatism in disguise, imposing its sentiments upon others under cover of sounding expressions which convey no reason for sentiment, but set up sentiment as its own reason. It had not struck me before, that Bentham's principle put an end to all this. The feeling rushed upon me, that all previous moralists were superseded, and that here indeed was the commencement of a new era of thought.

With this discovery of Bentham, Mill's formal education had ended. In the next five years he emerged as a new leader in the Benthamite movement. His acitivities on behalf of the movement were numerous. He formed a study group for the purpose of exploring the foundations of the Benthamite philosophy. Some of the members themselves, most notably J. A. Roebuck and Eyton Tooke, became prominent Benthamites. Mill named the group the Utilitarian Society. "Utilitarian" soon began to challenge "Benthamite" in common usage. (A movement which insisted on the importance of measures rather than men was, after all, more appropriately named after its principle than after its founder.) His father found him a position working directly under him at the East India Company where he too could begin to help shape the future of India. When the *Westminster Review* was founded, John Mill helped his father research the lead article for the first issue, and then he himself wrote a continuation of it which appeared in the second. Soon John Stuart Mill had become the most frequent contributor to the *Review*. He also contributed to another Benthamite organ, *Parliamentary History and Review*, a periodical devoted to showing, among other things, how the members of Parliament appealed "to the Passions, the Prejudices, and the Ignorance of mankind." And it was John Stuart Mill, not his father, who, when the *Parliamentary Review* began publication in 1825, was given the honor of the lead article in its first issue. John Mill, also, during this time, was preparing a five volume edition of Bentham's writings on legal evidence. He was also participating in, and helping organize, public debates on subjects of importance to utilitarians.

One of his speeches from such a debate, one given in 1823 before the Mutual Improvement Society, might be taken as representative. The speech, "On the Utility of Knowledge," argued against the "ascetic sophistry" which maintains that the progress of civilization has not increased human happiness, that "the Hurons and Iroquois are the happiest and the most enlightened of mankind." While admitting that such a position is "scarce worth refutation," Mill, nonetheless, supplied one. If we are only clear about what we mean by knowledge—the value of civilization, Mill assumed, is the value of its knowledge—then the issue virtually resolves itself. By knowledge Mill meant useful knowledge, that which "teaches men how to increase the sum of human happiness." If we understand this by "knowledge," then "to say that knowledge can be an enemy of happiness is to say that men will enjoy less happiness, when they know how to seek it, than when they do not." Of course, no one could sincerely argue such a position. Therefore, those who do must be attempting to promote their own self-interest at the expense of the common good—they are practicing the kind of sophistry that has been practised for centuries by priesthoods and aristocracies, by those who "would wish to see the great mass of mankind subject to the despotic sway of nobles, priests, and kings." But these forces of despotism and superstition are now finally in retreat, and, while much remains to be done, the future of mankind is secure. "Knowledge has triumphed. It has worked the downfall of much that is mischievous. It is in vain to suppose that it will pass by and spare any institution the existence of which is pernicious of mankind."

John Stuart Mill was, in short, being a very good utilitarian and, what was the same thing, a very good son. James Mill and Jeremy Bentham had expected nothing else. They certainly had not expected what came next.[2]

From the winter of 1821, when I first read Bentham, and especially from the commencement of the Westminster Review, I had what might truly be called an object of life; to be a reformer of the world. My conception of my own happiness was entirely identified with this object. The personal sympathies I wished for were those of fellow labourers in this enterprise . . . . This did very well for several years during which the general improvement going on in the world and the idea of myself as engaged with others in struggling to promote it, seemed to fill up an interesting and animated existence. But the time came when I awakened from this as from a dream. It was in the autumn of 1826. I was in a dull state of nerves, such as everybody is occasionally liable to; unsusceptible to enjoyment or pleasurable excitement; one of those moods when what is pleasurable at other times, becomes insipid or indifferent; the state, I should think, in which converts to Methodism usually are, when smitten by their first "conviction of sin." In this frame of mind it occurred to me to put the question directly to myself: "Suppose that all your objects in life were realized; that all the changes in institutions and opinions which you are looking forward to could be completely effected at this very instant: would this be a great joy and happiness to you?" An irrepressible self-consciousness distinctly answered, "No!" At this my heart sank within me; the whole foundation on which my life was constructed fell down. All happiness was to have been found in the continual pursuit of this end. The end had ceased to charm, and how could there even again be any interest in the means? I seemed to have nothing to live for.

This was how Mill in his autobiography described what he called "The Crisis in My Mental History." Whatever the cause of this crisis, it ended almost as unexpectedly as it began. He emerged from it while reading the memoirs of a minor French playwright—in particular, he was reading the passage where the playwright's father died. "I was reading, accidentally, Marmontel's 'Mémoires' and came to the passage which relates his father's death, the distressed position of the family, and the sudden inspiration by which he, then a mere boy, felt, and made them feel that he would be everything to them—would supply the place of all that had lost." Upon reading this, Mill, for reasons he never claimed to understand, began to weep. This weeping proved to him that he could experience deep emotion, that he had not yet been completely dried up by reason, that he was still a person and not a thing. "I was no longer hopeless: I was not a stick or a stone. I had still, it seemed, some of the material out of which all worth of character, and all capacity for happiness are made."

In discovering that he was not a stick or a stone, that he was not to be treated as a thing, John Mill, at least as he recollected it in his autobiography years later, believed he had discovered a limitation to utilitarianism. However useful logical analysis was in the creation of the greatest happiness for others, such analysis cannot be applied to oneself without killing all chance for happiness. This newly discovered importance of the emotions, of the feelings of the individual which for his own sake he must not submit to analysis, began to appear almost immediately in Mill's essays. In particular, it appeared as his insistence upon the importance of poetry.

Mill did admit that the opposition between poetry and science was fundamental. "The one addresses itself to the belief, the other to the feelings. The one does its work by convincing or persuading, the other by moving. The one acts by presenting a proposition to the understanding, the other by offering interesting objects of contemplation to the sensibilities." In admitting this, Mill felt he was just expressing an opposition which everyone already felt was there—and "where everyone feels a difference, a difference there must be." This was the new John Stuart Mill, allowing feeling to lead reason.

Everyone may well have felt the opposition, but not everyone, particularly among the utilitarians, chose to express this difference in a way that gave to poetry any positive function at all. If asked about poetry, most of the utlitarians would have answered as Newton is supposed to have—poetry is "a kind of ingenious nonsense." They would have concurred with Bentham's statement of the difference, as the difference between truth and falsity.

> Indeed, between poetry and truth there is a natural opposition . . . . The poet always stands in need of something false. When he pretends to lay his foundations in truth, the ornaments of his structure are fictions; his business consists in stimulating our passions, and exciting our prejudices. Truth, exactitude of every kind, is fatal to poetry.

A writer in the first volume of the *Westminster Review* was as uncompromising. Echoing James Mill's condemnation of infantile Hindu efforts at poetry, he asserted that the poet attempts to make the mind of man once again be "cradled in infantine weakness."

The utilitarian dismissal of poetry was taken to its extreme in "The Four Ages of Poetry" of Thomas Love Peacock, subordinate of Mill at India House and occasional contributor to the *Westminster*.

> A poet in our times is a semi-barbarian in a civilized community. He lives in the days that are past. His ideas, thoughts, feelings, associations, are all one with barbarous manners, obsolete customs, and exploded superstitions . . . . [I]t is a lamentable spectacle to see minds,

capable of better things running to seed in the specious indolence of these empty aimless mockeries of intellectual exertion. Poetry was the mental rattle that awakened the attention of intellect in the infancy of civil society: but for the maturity of mind to make a serious business of the playthings of its childhood, is as absurd as for a full-grown man to run his gums with coral, and try to be charmed to sleep by the jingle of silver bells.

How was Mill to account for this opposition to poetry by men of his own enlightened party? In his essay "The Two Kinds of Poetry," he attributed it to innate propensities—there were people who had a poetic nature, and there were people who did not.

> It seems undeniable in point of fact, and consistent with the principles of a sound metaphysics, that there are poetic *natures*. There is a mental and physical constitution or temperament, peculiarly fitted for poetry. This temperament will not of itself make a poet, no more than the soil will the fruit; and as good fruit may be raised by culture from indifferent soils, so may good poetry from naturally unpoetic minds. But the poetry of one, who is a poet by nature will be clearly and broadly distinguished from the poetry of mere culture.

Mill was speaking primarily about the writing of poetry, but the distinction between poetic and unpoetic natures could also, Mill believed, be extended to the poetic audience, the readers of poetry. Very few readers, he emphasized, will be able to distinguish the verse of a poet by nature from that of a poet by culture. To the many the natural poetry will not seem truer, will not be more useful; it will, however, be different for the few, and "in those few it will find a keener sympathy, and will yield them a deeper enjoyment." John Mill was here separating company with the bulk of his utilitarian brethren, but at least he was doing it in tone of voice that was familiar to them; it was the assured tone so often employed by his father.

How critical John Mill had become of his earlier philosophy was underlined by some "Remarks on Bentham's Philosophy," as he called them, which he wrote the year after Bentham's death. In these Mill did praise Bentham as the founder of the science of legislation; this achievement was "his exclusively and can be shared by no man." Yet the stature of this achievement was diminished when Mill proceeded to criticize Bentham for taking insufficient account of irreducible variety of government, a variety imposed by historical circumstance. Bentham did not realize that for a legitimate government, one that would have the support of the governed, historical continuity was more important than philosophical consistency. Severe as it was, this was not Mill's severest criticism of Bentham.

If as a philosopher of government Bentham was limited, as a moral philosopher he was, according to John Mill, simply a failure. The primary role for a moral philosopher was not that of a scientist enumerating, analyzing, and categorizing human motives. (Anyway, human motives, as Bentham failed to realize, were innumerable.) Rather it was to provide an example. The moral philosopher is to write to those whose "feelings of virtue are weak." The moral philosopher should inspire the morally weaker. He should manifest "in every sentence and every line, a firm unwavering confidence in man's capability of virtue." "A noble mind assimilates other minds to itself." Bentham, unfortunately, did not have a noble mind in that sense. "Upon those who *need* to be strengthened and upheld by a really inspired moralist . . . the effect of such writings as Mr. Bentham's, if they be read and believed and their spirit imbibed, must either be hopeless despondency and gloom, or a reckless giving of themselves up to a life of that miserable self-seeking, which they are there taught to regard as inherent in their original and unalterable nature."

Mill sent these remarks to a friend who was writing a popular book on their contemporary England. He later said he was surprised when the "Remarks on Bentham's Philosophy" appeared verbatim as an anonymous appendix to the book. He had also sent some remarks on his father. These appeared, although John Mill insisted substantially changed, as a second anonymous appendix.

The "Remarks on the Philosophy of James Mill" criticized him on the same grounds Bentham was criticized in the first appendix. James Mill was said to be unable to inspire mankind to be better because "something despondent and unelevating clings round his estimate of its powers." Poetry was even used to express James Mill's lack, his lack in effect of a poetic faculty.

> He possesses little of—
>   "the vision and faculty divine"—
> nor is it through his writings, admirable as they
> are, that we are taught—
>   "To feel that we are
>   greater than we know."

Mill might have mentioned, although he did not, that in describing the man who, having imbibed the spirit of Benthamism, was left in despondency, Mill was describing himself—or at least himself as he once had been. Mill might also have mentioned something else he did not. He might have mentioned that in describing the noble spirit who would assimilate lesser ones, he was also describing himself as he wanted himself to be, and perhaps already was beginning to be.

Bentham believed he could make mankind happy through his reason, and the body of laws which would be its natural fruit. Bentham, in short, wished to be a philosopher-king. Mill also wished to be a philosopher-king, but his kingship, unlike Bentham's, would be just partial, extending only over weaker men, then only until they reached maturity. And Mill would rule them not through laws, but through his person, through the nobility of his character. Jeremy Bentham, the fecund philosopher, was to be to mankind a lawgiver; John Stuart Mill, the fecund philosopher, was to be to mankind a father.[3]

In 1835, after James Mill was diagnosed mortally ill with tuberculosis, John Mill's own health suddenly began to deteriorate. He suffered headaches, facial tics, stomach pains, and breathing difficulties. After his father died in 1836, the son improved, although his stomach continued to bother him throughout the rest of his life. And he never lost the facial tics.

In fact, in 1836 one of his friends thought his physical condition so deteriorated that he described him as a "scrae," a Scottish name for anything shrivelled and stunted as if by heat. "Mill himself talked much, and not stupidly—far from that—but without emotion of any discernible kind. He seemed to me to be withering or withered into the miserablest metaphysical scrae, body and mind, that I had almost ever met with in the world. His eyes go twinkling and jerking with wild lights and twitches; his head is bald, his face brown and dry—poor fellow after all."

The description was that of Thomas Carlyle, one of Mill's recently made non-utilitarian friends. John Mill, since his recovery from his first mental crisis, had been investigating the work of a wide range of contemporary thinkers, both through their writings and, when possible, through personal contact. Carlyle was one of the few British thinkers whom Mill during this time had sought out to offset the narrowness of his utilitarian background. French thinkers, such as Auguste Comte, were more numerous among the list of new-found mentors. Carlyle and Comte each thought for a time that Mill was going to become a disciple. However, Mill was no longer to be the disciple of any other man. He was, in the end, looking for a balance to his father and Bentham, not a substitute for them. When he finally tried to express this balance he was attempting to achieve, he used Samuel Coleridge, a man who was esteemed at least as much as a poet as he was as a thinker, and, perhaps more importantly, a man who like Jeremy Bentham and James Mill had recently been put in his grave.

In Samuel Coleridge Mill could not have selected someone who appeared more opposite to Bentham. To be sure, John Bowring had tried to argue in the *Westminster Review* that Coleridge's poetry was, at least in spirit, whether the poet himself realized it or not, Benthamite. But, even in this attempt, with which few of his brethren would have agreed, Bowring had to admit that Coleridge's prose was anything but utilitarian. When Coleridge wrote prose, Bowring explained, he was "not his own man."

How else could Bowring, the conscious Benthamite, explain Coleridge, the purported Benthamite, writing a book entitled *The Statesman's Manual or the Bible the Best Guide to Political Skill and Foresight*? And the book which bore this title realized all the worst apprehensions the Benthamite might have had concerning it, from its epigraph, which implied that all law was pre-eminently traditional, to its appendix, which attacked the very attempt to make morals scientific. The epigraph was a selection from the Seventy-eighth Psalm which began, "For He established a testimony in Jacob and appointed a law in Israel; which He commanded our fathers, that they should make them known to their children." The appendix was even more painful.

> The commercial spirit, and the ascendency of the experimental philosophy which took place at the close of the seventeenth century, though both good and beneficial in their own kinds, combined to foster its corruption. Flattered and dazzled by the real or supposed discoveries which it had made, the more the understanding was enriched, the more did it become debased; till science itself put on a selfish and sensual character, and *immediate utility*, in exclusive reference to the caprices of the social, and the ambition of the political, man was imposed as the test of all intellectual powers and pursuits. Worth was degraded into a lazy synonym of value; and value was exclusively attached to the interest of the senses.

No readers of *The Stateman's Manual* could have been surprised at finding Coleridge elsewhere dismissing associationist psychology

as "neither tenable in theory, nor founded in facts." Nor could they
have expected otherwise when Coleridge said, "Newton was a great
man, but you must excuse me if I think that it would take many
Newton's to make one Milton." (Nor could they have been surprised to find even Coleridge's poetry singled out for ridicule in
Peacock's "Four Ages of Poetry".*)

So, Benthamites could not have been alone in seeing an opposition between what Bentham believed and what Coleridge believed.
No one had ever questioned that Bentham the radical and Coleridge
the conservative presented a remarkable contrast, that their opinions
on most subjects were not just different, but contradictory. Bentham
or Coleridge, radical or conservative, you had to choose between
them—or, at least, you could not choose both.

John Mill disagreed. In a pair of essays, one on Bentham, the
other on Coleridge, he wished to persuade his readers that Bentham
and Coleridge simply saw parts of a greater whole. Bentham perceived "those truths with which existing doctrines and institutions
were at variance"; Coleridge perceived "the neglected truths which
lay *in* them." Bentham's fault was that he did not trust the common
experience of mankind enough; Coleridge's that he trusted it too
much. Bentham's strength was that he saw opinions from the outside; Coleridge's that he saw them from the inside. Bentham saw
farther than most men because he saw less than they did; Coleridge
saw farther because he saw more. The followers of Bentham were
the first carefully to deduce from their assumptions about society;
the followers of Coleridge were the first "to inquire systematically
into the inductive laws ... of society."

The contrast, even as Mill presented it, could not seem more
complete. It was that between James Mill and Macaulay all over
again. It could not seem more complete, and yet it was phrased in

---

* There Coleridge's poetry was described as "visions in verse"—these visions
had as their sources "village legends from old women and sextons," "the dreams
of crazy theologians," "the mysticisms of German metaphysicians." "These
disjointed relics of tradition and fragments of second-hand observations, being
woven into a tissue of verse, constructed on what Mr. Coleridge calls a new
principle (that is no principle at all), compose a modern-antique compound of
frippery and barbarism, in which the puling sentimentality of the present time is
grafted in the misrepresented raggedness of the past into a heterogeneous congeries
of unamalgamating manners, sufficient to impose on the readers of poetry, over
whose understanding the poet of this class possesses that commanding advantage,
which, in all circumstances and conditions of life, a man who knows something,
however little, always possesses over one who knows nothing."

a way to leave no doubt that both Bentham and Coleridge *saw*. They
saw the corrupt state of British society, and they saw that an attention to first principles was the only hope for reformation. On this
basis Mill could conclude, "We hold that these two sorts of men,
who seem to be, and believe themselves to be, enemies, are in reality
allies. The power they wield are opposite poles of one great force
of progression."

Mill did not give a detailed description of this great force, apart
from his description of its two poles. But he did express his hope
for the future, and his conviction of the importance of these two
men for that future. "Whoever could master the premises and com-
bine the methods of both, would possess the entire English philosophy of his age."

The readers might not have yet mastered the premises of both,
nor have even begun to see how the methods of both could be combined. John Mill, however, obviously had, and had thereby gained
a vision of the whole, and of the great moral improvement of which
mankind is undeniably capable. He assured them he sees this, and
not a sentence, not a line showed any hesitance in this assurance.
So his noble mind assimilated his readers to himself, or at least
tried.[4]

CHAPTER NINE

JOHN STUART MILL
(from 1840)

The reaction among John Stuart Mill's utilitarian colleagues to his vision was not favorable. They did not see a force of progression so broad as to encompass the political pronouncements of Samuel Coleridge. All they saw was their most promising young philosopher straying, self-deluded, far from Bentham's philosophy. Francis Place wrote, "I think John Mill has made great progress in becoming a German metaphysical mystic." And Harriet Grote had begun to refer to him as "that wayward intellectual deity."

Mill was, however, undeterred by such carping. Moreover, he continued to regard himself as a utilitarian. He remained, for instance, a great admirer of his father's *Analysis of the Human Mind*—in particular, of its treatment of the principle of association. In reviewing a history of moral philosophy in 1833, John Mill became incensed that the historian had treated this principle as a trivial commonplace.

> So little does Mr. Blakey comprehend of the theory which resolves all the phenomena of the mind into ideas of sensations connected together by the law of association, that he does not even see anything peculiar in the doctrine. Association itself, he will not allow to be a distinct principle or fact in human nature. It is as the faculty of memory. Just so we may conceive, on the appearance of Newton's *Principia*, some mind of the same character objecting to the theory of *gravitation*, that there was nothing in it but the ancient and familiar fact of *weight*.

Mill recommended to Mr. Blakey to read James Mill's *Analysis*, the work which had done more to establish the principle of association that any other.

John Mill actually found in the conclusion to his father's *Analysis* a guide for his own future work. In that conclusion, James Mill had tried to assess what he had accomplished. "The phenomena which characterize man as a thinking Being, have been brought forward, have been carefully resolved into their component elements, and traced to certain general and indisputed laws." While James Mill did not claim to have finished this theoretical portion of psychology, he did make allowances for those readers who might disagree with him on this point. He reminded them that even if the theoretical branch of psychology were perfected, there would remain much to be done in "another great branch, the Practical." James Mill thought this branch could be conveniently treated in three books:

    I. The Book of Logic; containing the Practical Rules for conducting the mind in search after Truth:
    II. The Book of Ethics; or the Book of Rules for regulating the actions of human beings, so as to deduce from them the greatest amount of good, both to the actor himself, and to his fellow-creatures at large;
    III. The Book of Education; or the Book of Rules, for Training the Individual to the greatest excellence of his nature; that is, to his highest possible state of efficiency (ability and will included), as cause of good to himself, and to his species.

John Stuart Mill, in effect, accepted his father's public advice. He sought to reform utilitarianism from within, by working out the practical branch of the doctrine of the human mind. In the late 1820's he had already begun his first book, which also happened to be the first book on his father's list, *A System of Logic*.[1]

The System of Logic was finally published in 1843. John Mill claimed for it no originality save that required "to cement together the detached fragments of a subject matter never yet treated as a whole; to harmonise the true portions of discordant theories, by supplying the links of thought necessary to connect them, and by disentangling them from the errors with which they are always more or less interwoven." In treating the logic of the moral sciences, the final subject of *The System of Logic*, this meant harmonizing Bentham and Coleridge, supplying the links between Thomas Macaulay and James Mill.

Can there ever be a science of human nature? Some, such as Coleridge, with his emphasis upon art and genius, seemed simply to deny that there ever could be. Man is by nature free and, as such, is not a suitable object for scientific inquiry. The methods of science might be useful in the prediction of a planet or projectile, but they can lead only to misunderstanding when applied to persons. Such an application will make a person, who is by nature free, appear to be determined. Science in search of human nature can never come to a satisfactory end, for it can never find what it seeks. A science of man is not possible.

On this point, Mill was certain Coleridge and those who agreed with him merely misunderstood the question. The controversy over the freedom of the will, over the liberty or necessity of human actions, was itself the result of a simple misunderstanding, a misunderstanding about what is properly meant by "necessity." The libertarians object to necessity because they think it to be, as Mill put it, "inconsistent with everyone's instinctive consciousness," the consciousness that he is responsible for his own actions. In short, they believe that necessity is inconsistent with moral notions. This, Mill was sure, is not so.

All the doctrine of necessity requires is that "if we knew a person thoroughly, and knew all the inducements which are acting upon him, we could foretell his conduct with as much certainty as we can predict any physical event." Everyone, Mill was certain, believes this as much as he believes himself to be responsible for his own actions. Moreover, we do not feel these two certainties to be in conflict. That is to say, we do not feel them to be so until either the necessitarian or the libertarian overstates his portion of the truth, until one of them tries to make us mistake part of the truth for the whole of it. Hence both sides of this controversy are right, and neither of them is.

Of course, this might seem too simple, too easy, particularly to those on each side of the debate. They, both sides, might wish to insist that the debate is real. To be sure, we both feel ourselves free and feel others to be predictable. To be sure, we believe that we can shape both our own character and that of others. These are the conflicting appearances which occasion the debate; restating them does not resolve it. These appearances are inconsistent with one another. If we are to have a coherent philosophy of man, we must choose, we must decide, somehow, which of the alternatives is fundamental. Does a man ever shape his own character, or is his character really only an effect of external causes? Are a man's actions, in principle, always predictable, or does he sometimes make a choice which could not be expected? Argue, choose, they might say, or give up any hope for a coherent understanding of man's nature.

They might say this, but they would not be heard. All that was heard was the calm, confident voice of John Mill. The whole debate was "one of the most signal instances in philosophy of abuse of terms." The advocates of free will were closer to the truth in their practical feelings, Mill was sure; and not a line indicates the slightest doubt. The advocates of necessity, on the other hand, were closer to the truth in their theoretical doctrine, Mill was also sure; and his self-confidence was contagious. There was no fundamental conflict between the two positions, Mill was convinced; and not a sentence betrayed the slightest doubt. Who could demur?

Not all the opponents of Benthamism would directly deny that a science of man was possible. Some—a Macaulay, perhaps—might answer the Benthamite assertion with a doubt rather than a denial. They would doubt that we now do have a science of human nature and further doubt that, given past failures, such a science is a reasonable expectation for the near future.

Such doubts, however, were also based upon a confusion of ideas, Mill was certain. Mill was certain of this even though he admitted that we do not at present have a complete science of human nature, nor does it appear likely that we ever will.

> The impressions and actions of human beings are not solely the result of their present circumstances, but the joint result of those circumstances and of the characters of the individuals; and the agencies which determine human character are so numerous and diversified, (nothing which has happened to the person throughout life being without its portion of influence,) that in the aggregate they are never in any two cases exactly similar. Hence, even if our science of human nature were theoretically perfect, that is, if we could calculate any character as we can calculate the orbit of any planet, *from given data*; still, as the data are never all given, nor ever precisely alike in different cases, we could never make positive predictions, nor lay down universal propositions.

The science of man, therefore, could never be the perfect science Newtonian astronomy was. However, this did not mean that the science of man was a futile enterprise, for there are degrees of science. Mill, though it might seem so, had not conceded the main point of the objection. He had not. This, he thought, would be obvious to anyone who properly understood what constituted a suitable subject for scientific inquiry: "Any facts are fitted, in themselves, to be subject of science, which follow one another according to constant laws; although those laws may not have been discovered, nor even be discoverable by existing resources."

No one doubts that the weather is a suitable subject for scientific inquiry, even though the basic laws of meteorology are neither now known nor seem discoverable by existing resources. Therefore, no one should doubt that human nature is a suitable subject for scientific inquiry. In fact, we do already know a few fundamental laws of human nature. Any reader who doubted this Mill referred to "Mr. James Mill's *Analysis of the Phenomena of the Human Mind,* where the principal laws of association, along with many of their applications, are copiously exemplified, and with a masterly hand."

So some laws of human nature—namely, the laws governing the association of ideas—had been discovered by what Mill called "the ordinary methods of experimental inquiry." Therefore, although we do not now have, nor ever will have, a complete science of man, psychology does provide a foundation for such a science, and does make it, at least in principle if not in practice, possible to predict the formation of human character.

> Excepting the degree of uncertainty which still exists as to the extent of the natural differences of individual minds, and the physical circumstances on which these may be dependent (considerations which are of secondary importance when we are considering mankind in the average, or *en masse,*) I believe most competent judges will agree that the general laws of the different constituent elements of human nature are even now sufficiently understood to render it possible for a competent thinker to deduce from those laws, with a considerable approach to certainty, the particular type of character which would be formed in mankind generally by any assumed set of circumstances.

Except for the degree of uncertainty, most competent judges, Mill believed, would agree that a competent thinker could, with a considerable approach to certainty, practice the science of man, even though none has yet done so. Despite these qualifications, Mill insisted, ethology, the science of the formation of human character, "may be called an Exact Science of Nature."

It might be thought that Mill had given only lip service to the truth felt by Coleridge and those of like mind. The concessions made to them were only in practice, and not in principle. They were not concessions about the nature of man. But when Mill turned from talking of the individual in himself to the individual in his relation to social change, the importance of the freely creating individual of genius became central. Here Mill turned his back upon the utilitarian insistence on the importance of laws over men. It is great men, and not rational measures, which change the world.

> I believe that if Newton had not lived, the world must have waited for the Newtonian philosophy until there had been another Newton or his equivalent. No ordinary man, and no succession of ordinary men, could have achieved it . . . . Eminent men do not merely see the

coming light from the hill-top; they mount on the hill-top and evoke it; and if no one had ever ascended thither, the light in many cases, might never have risen upon the plain at all.

It is in social improvement that great individuals exercise the most decisive influence; in most cases "it is the existence of great men which decides even whether there shall be any progress." If such progress, even in astronomy, were only a matter of science, only concerned with matters of fact, then great men would not be so important. However, such progress is dependent upon something more; it is dependent upon art. To distinguish between the logic of art and that of science was the concluding task of Mill's *System*.

"Now, the imperative mood is the characteristic of art, as distinguished from science. Whatever speaks in rules or precepts, not in assertions respecting matters of fact, is art; and ethics and morality is properly a portion of the art corresponding to the science of human society." Science can tell us what will happen if we follow a certain course of action. Art can then tell us whether or not we should follow that course. Science supplies us with means; art with ends. The definition of ends constitutes the "peculiar province" of art.

It is the peculiar province of art, and it is the peculiar province of great men. It is the destiny of a great man to set the ends for which other men will strive; it is his destiny to call forth the dawn. John Mill concluded his *System of Logic* by modestly expressing his hope that he had set such an end, called forth the beginning of such a dawn.

> With these remarks we close this summary view of the application of the general logic of scientific inquiry to the moral and social departments of science. Notwithstanding the extreme generality of the principles of method which I have laid down, (a generality which, I trust, is not in this instance synonymous with vagueness,) I have indulged the hope that to some of those on whom the task will devolve of bringing those most important of all sciences into a more satisfactory state these observations may be useful, both in removing erroneous and in clearing up the true conceptions of the means by which, on subjects of so high degree of complication, truth can be attained. Should this hope be realised, what is probably destined to be the great intellectual achievement of the next two or three generations of European thinkers will have been in some degree forwarded.[2]

So John Mill tried in 1842 to communicate his vision of a unified philosophy through his *System of Logic*, and he tried again in 1859 in his *On Liberty*. This was the work which answered his father's call for a book on the second major subject of practical ethics, a book on ethics "for regulating the actions of human beings, so as to deduce from them the greatest amount of good, both to the actor himself, and to his fellow creatures at large." The subject was his father's but the thesis Mill defended was not.

> The object of this Essay is to assert one very simple principle, as entitled to govern absolutely the dealings of society with individuals in the way of compulsion and control whether the means used be physical forces in the form of penalties, or the moral coercion of public opinion. That principle is, that the sole end for which mankind are warranted individually or collectively, in interfering with the liberty of action of any of their number, is self-protection. That the only purpose for which power can be rightfully exercised over any member of a civilized community, against his will, is to prevent harm to others. His own good, either physical or moral, is not a sufficient warrant. He cannot rightfully be compelled to do or forbear because it will be better for him to do so, because it will make him happier, because, in the opinions of others, to do so would be wise, or even right. These are good reasons for remonstrating with him, but not for compelling him, or visiting him with any evil in case he do otherwise. To justify that, the conduct from which it is desired to deter him, must be calculated to produce evil to someone else. The only part of the conduct of any one, for which he is amenable to society, is that which concerns others. In the part which merely concerns himself, his independence is, of right, absolute. Over himself, over his own body and mind, the individual is sovereign.

While Mill had written in his *Logic* that the libertarians fostered a much higher sense of "self-cultivation"—their practical feelings were better—he had, in his resolution of the logical differences between the libertarians and the necessitarians, awarded the most fundamental point to the necessitarians: a science of man was possible. Now, when writing of self-culture, Mill gave the most fundamental point to the libertarians: over himself, the individual is sovereign, his integrity must be respected. "Human nature is not a machine to be built after a model, and set to do exactly the work prescribed for it, but a tree, which requires to grow and develop itself on all sides, according to the tendency of inward forces which make it a living thing."

The orthodox Benthamite would not have agreed. Should not, he would ask, the same means which proved useful to prevent an individual from hurting someone else be employed to make him do good for himself? Should not a Panopticon prisoner, for his own sake, be made to blow his nose on a handkerchief? Here, Mill was prepared with an answer which drew on Bentham's own careful enumerations of pleasures and pains, and of the circumstances which affect their intensity.

Men are, in fact, extremely different in their sources of pleasure and susceptibilities to pain. Men should be left to their own judgment as to what constitutes happiness for themselves individually, as long as that does not hurt any one else. "Different persons require different conditions for their spiritual development, and can no more exist healthily in the same moral, than all the variety of plants can in the same physical, atmosphere and climate."

Here, however, the Benthamite could propose an even more difficult objection. Unless Mill was giving up the principle of utility as the ultimate principle for moral judgments—which he stated explicitly he was not—then it might be that the total pleasure resulting from an imposed uniformity of ends would outweigh the pain suffered by those exotic individuals who required a different climate. After all, there was nothing sacred about any individual; what was sacred was the greatest good for the greatest number. One man must die that a nation might, in sum, be a little happier.

This objection could be put in a softer way. Of what general use was liberty? Even granting that some few individuals would benefit greatly from it, would it not in sum be disruptive to the happiness of society as a whole? Mill admitted that to make his point he had to show "those who do not desire liberty, and would not avail themselves of it, that they may be in some intelligible manner rewarded for allowing other people to make use of it without hindrance."

This statement of the problem was consistent with Mill's treatment of his readers from the very beginning of *On Liberty*. He assumed that his readers, while not against the doctrine of liberty, did not see it in general terms because its broader applications did not directly apply to them. Their own self-interest, as far as they understood it, was comfortably realized within the established rules of society. So they were in favor of, say, freedom of opinion, only as long as the opinions were moderate opinions moderately expressed. This was because they were not originators; they were rather the plains on which the light of a new dawn falls only eventually, and only falls at all because the new dawn has been called forth by someone on a peak.

Once they admitted that they were only the plains, then they would also recognize that it was in their own self-interest to allow liberty for those on the peaks. Liberty is useful because liberty is a necessary condition for genius. And it is genius, not tinkering, that improves mankind, that brings new dawns. Geniuses are, in Mill's phrase, "the salt of the earth; without them, human life would become a stagnant pool." This was an unpleasant truth for Mill's readers to have to admit. They had to admit that, without the influences of geniuses, they would become like a stagnant pool, that they would live their own lives, as Mill put it pointedly, "like cattle, not like human beings." This would not be a truth his readers wanted to hear, but Mill was firm in telling them it, in insisting upon it, in insisting upon it emphatically. "I insist thus emphatically on the importance of genius, and the necessity of allowing it to unfold itself freely both in thought and in practice, being well aware that no one will deny the position in theory, but knowing also that almost every one, in reality, is totally indifferent to it . . . . Originality is the one thing which unoriginal minds cannot feel the use of." Almost everyone is indifferent to it, everyone but the geniuses themselves who "can only breathe in an atmosphere of freedom."

The greatest number must, therefore, recognize, however humbling the recognition, that it was in their interest to allow the few who need liberty to have it—the greatest number must not "complain of the Niagara river for not flowing smoothly between its banks like a Dutch canal." They rather must support a state which permits such diversity; they must support it, as Mill emphatically insists in the last paragraph of *On Liberty*, because "the worth of a State, in the long run, is the worth of the individuals composing it" and "with small men no great thing can really be accomplished."[3]

James Mill had wished, as the third part of practical psychology, for a "Book of Rules, for training the Individual to the greatest excellence of his nature; that is, to the highest possible state of efficiency (ability and will included), as cause of good to himself, and to his species." And in his final act of filial obedience, John Mill produced, as near as he could, that for which James Mill had wished.

He could not produce exactly what James Mill had wanted, for John Mill had also to be true to the Coleridge side of his vision, and that side told him of the irreducible variety of individuals. He could not then write a book of rules for the education of all individuals; he could only write the story of one individual, an individual who perhaps had reached his own highest possible state of efficiency.

This John Stuart Mill did in his *Autobiography*, written when he was the most famous living British philosopher, and first published in 1872, the year after his death.

So Mill recounted his early education, and also acknowledged his debt to his father—the second chapter of the autobiography is entitled "Moral Influences in Early Youth. My Father's Character and Opinions." He also recounted his mental crisis, and acknowledged those such as Carlyle and Coleridge who helped him express the inadequacies he then saw in the Benthamite philosophy. Coleridge, Mill said, of all poets had described his feelings during his crisis:

> Work without hope draws nectar in a sieve,
> And hope without an object cannot live.

These two opposing forces in his education, these two opposing influences Mill believed he could synthesize into a consistent whole. He found he was, whatever his relative mental talents, "much superior to most of my contemporaries in the willingness and ability to learn from everybody; as I found hardly any one who had made such a point of examining what was said in defence of all opinions, however new or however old, in the conviction that even if they were errors, there might be a substratum of truth underneath them, and that in any case the discovery of what it was that made them plausible, would be a benefit to truth." So Mill recounted how he struggled to show the single substratum of truth he saw in both Bentham and Coleridge. In the midst of his struggle, according to his *Autobiography*, he discovered a person who embodied the new unity which he sought—he discovered his vision embodied not in an older man, but in a woman his own age. Mrs. Harriet Taylor was for more than a decade Mill's confidante and frequent companion, and then, after her husband died in 1850, his wife.

The closeness of his early relationship with her had caused consternation among his fellow Utilitarians. James Mill, in particular, disapproved, but the son would not yield. In fact, John Mill broke with all of his friends who disapproved of his relationship with Harriet Taylor, including Thomas Carlyle and one of the original members of the Utilitarian Society, J. A. Roebuck. As Roebuck later told it, he disapproved of Mill's relationship with Mrs. Taylor not just because of the scandal it caused the Utilitarian movement. "Mill's intellect bowed down to the feet of Mrs. Taylor. He believed her an inspired philosopher in petticoats; and as she had the art of returning his own thoughts to himself clothed in her own words, he thought them hers, and wondered at her powers of mind, and the accuracy of her conclusions."

Mill, who was struggling to reconcile the rational with the poetic, found in Harriet Taylor a poetic nature with whom he could become one. She was, he said, "a woman of deep and strong feeling, of penetrating and intuitive intelligence, and of an eminently meditative and poetic nature."

All that Mill himself had struggled for years to achieve by the efforts of hard intellect, Harriet Taylor, it seemed to him, had naturally intuited. No wonder he compared her to the, for Mill, most natural of poets, Shelley—at twenty-three, when Mill first met her, Harriet Taylor was Shelley's equal in natural poetic temperament. In intelligence, however, Shelley "so far as his powers were developed in his short life, was but a child compared with what she ultimately became."

What she became was partly influenced by Mill himself. He assisted in the development of her intellectual side. What she eventually became was a person who integrated both sides of human nature, a person who embodied the unification of these opposites in just the way Mill had said it could be done, but apparently never had quite achieved within himself.

His own role in Harriet Taylor's development into what she eventually became, Mill admitted but did not emphasize—"to her, who had at first reached her opinions by the moral intuition of a character of strong feeling, there was doubtless help as well as encouragement to be derived from one who had arrived at many of the same results by study and reasoning." Rather he emphasized Harriet Taylor's role in his own development—"the benefit I received was far greater than any which I could hope to give. "This benefit was not just from the poetic side of Harriet Taylor's nature. For, as Mill himself had predicted, when the two sides of human nature were unified, the result would dwarf the achievements of either side separately. And so Mill would insist that his intellectual debts alone to Harriet Taylor were "almost infinite." The point Mill made over and over and over again about Harriet Taylor is exemplified by what he said of her when writing of his relationship with Carlyle:

> I did not, however, deem myself a competent judge of Carlyle. I felt that he was a poet, and that I was not; that he was a man of intuition which I was not . . . . I never presumed to judge him with

any definiteness, until he was interpreted to me by one greatly superior of us both—who was more a poet than he, and more a thinker than I—whose own mind included his, and infinitely more.

Harriet Taylor proved in her person the truth of John Stuart Mill's vision of human nature, just as John Stuart Mill himself, it had been hoped by his father, was to have proven the truth of Bentham's vision of human nature. And if John Mill could get his readers to see Harriet Taylor as he saw her, then those readers would perhaps see the vision of mankind with which, in Mill's mind, she was associated.

John Mill and Harriet Taylor, after their marriage, continued to discuss, as Mill put it, "all subjects of intellectual and moral interest" —to discuss them in "much greater depths than are usually or conveniently sounded in writings intended for general readers." Out of such discussions in their married life came *On Liberty*, the work which, with the possible exception of his logic, Mill believed would prove to be his most lasting. Harriet Taylor was the inspiration for this work, and to her it was dedicated: "To the beloved and deplored memory of her who was the inspirer, and in part the author, of all that is best in my writings—the friend and wife whose exalted sense of truth and right was my strongest incitement, and whose approbation was my chief reward—I dedicate this volume."

Their married life together was not long. Harriet Taylor Mill died unexpectedly in 1858 during a trip they were taking through the south of Europe—and there she was buried. Mill, in his *Autobiography*, described what he had done to ease his lasting grief at her loss.

> Since then I have sought for such alleviation as my state admitted of, by the mode of life which most enabled me to feel her still near me. I bought a cottage as close as possible to the place where she is buried, and there her daughter (my fellow-sufferer and now my chief comfort) and I live constantly during a great portion of the year. My objects in life are solely those which were hers; my pursuits and occupations those in which she shared, or sympathized, and which are indissolubly associated with her. Her memory is to me a religion, and her approbation the standard by which, summing up as it does all worthiness, I endeavor to regulate my life.

Mill must have hoped that the readers of his *Autobiography* would understand why he gave homage at the grave of Harriet Taylor and not at the icon of Jeremy Bentham. He must have hoped that these readers would now understand the last line of his dedication of *On Liberty*—"Were I but capable of interpreting to the world one half the great thoughts and noble feelings which are buried in her grave, I should be the medium of a greater benefit to it, than is ever likely to arise from anything that I can write, unprompted and unassisted by her all but unrivaled wisdom." And that they would believe in his vision of Harriet Taylor even though they had never seen her, and that they would believe in his vision of human nature, even though John Stuart Mill, unprompted and unassisted, could never make them see it.[4]

Mill did try to communicate his vision in his system of logic, in his essay on liberty, in his autobiography. He tried, through these works, to communicate his vision. But, despite this lifetime of effort, the generation of philosophers who were coming to maturity at the time of his death, those of that generation who believed themselves to be evoking the dawn of a philosophical golden age—they, upon seeing the dawn, decided that John Stuart Mill could never have imagined it. They were certain it had occurred in spite of him.

PART III

HISTORY

CHAPTER TEN

THE OXFORD HEGELIANS AND T. H. GREEN
(to 1867)

The new generation of British philosophers were unsparing in their criticisms of Mill. They felt justified in being ungenerous because they saw clearly how all the contradictions with which Mill had lived for so long could be resolved. They saw clearly because they now understood the meaning of history. And when they understood this, then they understood how all the principles which previous generations of philosophers thought irreconcilable were but the opposite poles of the one great force of progress. This force Mill, despite his pretences to the contrary, had never seen, for he had never seen that history was the process whereby the Ideal becomes conscious of itself as the Real.

Of all this new generation of British philosophers, none could explain the meaning of history with greater clarity than Edward Caird. And nowhere is Caird's explanation of history more accessible than in his collected *Essays on Literature*. In particular, Caird had used his understanding of history to explain something which had deeply troubled Mill, what Caird called "the old quarrel of poetry and philosophy."

Caird admitted that the procedures of the poet and the philosopher do seem irreconcilably opposed. Poetry is, of its essence, "spontaneous and even unconscious." Here philosophical reflection seems to have no place.

> The poet cannot be one who has had to trample upon his natural life in order to make room for moral freedom, or one who has lost the vividness of the sensuous present in order to grasp at an idea. He must remain at one with himself as in happy childhood, and maintain an unbroken life in spite of all fightings within and contradictions without. For if he does not, a false note will get into his song; it will become a wail for a lost past, a complaint against time and fortune, or an aspiration after the unattainable, instead of an echo of the divine word that "all is good."

Because of this spontaneity, this happy childishness, this confidence that all is good, the poet become "a free channel for a power that works in him like a natural force." Living in fruition, the poet is certain that nature, if allowed her fullest expression through his voice, will resolve "all fightings within and contradictions without." He will, in short, "be able to see good in the heart of evil."

According to Caird, the true contrary of poetry is not philosophy but science. The scientist is always dividing, analyzing the world, searching for the atoms which he assumes are its essence. In his procedures he always assumes that the world is mechanical not organic, dead not living, indifferent to good and evil, purposeless. The poet, faced with the scientist's analysis of the world, will simply assert that it is false, that there is a deeper truth, one to which the scientist is blind.

> The Atoms of Democritus
> And Newton's Particles of Light
> Are sands upon the Red sea shore
> Where Israel's tents do shine so bright.

So wrote the poet William Blake, but such eloquence could scarcely be expected to convince the proponents of scientific analysis. They will not accept the poet's private vision, no matter how beautiful; they require arguments. And here the philosopher can complement the poet, at least according to Caird.

The philosopher, the true philosopher, does not mistake science for philosophy. He does not regard himself as a kind of scientist. Unlike the scientist, and like the poet, he is always "in search of a deeper truth in things than that which is the object of science." He is like the poet, but he is also different. Like the poet, he knows that however promising the scientist's procedures appear for a time, they must always end in failure, in self-contradiction. But, unlike the poet, he knows this rationally. He can demonstrate the limitations of science by arguments the scientist, however reluctantly, must accept.

However, philosophy in its results is not just negative. It is, more importantly, the positive synthesis of the reason of science with the intuition of poetry. Philosophy uses the means of science to arrive at the insights of poetry. It is "nothing more than an attempt to prove that which poetry assumes as given, or to enable us by reflection to recognise as the universal principle of reality that ideal which poetry exhibits to us in special creations." The poet expresses to man an ideal which the philosopher then attempts to prove real.

But is the ideal real? Even granting that poets do express a belief in a good order or providence which true philosophers then try to prove to exist, the question still remains how one can ever be sure that the poet's seeing good in the heart of evil is not just wishful thinking. The incessant quarreling among philosophers themselves seems to indicate that no agreement as to the ultimate order or disorder of the world is possible.

Caird recognized the apparent difficulty of this objection. He conceded that it appeared unanswerable—until, that is, one understands what is really happening in history. All the systems of philosophers do seem a chaos if we place them side by side, if we treat them mechanically. However, we need not do that. We can treat them organically by studying how one grew into the other. When we do this, we will see that the history of man, despite its apparent vicissitudes, actually has a direction, a purpose, a providence. In particular, we will see that successive generations of philosophers have come closer and closer to understanding that the ideal is in fact in the process of becoming the real—that the world is at its heart spiritual. Such a confidence in past achievements can alone give us true confidence in the future. It alone "can justifiably raise us above the feeling of our weakness for the task which is laid upon philosophy in our time, and can save us from the intruding suspicion, that in his religions and his philosophies man had been perpetually renewing the history of Babel—attempting to build a tower that shall reach to heaven, only to find the work again and again stopped by the confusion of languages among the builders."

In short, the first evil in which the philosopher must find good is Babel of past philosophies. They must be seen as necessary steps in man's recognition of the ideal in the real, the spiritual in the material. Caird invited his readers to see the history of philosophy as a series of attempts to prove the rationality, the ideal character, of the world, each attempt partially successful, each attempt implying and being improved by its successor.

In Caird's account of the development of Western philosophy, Christianity occupied a central position. Christianity had brought together many of the "inconsistent elements of thought and feeling" which doomed Greek philosophy to scepticism. Nonetheless, these elements were not entirely synthesized; within Christianity they were "combined only by distributing them between two worlds." So the medieval Church taught that the present life was but a preparation for a future one, a doctrine which acted as an "anodyne to reconcile men to the injustices which they were suffering." The best of men, rather than spending their lives making the ideal real in the world, would withdraw from the world as monks. Hence Christianity, at least as it was embodied in the medieval church, became mired in its own contradictions—the contradiction between faith and reason, the contradiction between this world and the next, the contradiction between the city of God and the city of man, the contradiction between the natural and the spiritual, the contradiction between a morality of self-denial and a morality of self-realization.

In the modern world, these series of contradictions had been resolved, but only by denying the reality of the spiritual. According to Caird, much modern philosophy, and virtually all modern science, had focused exclusively upon the natural, the material, the secular. As a result, we have made much progress. We have a "knowledge of the greatness of the universe ... and the complexity of finite interests, both practical and scientific, which seem to stand on their own merits, and to need no reference to anything higher, in order to recommend them as sufficient objects of our lives."

Has the final synthesis of philosophy been achieved in this modern scientific materialism with its emphasis upon self-interest? No, Caird insisted, it has not, for this system has within itself fundamental contradictions, arising from its denial of the spiritual, the ideal. Even physical science, the one area in which a materialistic view would appear completely secure, is not immune from the incompleteness caused by the denial of the ideal. This is shown by the fact that, under the present system, no consistent account can be given of the foundations of science.

> The scientific impulse itself presupposes the presence in our own minds of an idea of truth as the ultimate unity of being and knowing, which in all our inquiries into the laws of the universe we can only develop and verify. For it is just because we are obscurely conscious, even from the beginning, of this unity that we regard every apparent discord of things with each other as a mystery and a problem, and so are continually seeking law and unity—in other words, seeking thought in things, with the confidence it must be found there.

That we can now clearly see this contradiction means that the time is now ripe for a new synthesis. And Caird believed that it is coming, and will be the fruition of all that has gone before. This synthesis will "awaken men to the reality of spiritual things." It will also do more. It will follow out the spiritual principle in its application to all the details of our condition "till we have seen how the life of each human being, and every part of that life, may be made worth living for itself." The ideal will become the real.

Caird never said that this will be the final synthesis of history. Nonetheless, his readers could scarcely avoid that conclusion. We are now entering the final phase of history. Past philosophers, however acutely conscious they were of their predecessors, did not see to the essence of the historical process of which all philosophers were a part. They did not see how the life of each philosopher was worth living for itself. They could not have seen this because they did not see how every system of thought had contributed to the ideal becoming one with the real. Now and now alone, the old quarrels, quarrels at the heart of human experience, are being laid to rest—the quarrels between the Greek and the barbarian, between the rich man and the slave, between the Christian and the world, between religion and science, between poetry and philosophy. All these quarrels are being laid to rest. Who can deny that, when all this is finished, the lion will lie down with the lamb?[1]

It is perhaps inappropriate to speak of the historical origins of a philosophical movement which sees itself as the fulfillment of all history. Even so, part of the harshness with which Mill was treated by philosophers of the next generation was perhaps due to their resentment that this greatest of philosophical discoveries, the discovery of the meaning of history, had not been made by a British thinker. While Jeremy Bentham and James Mill were espousing self-interest, German philosophers, led by Immanuel Kant and then Georg Friedrich Wilhelm Hegel, were re-introducing the ideal. And Hegel, who died a year before Bentham, had been the one who had finally discovered the meaning of history. In Kant and Hegel combined, Germany had its Newton.

The importance of German philosophy of the late eighteenth and early nineteenth centuries had been appreciated by both Carlyle and Coleridge. Nonetheless, they failed to found a movement in Britain which would sweep away the out-dated trivialities of utilitarianism. This failure seemed due, in part, to the indecisiveness of John Stuart Mill, who stood blamed by the next generation both for his lineage and his misplaced loyalty to it.

The new generation of philosophers, who intended to sweep aside utilitarianism, could not trace their British origins quite so far as to

Carlyle and Coleridge. For most of them, their British line stretched
only to mid-century, and then only to one place—Balliol College,
Oxford—and there only to one man, Benjamin Jowett.

> My name is Benjamin Jowett
> Whatever's to be known, I know it
> I am the Master of this College
> And what I don't know is not knowledge.

This was a popular Balliol rhyme of the 1870's. However, in the
1850's Jowett was not yet master of Balliol. Nor did it look as if
he ever would be because of his suspect religious views. The suspicion was that he had few if any. And Jowett, to the annoyance of
those who suspected, refused to take firm positions on doctrinal
questions. In fact, he objected to the very idea of systematic theology; systems of theology made it "difficult for us to see anything
in Scripture but themselves." Theology itself Jowett seemed to
regard more as a burden than an advantage for the educated believer.

> To the poor and uneducated, at times to all, no better advice can
> be given for the understanding of Scripture than to read the Bible
> humbly with prayer. The critical and metaphysical student requires
> another sort of rule for which this can never be made a substitute.
> His duty is to throw himself back into the times, the modes of thought,
> the language of the Apostolic age. He must pass from the abstract
> to the concrete, from the ideal and intellectual to the spiritual, from
> later statements of faith or doctrine to the words of inspiration which
> fell from the lips of the first believers. He must seek to conceive the
> religion of Christ in its relation to the religions of other times; and
> if in this effort his mind seems to fail or waver, he must win back
> in life and practice the hold on the truths of the Gospel which he
> is beginning to lose in the mazes of speculation.

The poor and educated should read the Bible humbly with prayer.
Those of a metaphysical bent could try to improve upon this humility.
They should be allowed to use all the tools of reason possible. Then,
when they finally begin to become lost in the mazes of speculation,
they should return to do what the poor and uneducated have done
all along—read the Bible humbly, and find its truth in their lives.
For those followers of Christ who thought themselves better than
the poor and uneducated, the mazes of speculation were perhaps
an indispensable digression.

This attitude also governed Jowett's teaching of philosophy. He
would lead his students through the mazes of speculation until they
were ready to return to life and practice without any commitment

to any particular system, and with an abiding suspicion of system-making in general. Edward Caird, himself a student of Jowett, observed:

> His treatment of great questions never took the form of an attempt to think them out consecutively but of a series of glances at truth from various points of view somewhat inconsistent with each other . . . . Hence what was for him a satisfactory expression of his convictions might seem to others like a collection of aporias or conflicting views that want for reconciliation.

Milton in one of his shorter poems had described fame as "that last infirmity of a noble mind." Jowett was fond of adapting this phrase to his own purposes. "System," Jowett would say, "is the last infirmity of a noble mind."

During the 1840's Jowett had twice summered in Germany. He had done so primarily to get first-hand knowledge of contemporary movements in German philosophy. For a time, he studied with a close disciple of Hegel. The new philosophy attracted him. It seemed more conducive to Christian morality than did the indigenous British philosophy with its insistence on self-interest as the only possible human motive. Moreover, this German philosophy provided a nice counter-weight to the British. Here was a point of view inconsistent with that to which his British students would naturally incline by default.

For Jowett, German philosophy was a counter-weight to British philosophy, not a substitute for it. Jowett could be as caustic about German system-building as he was about British. The following were Jowett's remarks on his meeting of perhaps the most famous living German philosopher of the period, Friedrich Schelling.

> We were greatly flattered by a visit from Schelling, courtier and philosopher, who about that time transferred himself from Munich to Berlin. He had already had six systems of philosophy, and was revealing the seventh and newest to a Berlin audience. He was very kind to us, and we regarded him with immeasurable respect. All his systems of philosophy were the creation of a man of genius, and showed a great deal of thought and insight, but they had no definite relation to history or fact. All of them claimed to be based on first principles and eternal truths. In a few years they were no longer remembered.

Jowett's assessment of Schelling's career is not very different from his assessment of the much longer, wider career of western philosophy. System succeeding system, each the result of a great deal of thought and insight, each final according to the best estimates of its day, each based upon immortal truths which in the end do not seem to live quite as long as expected.

To this generalization Jowett made one important exception, Plato. Jowett's major published contribution to philosophy would be not an original work of his own. He was not going to build yet another dead end for the maze. He produced rather a translation of Plato's dialogues. Jowett explained in the preface to his translation why he so admired the dialogues.

> There is a common spirit in the writings of Plato, but not a unity of design in the whole, nor perhaps in any single Dialogue. The hypothesis of a general plan which is worked out in successive Dialogues is an after-thought of the critics who have attributed a system to writings belonging to an age when system had not as yet taken possession of philosophy.

This was Jowett's Plato, a man of dialogue not of system. What Jowett had tried to do, as he put in the last volume of his translation, was to portray Plato "as a great original genius struggling with unequal conditions of knowledge, not prepared with a system nor evolving in a series of dialogues ideas which he had long conceived, but inconsistent, contradictory, inquiring as he goes along."

This was what Jowett hoped to convey in his translation of Plato. And it was what he hoped to convey by his own example in his teaching. He hoped to show his students how to deal with the unequal conditions of knowledge characteristic of human life, how to deal with them without resorting to the noble escape of system. It was practice with which he was most concerned, the dealing with human life as he found it.

By all accounts, Jowett's influence over many of his students was striking. And in no instance was his influence more striking than in the case of the undergraduate career of Thomas Hill Green. Before coming to Balliol College, Oxford, Green had never distinguished himself academically. Green later attributed this lack of success to simple laziness; only with great difficulty could Green bring himself to do work he did not like. During his first year at Oxford, despite the efforts of his tutor Jowett, this pattern continued. Then Jowett found the key. He told Green that if he did not get a first, the highest possible grade, on his next set of examinations, "I will have a great deal to answer for." In retrospect, Green believed that this appeal to his loyalty to Jowett changed his life.

Green was at the top of those awarded firsts in philosophy in 1859. After Green received his B.A., Jowett began to manage his academic career. By 1866, Green had become senior dean of Balliol. And by the time Jowett himself became master of Balliol, most of the actual administration of the college had been placed in Green's hands. In Green, Jowett had found, and helped create, not only another success for himself as a teacher, but also a worthy successor. Here was someone who could follow along the same path Jowett had chosen for himself. So it appeared at first; but soon the younger man's path began to diverge farther and farther from his mentor's. The divergence came over German philosophy. Whereas Jowett had found in it a useful tool, Green had found the Truth.[2]

T. H. Green saw that Jowett himself had been attacked by two groups. He was attacked by those who would denigrate faith in the name of reason; and he was attacked by those who would denigrate reason in the name of faith. Jowett, in the name of faith and reason, had denigrated both and neither. The two groups found themselves at least in agreement about Jowett. Only a lack of candor allowed him not to take sides. To this, Jowett would in effect reply that his critics were suffering from that last infirmity of noble minds.

Green, even before he traveled to Germany, believed he had discovered the solution to his teacher's troubles. There was no real tension between faith and reason, if only they were properly understood—that is, understood historically. Green summarized his discovery in "An Essay on Christian Dogma."

> The progress of thought in general consists in its struggle to work itself free from the mere individuality and outwardness of the object of intuition. The thing as sensible, i.e. as presented in an individual moment of time and space, must become the thing as known, i.e. as constituted by general attributes. Again, from being supposed to be known only so far as it exists, it must exist only so far as it is known.

The development of Christian doctrine exemplified this more general process. The first apostles knew Christ initially as an historical individual, and then as the saviour of the Jews. For Paul, Christ, while still an historical individual, had become the saviour of all mankind, the light of the world. Now, centuries later, we see that the real Christ, the Christ who has emerged from the history of Christianity, is Christ the ideal, the Christ who exists insofar as he is known.

This result might seem opposed to the original belief in Christ as
an individual person. But this opposition is merely apparent. Christ
the individual finds his necessary historical fulfillment in Christ the
ideal; and the history of Christianity is the history of this ideal forming a more and more adequate conception of itself.

At each stage of this progressive movement, not surprisingly,
some hardened their hearts against it, preferring to remain behind
with the ossified formulae of the past. Needless to say, history was
not on their side.

> Orthodox dogmatists . . . proscribe the rational evolution of the
> content of that dogmatic system which has itself been rationally
> evolved from the acts and utterances to which it appeals. Therefore
> they are witnesses against themselves that they are the children of
> them that stoned the prophets. Like them, in their zeal for the truth
> once delivered to the saints, they shut the door upon the power of
> infinite expansion in virtue of which alone it can claim to be absolute
> truth at all.

Green in his writings continually challenged his readers to see
reason historically. The rational is usually believed to be a static
system of logically connected truths which a man can passively
comprehend. Green challenged his audience to believe the rational
to be a half-seen ideal toward which all history is moving inevitably
despite what at times appear to be insuperable obstacles. To believe
otherwise is to risk being numbered among those who would stone
prophets.

The obstacles to progress Green once described as "the force of
circumstances." This phrase, capturing as it does "some want of
harmony between ourselves and the outer world," is one Green
believed no child could understand. The force of circumstances,
the force of history is that in terms of which the mature man must
define himself as a moral being. Does he withdraw from it, hiding
in the gardens of his childhood, or does he go out to meet it, confident
that it is good and he can help it in the realizing of the ideal? If he
goes out to meet it, he will somehow become part of the ideal itself,
"raised above that atmosphere of circumstances on which he throws
the light of his own being, penetrating even to those who still wander
beneath it."

Contemporary descriptions of Green are remarkably consistent.
One who had heard him wrote that he "preached Hegel with the
accent of a Puritan." Another that he had "that religious earnestness

in politics which in Carlyle is a kind of revival of Puritanism: and he also had a certain aloofness from his fellows and a sense of unlikeness." Yet another noted that "his habitual dress of black and grey suited him well and was true to his character." Of his effectiveness as a lecturer the most florid account appeared in a novel of the period, *Robert Elsmere*, where Green, as "Mr. Grey," was an influential character.

Young Robert Elsmere, hearing Grey for the first time, did not understand his argument since it was "clothed, throughout a large portion of the lecture, in metaphysical language, which no boy fresh from school, however intellectually quick, could be expected to follow with any precision." Nonetheless, he was profoundly moved.

> To the boy sitting among the crowd at the back of the room, his face supported in his hands and his gleaming eyes fixed on the speaker, it seemed as if all the poetry and history through which a restless curiosity and ideality had carried him so far, took a new meaning from this experience. It was by men like this that the moral progress of the world had been shaped and inspired; he felt brought near to the great primal forces breathing through the divine workshop; and in place of natural disposition and reverent compliance, there sprang up in him suddenly an actual certainty of belief. "Axioms are not axioms," said poor Keats, "till they have been proved upon our pulses;" and the old familiar figure of the Divine combat, of the struggle in which man and God are one, was proved once more upon a human pulse on the May night, in the hush of that quiet lecture room.

Even some of those boys who were not fresh from school found Green's metaphysical reasoning difficult to follow. The Balliol rhyme about Green was:

> I'm the self-distinguishing
> consciousness in everything;
> the synthetic unity
> one in multiplicity,
> the unseen nexus of the seen,
> sometimed known as Tommy Green.

Jowett, for his part, was deeply disturbed by Green's obviously metaphysical turn of mind. As Jowett's nineteenth century biographers put it, "Himself a critic of philosophy rather than a philosopher, it gave him real pain to see any of his friends fall, as he thought, under the dominion of a system." Jowett is supposed to have once left a lecture of Green muttering to himself, "Foolish man! Foolish man!"

Jowett particularly objected to Green using his position as tutor to impose his philosophy. In lectures one might be free to defend what one wished, but tutorials should not be used to present one point of view. So Jowett had Green removed as a tutor. This fundamental difference of opinion does not seem to have caused personal rancour between the men. They still agreed on many practical issues. With Master Jowett's help, Green founded an inexpensive residence hall for poor Balliol students. Both Jowett and Green supported the movement for a University Extension which would promote adult education. Both were active in the formation of what was to become Bristol University, and for a time helped fund the new institution out of their own pockets. Like Mill and Macaulay before them, they agreed on many practical issues. It was just that Jowett and Macaulay did not ground their decisions on philosophical first principles. Jowett could not help but be proud when Green was the first don to be chosen by the general electorate for the Oxford City Council. He would not, however, have put a metaphysical interpretation on the event. He would not have thought that here once again history was achieving the synthesis of opposites, this time the opposition of Town and Gown being transcended in the person of T. H. Green.

Green soon became more influential than Jowett with the brightest of Balliol undergraduates. They formed a club called the "Essay Society"; and in their letter to Green asking him to join, they pledged their allegiance. The allegiance was not to Green personally, but to philosophy as an end in itself. Philosophy should not be made subservient to other educational aims; it should be pursued for its own sake. As a group, they shared a "belief in principles, instead of the present eclecticism."

Green, of course, was not able to convert all the brightest of Balliol undergraduates to his pursuit. In fact, the student who was eventually to become perhaps the most famous—famous not as a philosopher, but as a poet—left Oxford to enter the Jesuits. He was Gerard Manley Hopkins.

Hopkins appears from the first not to have seen things as Green saw them. In an essay on Plato he had written for Green in 1865, the Plato who emerges is more the Plato of Jowett than the systematic Plato Green would have. Plato "asked the questions which philosophy has since been trying to answer." His was "that philosophy which never could be a system."

Nonetheless, Hopkins' Plato was not simply Jowett's. Hopkins was not content with the unanswered questions; he was not amused by the inevitable lack of final system. "Plato was able to feel the sadness of complex thought running freely to different conclusions when the old unity of belief which gives meaning to every subordination of thought and action was gone." Hopkins even found within Plato a philosophical despair—"despair at the multiplicity of phenomena unexplained and unconnected." (To the phrase "unexplained and unconnected," Hopkins added in the margin of his paper "the heavy and the weary weight of all this unintelligible world.") Finding himself in such a world, Plato could only make his ideals persuasive by "the images he gives us for them," by "the indefinite suggestions of metaphor." His teaching succeeds only when it "goes beyond rhetoric into poetry."

That Hopkins could not have expected Green to sympathize with such conclusions, he had already concluded before they met. When he was first at Oxford, he wrote home about a "wicked thing" Green and another fellow had insisted be done. They had arranged to have "cut down the beautiful beech in the Garden . . . because it was said to darken their rooms." Hopkins thought then he knew why Green, in particular, did not appreciate the tree. Green, because of his "infidelity" (rationalism), "naturally dislikes the beauties of nature."

After Hopkins left Oxford, Green wrote, "I imagine him—perhaps uncharitably—to be one of those . . . who instead of simply opening themselves to the revelations of God in the reasonable world, are fain to put themselves into an attitude—saintly, it is true, but still an attitude." Green would, had he known it, probably have taken a Hopkins' poem like the following to epitomize the assumption of a saintly attitude.

> Thou art indeed just, Lord, if I contend
> With thee; but, sir, so what I plead is just.
> Why do sinners' ways prosper? and why must
> Disappointment all I endeavor end?
>
> Wert thou my enemy, O thou my friend,
> How wouldst thou worse, I wonder, than thou dost
> Defeat, thwart me? Oh, the sots and thralls of lust
> Do in spare hours more thrive than I that spend,
> Sir, life upon thy cause. See, banks and brakes
> Now, leavèd how thick! lacèd they are again
> With fretty chervil, look, and fresh wind shakes
> Them; birds build—but not I build; no, but strain,
> Time's eunuch, and not breed one work that wakes.
> Mine, O thou lord of life, send my roots rain.[3]

Gerard Manley Hopkins was a disappointment to T. H. Green.
Green regarded his decision to enter the Jesuits to be precisely the
kind of turning away from the world against which the older man
had consistently preached. It vexed Green "to the heart," as he put
it in a letter to a mutual friend, that so fine a person as Hopkins
would go against his "historical conscience." How could he not see
that Catholicism was not a force for the future, but a residue of the
past?

> The real movement of the world has passed it by. It lets the muddy
> tide have its way and merely picks up a few stones thrown on the
> shore, which will take the saintly polish—not without satisfaction
> that the tide should be muddy as it is by contrast. Nor is this weak-
> ness accidental. It results from the wrong principle, of the antithesis
> between Church and World, the religious and the secular, etc. This
> antithesis, doubtless, had its work to do, but the rational movement
> of mankind has got beyond it.

Gerard Manley Hopkins had neglected T. H. Green's well-devel-
oped interpretation of modern history, or just rejected it. The Protestant Reformation, according to Green, was the beginning of the
resolution of all those contradictions which had beset medieval
Christianity. "The opposition between the inward and outward,
between reason and authority, between the spirit and the flesh,
between the individual and the world of settled right, no longer a
mere antithesis of the schools, was being wrought into the political
life of christendom." Ideas had left the monastery and were making
their way in the world. The Ideal was making itself the Real. So the
rational movement of mankind left the Catholic Church behind. It
had done its work. History was now on the side of the Protestants.
Or so Green thought.

The historical record presented some difficulty for this interpretation, however. The forces of reaction, led by the Jesuits, did rally, and
the Protestant Reformation never fully succeeded. Some countries
never became Protestant. A few, after having enjoyed Protestantism,
then reverted to Catholicism. By way of explaining this, Green would
point out that forces of reaction tended to be successful only in the
Romance nations which, as "has often remarked, have not the same
instinct of spiritual completeness as the Teutonic." But this still did
not answer the difficulty.

Perhaps the retention of Catholicism was a sign of spiritual incompleteness, but how could one be certain that History was on the side of

spiritual completeness? The history of England itself presented a striking example of the apparent indifference of History to any particular set of spiritual values. In the Great Rebellion and the Commonwealth which was its fruit, the Puritans, led by Oliver Cromwell, sought to impose on England the Protestant spirit in its purest form. And how did History repay those who fought on the side of spiritual completeness?

By 1660, Cromwell was dead, and with him the Christian Commonwealth. The monarchy was restored. In 1661, on the twelfth anniversary of the execution of Charles I, the bodies of Cromwell and two other of the Puritan leaders who had died before the restoration were exhumed and hung on a gallows. In 1662, the judge at the trial of Charles I, Henry Vane, who had lived to see the monarchy restored, was himself executed as a regicide. What kind of providence was this that delivered the godly Puritans into the hands of their enemies?

Late in the seventeenth century, John Milton himself tried to supply an answer in his play *Samson Agonistes*. Having seen the blinded Samson, now a slave of the very Philistines whom he was supposed to vanquish, the chorus could not help but question the wisdom of divine providence.

> God of our Fathers, what is man!
> That thou towards him with hand so various,
> Or might I say contrarious,
> Temper'st thy providence through his short course,
> Not evenly, as thou rul'st
> Th'Angelic orders and inferior creatures mute,
> Irrational and brute.
> Nor do I name of men the common rout,
> That wand'ring loose about
> Grow up and perish, as the summer fly,
> Heads without name no more remember'd,
> But such as thou hast solemnly elected,
> With gifts and graces eminently adorn'd
> To some great work, thy glory,
> And people's safety, which in part they effect:
> Yet toward these, thus dignifi'd, thou oft,
> Amidst thir height of noon,
> Changest thy count'nance and thy hand, with no regard
> Of highest favors past
> From thee on them, or them to thee of service.
> Nor only dost degrade them, or remit
> To life obscur'd, which were a fair dismission,

> But throw'st them lower than thou didst exalt them high,
> Unseemly falls in human eye,
> Too grievous for the trespass or omission,
> Oft leav'st them to the hostile sword
> Of Heathen and profane, thir carcases
> To dogs and fowls a prey, or else captiv'd:
> Or to th' unjust tribunals, under change of times,
> And condemnation of th' ingrateful multitude.
> If these they scape, perhaps in poverty
> With sickness and disease thou bow'st them down,
> Painful diseases and deform'd,
> In crude old age;
> Though not disordinate, yet causeless suff'ring
> The punishment of dissolute days: in fine,
> Just or unjust, alike seem miserable,
> For oft alike, both come to evil end.

However, by the end of the action, the chorus finally saw that the degradation of Samson was but a subtle means for God to work His Will. So the chorus could conclude the play with an expression of faith in the ways of God.

> All is best, though we oft doubt,
> What th' unsearchable dispose
> Of highest wisdom brings about,
> And ever best found in the close.

This was the attitude Milton wished his readers to assume to the apparently planless course of history, and it bore remarkable similarity to the attitude T. H. Green offered his followers almost two hundred years later when in 1867 he delivered a series of lectures on the Great Rebellion. For Green the Great Rebellion exhibited the essental dynamics of all history, the "tragic conflict between the creative will of man and the hidden wisdom of the world, which seems to thwart it."

Green did not deny that the world seems to have thwarted the Great Rebellion. According to Green, one need only compare two descriptions of the British people, both given by John Milton, "the true exponent of the higher spirit of the republic." One description Milton gave near the beginning of the Commonwealth, the other after its end. At the beginning Milton had written of "a noble and puissant nation arousing itself like a strong man after sleep"; at the end Milton had described a people who "with a besotted and degenerate baseness of spirit . . . are ready to fall flat and give adoration to the image and memory of this man, who hath more put tyranny into an act than any British king before him."

Green was most interested in the creative Puritan will as embodied in two men, Oliver Cromwell and Henry Vane. As Cromwell was the ablest military man, so Vane was, in Green's opinion, "the ablest civilian of the time." Green praised the lesser known Vane perhaps more highly than Cromwell himself. What seems to have attracted Green to Vane was what he described as "a strange intensity of intellectual aspiration, which, if his secondary gifts had been those of a poet instead of a politician, might have made him the rival of Milton."

Before the rebellion, Vane had for a time served as Governor of the Puritan colony of Massachusetts. He, almost alone among the English Puritans, seemed to Green to have understood fully the openness to the world, the new spiritual freedom which was at the heart of Puritanism, a freedom Green found most aptly expressed in an exortation given by a Puritan divine to a segment of his congregation leaving England to colonize the New World. "If God reveals anything to you by any other instrument of his, be as ready to receive it as ever you were to receive any truth by my misery; for I am verily persuaded the Lord has more truth yet to break forth out of his holy word . . . for it is not possible the christian world should come so lately out of such thick anti-christian darkness, and that perception of knowledge should break forth all at once." They and those who followed did not heed this advice; if they had, Henry Vane would not have lost his office as Governor of Massachusetts for having tried to institute a limited degree of religious tolerance.

Vane had, it seemed, failed in Massachusetts. And then both Oliver Cromwell and Henry Vane together failed in England. They had been thwarted by the world in their creative efforts to realize their ideals. And so their lives, and the Great Rebellion itself, might be taken as evidence that such ideals are not of this world, or at least will never be fully realized within its confines. This is the view which Green in his lectures was seeking to refute.

Green insisted that we must see the hidden wisdom of the world. We must see that this hidden wisdom makes men like Vane and Cromwell fail only to ensure that their ideals will eventually triumph.

> The higher enthusiasm, however, which breathed in Cromwell and Vane, was not puritanic or English merely. It belonged to the universal spiritual forces which as ecstasy, mysticism, quietism, phil-

osophy, is in permanent collision with the carnal interests of the world, and which, if it conquers them for a moment, yet again sinks under them, that it may transmute them more thoroughly to its service.

Ecstasy, mysticism, quietism, philosophy are not all equal manifestations of the great spiritual forces. Ecstasy, mysticism, quietism are unequal to the task of making these forces real. They are but preliminary to philosophy. As Green put it, "It is the true nemesis of human life that any spiritual impulse, not accompanied by clear comprehensive thought, is enslaved by its own realisation."

This was the tragedy of the Great Rebellion, why the world in its hidden wisdom had resisted the creative wills of Oliver Cromwell, Henry Vane, and those like them. They lacked a comprehensive philosophical system. As a result, the Commonwealth crumbled after Cromwell's death. And after the Restoration, Vane was executed. It was with the execution of Henry Vane that Green closed his lectures.

> "Death," said Vane on the scaffold, "is a little word, but it is a great work to die." So his own enthusiasm died that it might rise again. It was sown in the weakness of feeling, that it might be raised in the intellectual comprehension which is power. "The people of England," he said again, "have been long asleep. I doubt they will be hungry when they awake." They have slept, we may say, another two hundred years. If they should yet wake and be hungry, they will find their food in the ideas which, with much blindness and weakness, he vainly offered them, cleared and ripened by a philosophy of which he did not dream.

The ripening philosophy was, of course, that which Green had found in Germany. Once again Teutonic Germany had taken the lead in a spiritual Reformation. There now existed, almost complete, a clear comprehensive philosophy. Now at last, the spiritual impulse need not be enslaved by its own realization. At one point, Cromwell had epitomized the troubles of the Commonwealth: "Every sect saith, 'O give me liberty.' But give it him, and to the best of his power he will yield it to no one else." This could not happen if the call for liberty was based on a rational philosophical system. Green believed that Europe, now having such a philosophy, was on the verge of a new awakening.[4]

CHAPTER ELEVEN

T. H. GREEN AND F. H. BRADLEY
(1867-1876)

In his lectures on the English Commonwealth T. H. Green had pleaded with his listeners not to dismiss the Puritan thinkers because they believed in miracles. This belief was perhaps irrational; but, he reminded them, it was no less irrational than the nineteenth century belief that reason supports irreligion.

> It is a notion which governs much of the popular thought of the present day, and which the most cultivated "men of feeling" are not ashamed to express, that the world is atheised when we regard it as a universe of general laws, equally relentless or equally merciful to the evil and the good. If such a notion, through mere impatience of thought, can dominate an educated age, we may well excuse uncultivated men, who cling close to God, for believing him to manifest himself to his favoured people by sudden visitation and unaccountable events.

Green's followers would have known to whom he was referring. They had probably heard him in other letures attack the shallowness of the utilitarians. "Men of feeling," such as the utilitarians, presumed that a disbelief in miracles was tantamount to a disbelief in God, that a proof of scientific laws governing nature was a disproof of a Divine Providence governing history. They would have us believe that Newton, who had dispelled the miraculous, had also dispelled the divine, the spiritual. The utilitarians, in particular, would claim that men could be understood in much the same way that planets and stars were. They claimed, in fact, that the foundations of such a science of man had already been laid. Some psychological laws which governed man's mind as surely as the astronomical laws governed the planets had been discovered through introspection. The philosophers who had made these discoveries were, in the utilitarian account, working in a tradition which stretched all the way back to John Locke in Newton's own time.

So scientific philosophers could look back with condescension upon those Puritans of old who believed in the miraculous as the proof of the spiritual realm. These beliefs had long since been superceded by a more rational philosophy. Or so the utilitarians thought.

Green did not think their smugness justified. What these thinkers did not realize—or at least seemed unwilling to admit—is that they too have been superceded. Their own philosophy was now as much a relic of the past as was the Puritan's belief in the miraculous. This was what Green announced in his first book-length work. This work began:

> There is a view of the history of mankind, by this time familiarised to Englishmen, which detaches from the chaos of events a connected series of ruling actions and beliefs—the achievement of great men and great epochs, and assigns to these in a special sense the term "historical." According to this theory—which indeed, if there is to be a theory of History at all, alone gives the needful simplification—the mass of nations must be regarded as left in swamps and shallows outside the main stream of human development. They have either never come within the reach of the hopes and institutions which make history a progress instead of a cycle, or they have stiffened these into a dead body of ceremony and caste, or at some great epoch they have failed to discern the sign of the times and rejected the counsel of God against themselves. Thus permanently or for generations, with no principle of motion but unsatisfied want, without the assimilative ideas which from the strife of passions elicit moral results, they have trodden the old round of war, trade, and factions, adding nothing to the spiritual heritage of man. It would seem that the historian need not trouble himself with them, except so far as relation to them determines the activity of the progressive nations.

Here Green's British readers might have been left thinking about the inhabitants of India who were really only important insofar as they contributed to British progress—or perhaps about the Romance nations who failed to see the counsel of God against themselves in the Reformation, and hence fell under the spell of Jesuitry. But his readers would probably have thought of Britain only as one of the progressive nations. Falling outside the mainstream of history was something that happened to other nations. Neither at the present nor in the foreseeable future was there any danger of such a fate befalling Great Britain. Was there?

Here Green gave his readers an unwelcome surprise. Britain already, for more than a generation, had been left in the swamps and the shallows, unable to add to the spiritual heritage of mankind. She had been left there because she had been betrayed by her philosophers.

The beginning of a new dawn had been called forth late in the eighteenth century by Immanuel Kant. Upon reading the Scottish philosopher David Hume (whom the utilitarians still numbered as one of their precursors), Kant realized that the foundation of the Newtonian philosophy was inadequate. He was awakened, as he himself described it, from a dogmatic slumber. Kant attempted a new synthesis.

Now, almost a century later, Britain still slept, besotted with utilitarianism. Green wished to rouse Britain to make her once again a noble and puissant nation. And the instrument he chose was the same instrument History itself had chosen to awaken Kant: David Hume.

Green's new publishing venture was a new edition of the philosophical works of David Hume. (There had not been one since the eighteenth century.) Green's discussion of the nature of human history, with its shallows and swamps, is the beginning of his introduction to that collected edition, which first appeared in 1876. His introduction itself was over three hundred pages. He wished to take no chance that the British, in their drunken stupor, would miss the significance of Hume this time, as they had the first time. The thesis of Green's introduction was that nineteenth century British philosophy "has been unprofitable because its representatives have persisted in philosophising upon principles which Hume had pursued to their legitimate issue and had shown, not as their enemy, but as their advocate, to render all philosophy futile." In short, British philosophers had failed to admit the significance of Hume; they had failed to discern the sign of the times and rejected the counsel of God against themselves. "They have either thrust their heads in the bush of uncriticised belief, or they have gone on elaborating Hume's doctrine of association, in apparent forgetfulness of Hume's own proof of its insufficiency to account for an intelligent, as opposed to a merely instinctive, or habitual, experience."

Such a work as Hume's, like the work of the Puritans, "could not be in vain." And so Hume led to Kant, and eventually to Hegel and a philosophy which "claims to set man free from the artificial impotence of his own false logic, and thus qualify him for a complete interpretation of his own achievement in knowledge and morality." Green wished to induce his readers to take the first step along that path toward Hegel. He wished, by an exposition of Hume, to make his readers see the insufficiency of associationism.

In his *A Treatise of Human Nature*, published in 1740, David Hume had, in fact, anticipated many of the doctrines defended by James Mill in his *Analysis of the Phenomena of the Human Mind*, published almost a century later. Like Mill, Hume observed the workings of his own mind. Like Mill, he observed that all his ideas were nothing but faded copies of sensations. Like Mill, he observed that the ways in which these ideas associated with each other were also traceable back to the sensations. However, unlike Mill, Hume did not think that these observations demonstrated the mind to be causally determined.

To Mill the demonstration was obvious. All other mental phenomena are caused by sensations. Sensations are caused by objects in the physical world. Newton had proven that the physical world itself was causally determined. To Mill the demonstration was obvious. Hume, almost a century earlier, was not so sure. Hume, as the Scot made clear in another work, was not so sure that Newton had proven any such thing. Newton, in Hume's opinion, had demonstrated more our ignorance of causes than our knowledge of them. "While Newton seemed to draw off the veil from some of the mysteries of nature, he showed at the same time the imperfection of the mechanical philosophy, and thereby restored her ultimate secrets to that obscurity in which they ever did and ever will remain."

Hume was not convinced that the physical world had been demonstrated to be determined. Nor was he confident that he himself could demonstrate that his own sensations were caused by objects in that physical world. Everything in his mind came from sensations. These sensations were what he knew for certain, these and these alone. The physical objects which were supposed to be causing these sensations were themselves merely inferences from the sensations. Hume did not think he could ever be certain that these hypothetical objects were really out there, for he knew of them only through the sensations.

Needless to say, the utilitarians, while acknowledging Hume as a forefather, never completely approved of him. James Mill attributed Hume's scepticism to a lack of judgment—Hume "was misled by the pursuit of a few surprising and paradoxical results." John Stuart Mill simply questioned Hume's philosophical seriousness: "Hume, the prince of dilettantes, from whose writings one will hardly learn that there is such a thing as truth, far less that it is attainable."

This lack of earnestness was for the utilitarians perhaps Hume's most annoying characteristic. Hume, when faced with the shambles in which he had left systematic philosophy, would joke. He even repudiated his massive *A Treatise of Human Nature* because it was too earnest. He said he had made "a very great mistake" ever publishing the book: "the positive aire which prevails in that book . . . so much displeases me that I have not the patience to review it." To make amends, he re-worked the *Treatise* into two shorter, lighter works. In these he did not take his role as a philosopher too seriously.

For instance, at the beginning of one of them, *An Enquiry Concerning Human Understanding*, he pretended that he did not know how the inquiry was going to turn out—he and his readers were going to conduct this inquiry together. Having established this fiction, Hume happily expressed expectations that he had no intention of fulfilling. Hume hoped that through this inquiry he and his reader would gain a certainty about the movements of the human mind comparable to that obtained by astronomy about the movements of the planets. While the readers would think this means that psychology is going to be raised to the level of astronomy, Hume knew that it is astronomy which is going to be lowered to the level of psychology. And when Hume suspected his readers were beginning to surmise as much, he would turn to reassure them of his good faith. For example, after Hume had shown that no good reason seems to exist for believing in causality, he turned to his readers and said: "My practice, you say, refutes my Doubts. But you mistake the Purport of my Question. As an agent, I am quite satisfied in the point: but as a Philosopher, who has some share of Curiosity, I will not say Scepticism, I want to learn the Foundation of this Inference."

By the end of the inquiry, after he and his readers had somehow been unable to find a rational basis for any of their common sense beliefs, Hume was no longer referring to himself as a philosopher. He had in the course of the inquiry, much to his professed surprise, lost his own share of curiosity. So, too presumably, had his readers. And the readers had also learned the fundamental requirement of a successful sceptic. A successful sceptic, Hume had told them, must always be "the first to join in the laugh against himself."

Needless to say, this attitude was as annoying to T. H. Green as it had been to John Stuart Mill. Green solemnly recounted Hume's unsolemn destruction of the assumptions of the still prevalent British philosophy. Green was confident that his readers, having been exposed to Hume, could not long remain utilitarians. Nevertheless, to use Hume, however diluted, was to risk infecting his readers with Hume's ironic attitude toward philsophy. Nothing could have been more contrary to the attitude Green wished his readers to have than one of self-deprecation.

The work of the Great Rebellion had remained unfinished precisely because the Puritans had lacked a philosophy with which they could convince the public at large of the truth of their vision. The completion of the Puritan's work awaited the new age of philosophy. This should be an ennobling vision for a philosopher. Yet there was David Hume who more than anyone had brought philosophy to the threshold of the new age—David Hume who, having reached that threshold, grinned and turned his back. There was something wrong with Hume. Green had to make his readers see that.

> The pity is that having carried his speculative enterprise so far before he was thirty, he allowed literary vanity to interfere with its consistent pursuit caring only to think out the philosophy he inherited so far as it enabled him to pose with advantage against the Mystics and Dogmatists, but not to that further issue which is the entrance to the philosophy of Kant.

A poet like Gerard Manley Hopkins might be content to pose with advantage against the world, but how could Hume do that? Hume who was a great philosopher, who had almost seen the vision that Green had seen? Did not the doing of philosophy make men better? Did it not free them from vanity and self-interest? If a great philosopher failed to discern the sign of the times and rejected the counsel of God, how could we be sure that there were signs and counsels?

Green had anticipated all these questions in his original characterization of Hume's achievement; Hume philosophized, according to Green, "as one could who had neither any twist or vice nor bias for doing good, but was a philosopher because he could not help it." Hume had no bias for doing good, no predilection to help the eternal be realized in history. He did not become a philosopher as the result of a moral decision to assist the good in its realization. He could not have. He was amoral; he lacked the moral vision by which those who consciously participate in the progress of the world attempt to guide their actions. Hume, as his actions showed, was a moral invalid, not a complete man.

How would such a man have reacted if he had lived to see the new age he had helped create? What would he have said if he had lived to read the sublime philosophy of Hegel? Green would not have expected much from Hume. Hume was constitutionally unable to see what Green and Hegel saw so clearly. Green would probably not have been surprised if Hume, after reading Hegel, merely shook his head, saying "Foolish man, foolish man."

There was just one way to silence a Hume, or even a Jowett. This was to demonstrate, once and for all, that Reason does in fact govern the world, and that men exist as manifestations of this one Reason. This is just what Hegel had tried to do. But had he really succeeded?

At the time of his edition of Hume, Green appears to have thought so. But by 1880 he had changed his mind. By 1880 he had decided that Hegel had failed. In a review written in that year, Green admitted, "Hegel's doctrine has been before the world now for half a century, and though it has affected the current science and philosophy to a degree which those who depreciate it seem curiously to ignore, yet as a doctrine it has not made its way in the world. It may be doubted whether it has thoroughly satisfied even those among us who regard it as the last word of philosophy."

Green did not mean to imply by this that Hegel's doctrine was false. He still believed it to point to the true frame of the world. What Green meant was that Hegel had not demonstrated his system to be true. Much like the Puritans before him, Hegel had talked of his vision but had failed to supply the proof.

> That there is one spiritual self-conscious being of which all that is real is the activity or expression; that we are related to this spiritual being, not merely as parts of the world which is its expression, but as partakers in some inchoate measure of the self-consciousness through which it at once constitutes and distinguishes itself from the world; that this participation is the source of morality and religion; this we take to be the vital truth which Hegel has to teach. It still remains to be presented in a form which will command some general acceptance among serious and scientific men.

It still remained to be done, but there are hints in this review that Green had come to think of it as an ultimately impossible task. He believed the spiritual nature of the world could be demonstrated because "on no other supposition is its unity explicable." If we assume that the world is one, if we assume that it is a single rational system, then we must suppose that it has a spiritual nature. But supposing is not knowing, and Green seems to despair of ever knowing the world in its spiritual nature.

> When we have satisfied ourselves that the world in its truth or full reality is spiritual, because on no other supposition is its unity explicable, we may still have to confess that a knowledge of it in its

spiritual reality—such a knowledge of it as would be a knowledge of God—is impossible to us. To know God we must be God. The unifying principle of the world is indeed in us; it is our self. But, as in us, it is so conditioned by a particular animal nature that, while it yields that idea of the world as one which regulates all our knowledge, our actual knowledge remains a piecemeal process. We spell out the relations of things one by one; we pass from condition to condition, from effect to effect; but as one fragment of truth is grasped, another has escaped us, and we never reach that totality of apprehension through which alone we could know the world as it is and God in it. This is the infirmity of our discursive understanding. If in one sense it reveals God, in another it hides him. Language which seems to imply its identification with God, or with the world in its spiritual reality, can lead to nothing but confusion.

We will never know God. We will never be God. There is an infirmity in our understanding. Crippled thus, our understanding can but lead us to confusion. Hume would not have shaken his head at this, though he might have grinned.

In the same year this review appeared, Green, sounding older than his forty-four years, admitted in a letter to a friend, "Writing now is very different from what is was ten years ago. Then there were much larger vistas of possibility, and I thought I had got hold of a key which I find now will not unlock so much as I fancied it would." In that year of 1880, Green became very ill. When he had only partly recovered, he insisted upon resuming his very active life. He would not allow weakened health to curtail his efforts at reform. Two years later he was dead.

Benjamin Jowett, as master of Balliol, gave the eulogy. In it he praised Green's contributions to his college and to his city. Jowett could only suspend judgment on his achievements as a philosopher.

> No one without metaphysics can get rid of metaphysics. . . . To this most important but precarious branch of knowledge our departed friend devoted the best energies of his mind and life. He soon gathered around him a band of disciples. . . . They seemed to wait for some new exposition of the truth which should deliver them from the lowering tendencies of the age. Whether this hope would have been altogether realized, or realized in the way in which they expected, or whether any such hope was entertained by himself, I cannot tell. His memory and his reputation do not depend on the completeness of his system.[1]

T. H. Green's disciples were understandably distraught at his parting. (Edward Caird, for instance, had to make the trip from Edinburgh to Oxford to attend the funeral; at the Edinburgh station,

Caird was so obviously distressed that a friend thought someone should accompany him to assist him make the necessary change of trains.) They were distraught not just by their personal loss.

Green's death exemplified the apparent irrationality of history. Green was a man who might have been able to complete the work begun in England by the Puritans, a man who might have been able to prove Hegel true—or at least who could have made further steps toward this end. If only he had lived longer.

Green died with a book almost finished, his *Prolegomena to Ethics*. The first part of this he had already begun to publish as a series of articles entitled "Can there be a natural science of man?" The answer was, of course, negative. It was negative, that is, unless one supposed the existence of a spiritual principle governing nature. Unless we admit such a principle, our knowledge of nature, to say nothing of our own intrinsic moral sense, is a figment of our imaginations. Unless we see that the world is of the same spiritual substance as man, then all the striving to comprehend the unity of the world is but a projection of our fabrications: "Man weaves a web of his own and calls it a universe." The progress which history shows man to have made in his attempt to comprehend the cosmos is nothing but man's gradual discovery of the eternal intelligence both in the world and in himself—his discovery that the world and himself and the eternal intelligence are all one.

> The growth of knowledge on our part is regarded not as a process in which facts or objects, in themselves unrelated to thought, by some inexplicable means gradually produce intelligible counterparts of themselves in thought. The true account described indifferently as an eternal intelligence realized in related facts of the world, or as a system of related facets rendered possible by such an intelligence, partially and gradually reproduces itself in us, us communicating piece-meal, but in inseparable correlation, understanding and the facts understood, experience and the experienced.

Green was here trying to force language to do what perhaps he knew it could not. His readers, however, had to be made to believe that any desire for universal knowledge supposed the spirituality of the universe, and man's oneness with God. In the remainder of his *Prolegomena to Ethics*, Green did not try to give his readers any knowledge of this spiritual reality he had led them to suppose. Rather, he began to describe how they should assist in the realization in the world of the eternal spiritual intelligence they can never know. Men had to see that the eternal intelligence was reproducing itself through us, and hence we had an obligation to assist in whatever way we could in its realization.

A. C. Bradley, one of Green's younger disciples, was chosen to edit the *Prolegomena to Ethics* for publication. R. L. Nettleship, who himself had become the most influential tutor at Balliol after Jowett removed Green, was chosen to edit a collection of Green's works, including many lectures and sermons not previously published. This would make Green's life work, however unfinished, available to a wider audience than Oxford alone. R. L. Nettleship was given the important task of writing a memoir of Green to be published with Green's collected works.

In this memoir Nettleship surveyed Green's life, emphasizing his achievements both as a philosopher and citizen. He also attempted to characterize Green as a man—and, in particular, he attempted to describe what it was about Green that enabled him to have such influence over other men. Nettleship found the key in an enigmatic sentence Green had written near the end of an unpublished fragment on immortality: "he let the world have its way, not from the hopelessness of the sceptic or the indifference of the epicurean, but because he knew that his own way, however lamely and blindly he pursued it, was yet that to which all the world's ways converge, and it was the way that leadeth to eternal life." This, Nettleship believed, expressed exactly Green's view of himself.

Like the Puritans he so much admired, Green knew that he, however blindly he followed his own way, was predestined to eternal life. This was so because he had a vision of the divine in things, of the eternal in the temporal, the spiritual in the material. And he knew, he just knew, that the day was soon coming when all men would see what he saw—when, in Nettleship's words, "the secret existence, which the poet now speaks to the inward ear of few, will be proclaimed on the housetops to the common intelligence."

Green's vision, Nettleship was certain, "made him what he was." And Green could convince others, as much by his demeanor as by his words, that he did indeed see it. This was the source of his remarkable hold over them. They would work for the realization of the vision which Green saw. Green saw that history was neither blind or lame. And he saw that the time was coming when this truth would be available to the common intelligence of mankind, and so he and his followers worked for wider education of men so that they would by ready for this truth.

Nevertheless, despite Nettleship's great admiration for Green, he had to make an admission. The time when this vision was to be available to the common intelligence had not arrived with Green. Green himself had never made the substance of his vision clear, even to the closest of his disciples. And so, when Nettleship in the conclusion of his memoir looked for an epic hero with whom to identify Green, he chose Sir Bors of the Round Table. Of the Knights of the Round Table, Sir Bors alone had seen the Holy Grail for which they all quested. Sir Bors alone had seen it, and yet when asked to describe it he refused. When asked he would only reply, "Ask me not, for I may not speak of it; I saw it."

Green's disciples, on the whole, were not for giving up the quest. Despite Green's death, they did have some firm ground for hope. Green may not have communicated his vision, but he had seen it; and he had pointed his disciples in the direction they should seek it. And they, even before Green's untimely death, were beginning to make some progress.

Edward Caird, who was to succeed Jowett as master of Balliol, had already published his monumental *Philosophy of Kant*, which showed how the whole history of modern philosophy rationally led to the thought of the German philosopher. Edward's brother, James Caird, had already published his *Philosophy of Religion* which clarified Hegel's thought on this most important subject. William Wallace, who suceeded Green as Professor of Moral Philosophy at Oxford, had already published the first of his English translations of Hegel. Still, someone was needed to bring this preliminary work to fruition.

Bernard Bosanquet could not assume leadership, despite his promise as a philosopher; he had moved to London in 1881. Arnold Toynbee, although he did edit a selection of Green's sermons, did not pick up his mantle; he died only a year after Green. A. C. Bradley himself had already begun to work out the implications of Hegelian philosophy for literary criticism; as important as this might be (and it would eventually lead to Bradley's assuming the Oxford Chair of Poetry), it was not the fundamental work that was still required.

What of R. L. Nettleship? The very choice of him to write the official memoir of Green indicated great confidence in him and perhaps also great hope for his future. Yet Nettleship had always remained independent of Green. (Jowett, not Green, had been his tutor.) While he was sympathetic to Green's philosophy, unlike others he did not, in Bradley's words, "regard Green's teaching as a kind of gospel which it was his mission to spread." (Bradley, in contrast, had been so evangelical that Jowett had him virtually banished from Balliol and Oxford.) Nettleship had not even entirely committed himself to philosophy. At the time of Green's death, he had been working on the history of a country most unlikely for a truly devoted follower of Green, Italy, in a period even less so, the Middle-Ages—and, to make matters worse, Nettleship was most interested in *southern* Italy.

Perhaps the assignment of the memoir was intended to bring the talented individualist back toward the center of the group. Nettleship, seeing the great but unfinished work of Green, would take it up himself. If this was the intention, it failed. After Green's death, Nettleship, although he gave up all plans for his history, only drifted farther from the group. Within a year he had given up his rooms at college. The very memoir of Green which hopefully was to lead to greater things led nowhere. It was, in fact, the last thing he published. Green's death only hardened Nettleship's characteristic emphasis on the personal rather than the public side of ethics.

This had always been a difference between himself and Green. While Green was still alive Nettleship had tried to explain to him in a letter an attitude of which the older man could scarcely have approved. "I suppose the only hope lies in patience and courage, patience to recognize fairly what has been lost (by me, I mean, not by mankind), and courage not to be afraid that all is lost." Courage against despair had little place in Green's ethics, and recognition of personal failure had none. History did not fail, and hence there was nothing that could tempt us to despair. Courage, nonetheless, was central to Nettleship's personal ethics. Bradley wrote:

> In all things that which called for courage, as well as effort and skill, appealed to him most. One might even say that in Nettleship's experience all the virtues appear in the shape of courage, just as to another they may all appear as forms of unselfishness; and it was natural to him to think of moral weaknesses as kinds of fear.

Consistent with Nettleship's identification of virtue with courage in the face of danger or the unknown was his love of mountain climbing. In a few of his letters his descriptions of his experiences in the mountains bear some similarity to his description of Green's vision of the divine in things. In one of these letters he wrote:

Few things are more disgusting at the moment than grinding along a whole day over a pass on a sick stomach, feeding on brandy and water. Yet gradually "the outward man perisheth"—the stomach fades away—and there remain the unimagined glories of snowy plain or towering peaks or garden-like valleys, tinged with the sense of pleasant fatigue . . . . Mount Blanc stood as if cut out of ethereal marble against an azure sky, and flashed from white to gold and from gold to rose every evening . . . . It is a most strangely unearthly thing that apparition of a peak of far-off snow field through the breaks in the clouds.

In the summer of 1892, an unexpected storm hit Mount Blanc while Nettleship was attempting an ascent. He froze to death.[2]

The man who did emerge as the new intellectual leader of Green's Oxford disciples was A. C. Bradley's brother, Francis Herbert Bradley. He, too, had been educated at Balliol College. He was one of the original members of the Essay Club. He, like Nettleship and others, failed to get a "first" on his final undergraduate examinations in philosophy, presumably because of a prejudice against the philosophical positions he advocated. Despite the second class degree, Bradley was awarded a life-tenured fellowship at Merton College, Oxford. That this fellowship was for life, and required no official duties on Bradley's part, soon became a fact of importance.

Of course, it was expected that Bradley would do his share of tutoring, lecturing, and administering in the college. And no one could have doubted that Bradley, imbued as he was with Green's example, would do more than his part. Nevertheless, it was not required for his continuing to hold his fellowship. Scarcely a year after he had received this fellowship, Bradley's health failed; a kidney disease left him unable to lead an active life. He could not lecture or even tutor, and he certainly could not shoulder any major administrative position in the college. His health generally did not even permit him to spend the winters in Oxford.

Bradley could not live the energetic life of citizenship Green had advocated. He could, however, contribute his part since his isolation did leave him with more opportunity to think and write. His life was to be almost exclusively that of a philosopher. Within two years of Green's introduction to Hume's works. Bradley had published his own attack upon the utilitarians in a work entitled *Ethical Studies*.

"Vanity of vanities; all is vanity . . . . I have seen all the works that are under the sun; and behold, all is vanity and vexation of spirit."

This central preaching of *Ecclesiastes* Bradley evoked at the beginning of his critique of utilitarian ethics.

> It is an old story, a theme too worn for the turning of sentences, and yet too living a moral not to find every day a new point and to break a fresh heart, that our lives are wasted in the pursuit of the impalpable, the search for the impossible and the unmeaning. Neither to-day nor yesterday, but throughout the whole life of the race, the complaint has gone forth that all is vanity; that the ends for which we live and we die are "mere ideas", illusions begotten on the brain by the wish of the heart—poor phrases that stir the blood, until experience or reflection for a little, and death for all time, bring with it disenchantment and quiet.

Bradley began with the theme that all is vanity because he believed it to account for much of the popularity enjoyed by utilitarianism. Utilitarian philosophy seemed to recognize the truth of this age-old insight, for it rejected the pursuit of anything but the palpable. Pleasure was to be our only guide. With it we would perhaps enter a new life. The forest would become a garden.

> We have said good-bye to our transcendent longings, we have bidden a sad but eternal farewell to the hopes of our own and of the world's too credulous youth; we have parted for ever from our early loves, from our fancies and aspirations beyond the human. We seek for the tangible, and we find it in this world; for the knowledge which can never deceive, and that is the certainty of our own well-being; we seek for the palpable, and we feel it; for the end which satisfies us as men, and we find it, in a word, in happiness.

If the utilitarians are right, we will find our happiness in pleasure, and the old story will never be told on us. Or will it? If all is vanity, then so is the pursuit of pleasure. Bradley reminded his readers that the age-old wisdom dismissed the pursuit of pleasure as the most vain of all. As Bradley put it, "The pursuit of pleasure is a phrase which calls for a smile and a sigh, since the world has learnt that, if pleasure is the end, it is an end which must not be made one, and is found there most where it is not sought."

Bradley could have documented this point by quoting the section of Mill's *Autobiography* where he recounts his discovery that utilitarian analysis prevents individual happiness. Bradley did not choose to give his English predecessor credit for having come to this insight; he chose rather a stanza from a poetic forerunner of German metaphysics, from Goethe's *Faust*:

> The highest might
> Of Science quite
> Is from the world concealed.
> But whosoe'er
> Expends no care,
> To him it is revealed.

Moreover, utility not only fails as an effective practical guide, it also fails as a description of the goals for which "moral persons without a theory" strive. Bradley tried to make his readers see that all their moral aspirations could not be reduced to the pursuit of pleasure. He tried to make them recognize as their own the belief "that there are things 'we should choose even if no pleasure came from them'; and that if we choose these things, being good, for ourselves, then we must choose them also for the race, if we care for the race as we do for ourselves."

Bradley was reversing the process whereby James Mill had tried to get his readers to see that all their ideas were derived from sensations. He was trying, through the same means of introspection, to get them to admit that their moral ideas transcended the sensations of pleasure and pain. Like Mill, Bradley had to go slowly, for all he could do was point and then point again. "At the cost of repetition, and perhaps some weariness, I must dwell a little longer on the ordinary consciousness." And two pages later, "This, we repeat once more, is absolutely irreconcilable with ordinary beliefs."

Utility was neither an effective practical guide nor an accurate description, but it could be a pernicious rationalization for immoral conduct. Bradley did not descend to pointing out moral improprieties in the private lives of the utilitarian philosophers themselves. He rather took a hypothetical case.

> The rule says, Do not commit adultery. I wish to commit adultery. I am sure I do not want to please myself at all; in fact rather the contrary. I am as positive as I can be of anything, that the case is either not contemplated by the rule, or, if it is, that the rule is wrong, that the proposed act must diminish the sum of the pain and must increase the sum of pleasure of the sentient world as a whole, and this too after all consequences that I can reckon (and I can reckon no more) have been counted in. Is it immoral to break the rule; or rather is it not immoral to keep it, to sacrifice a real good to a mere idea? My conscience is clear; and my dreams will not be broken by "the groans" of an "abstraction."

"The groans of an abstraction," so apt a concluding phrase for this rationalization of adultery, was not F. H. Bradley's. It was John

Stuart Mill's—and Bradley, being fair, gave Mill full credit for it.

The readers' recognition that utilitarianism was not adequate to their moral aspirations was more important than simply a refutation of utilitarianism. It provided the pattern for the rest of *Ethical Studies*. A moral ideal would be proposed. Bradley's readers, with his help, would soon find inadequacies, contradictions within it. The readers would then grow dissatisfied with it. They would desire a better one. Another would be proposed, and the process would start over again.

Slowly the readers were to realize that their moral aspirations somehow always exceeded the grasp of their ideas. Slowly they were to discover within themselves a perennial dissatisfaction, a Faustian passion for transcendence—and, in so doing, they were to find within themselves exactly the same insatiable desire which Green and his followers believed to govern history, our desire to have the eternal intelligence reproduce itself through us.

At the conclusion of his *Ethical Studies* Bradley described the book as a journey, a journey through the inadequacies of moralities to a place "where morality is removed and survives in its fulfilment." This place is, of course, the same place where Green's vision is real. "Here our morality is consummated in oneness with God, and everywhere we find that 'immortal Love', which builds itself for ever on contradiction, but in which contradiction is eternally resolved."

In the sorrow following their master's death, the disciples of Green could have found some consolation in the conclusion of Bradley's *Ethical Studies*. Perhaps they still had among them one who could see Green's vision. If they did, then they could still hope that he would be able to make this vison available to the common intelligence of mankind. He would make accessible to the common intelligence the eternal love in which the human contradiction is eternally resolved.

There was cause for hope, but not yet joy. A morality described as simultaneously removed and fulfilled was a morality not yet accessible to the common intelligence. The vision of an immortal love in which the contradictions are eternally resolved had to be made accessible or else the spirit of *Ecclesiastes*, once invoked, would remain to haunt, for *Ecclesiastes* had seen this very longing to transcend reality as but another of the vanities of life.

> The eye is not satisfied with seeing,
> Nor the ear filled with hearing.

The thing that hath been,
It is that which shall be;
And that which shall be is that which shall be done:
And there is no new thing under the sun.

The failure is inevitable, the hunger will never be satisfied, the future will be the past—Bradley had to show that this was not so. The contradictions in the world build; they do not destroy. The pursuit of first principles is more than a vexation of the spirit.[3]

CHAPTER TWELVE

F. H. BRADLEY
(from 1876)

F. H. Bradley's second major work, *The Principles of Logic*, was almost ready for publication at the time of Green's death. It was published in 1883, the same year as Green's *Prolegomena to Ethics*. In *The Principles* Bradley had not yet assumed the role of leader. He modestly described his task much as Green had described his own in the introduction to Hume years before. Bradley was simply clearing the ground for a philosophy of the future.

> What we want at present is to clear the ground, so that English Philosophy, if it rises, may not be choked by prejudice. The ground cannot be cleared without a critical, or, if you prefer it, a sceptical study of first principles.... I am persuaded that a movement which keeps to this line will not be turned back.

This tone of confidence would have pleased Green. Nonetheless, there were certain statements made in this same preface that would probably have disturbed him, for they would have reminded him of his own teacher, Benjamin Jowett. First there was a condemnation of system-making: "We want no system-making or systems home-grown or imported. This life-breath of persons who write about philosophy is not the atmosphere where philosophy lives." Perhaps Bradley meant *premature* system-making. But then there was also Bradley's admission that he possessed no certainty about what he says—"On all questions, if you push me far enough, at present I end in doubts and perplexities." However, he did say *at present*. Presumably, with a little more thought, he could remove this uncertainty. But, if he thinks he can, why does he say concerning his uncertainty, "on this account at least no lover of metaphysics will judge of me hardly"? Is he implying that uncertainty is inevitable in foundations of philosophy? If he is, this is certainly not a matter to be discussed in so playful a tone. Green would have found much the same ambiguity throughout *The Principles of Logic*, things of which he would have approved closely mixed with those he would have thought questionable.

Green would have approved of Bradley founding his logic on a denial of a central tenet of the psychology the utilitarians had advo-

cated. Ideas are not, Bradley argued at length, merely faded sensations. Our ideas are as fully factual as are the sensations from which
utilitarians mistakenly think they are derived. Ideas are simply mental
facts which we use to stand for other facts. They are signs for the
other facts, not faded residues of them.

Bradley developed his point by using the example of what he called
the language of flowers. In the language of flowers one type of flower
is used to stand for each of the virtues. One stands for hope, another
charity, and so on. The flowers have the same logical relationship to
their signified virtues as do our ideas to their signified facts. The
flowers and our ideas fully exist in their own right, independently
of their virtues or facts. Both of their relationships to the signified
are purely arbitrary, established by custom or convention. There is no
intrinsic reason why a particular flower signifies a particular virtue,
and the same word can be used to denote quite different objects.

Green would have approved of this point. He had himself devoted a
whole series of lectures to enumerating the many mistakes of Mill's
System of Logic. So Green would have approved, fully expecting the
next step to be the demonstration that sensations were themselves
really ideas. Here Bradley would have disappointed him. Bradley had
no love for ideas as such.

The flowers as themselves were things of delight, but as signs for
virtues they were imposters. Flowers could never be virtues; no more
could my idea of green be itself green. A sign, although having an
existence in its own right, could never assure the existence of the
signified. In short, ideas were logical freaks which could never be
adequate to the sensuous reality they purported to signify. We can
never be sure that any virtues really exist, even though we have flowers
and words aplenty to signify them. Signs are facts which have been cut
off from the one thing that makes them valuable, their own factuality.

As if to emphasize this freakish character of ideas, Bradley multi-
plied the metaphors through which he tried to express it. On a single
page of the *Principles* ideas are called paradoxical shadows, ghosts of
facts, divorced adjectives, cutloose parasites, spirits without bodies,
mere possibilities. They are called fleeting, self-destructive, mutilated,
condemned to live under other skies and changing seasons.

If anyone objected that such metaphors were inappropriate for a
treatise on logic, Bradley would probably have agreed. Metaphors
are, by their very nature as metaphors, always inadequate to the
reality which they pretend to represent. An idea is not a ghost, but

an idea. To call it a ghost is to call it what it is not. But, then again, an idea is not really an idea but a fact. It is a fact which is being used to stand for what it is not. All metaphors are, by their very nature as metaphors, always inadequate to the reality which they purport to represent—and all ideas, all signs are metaphors. Could there be any more obvious metaphor than representing a virtue by a flower? And could there be any more obviously inadequate metaphor than representing a virtue by marks upon a page or sounds upon the wind?

Here Green would have become worried. Bradley was leading his readers dangerously close to the place Hume had been content to stay, the grave of philosophy itself. "To sum up the result—if reality consists in an actual sequence of sensuous phenomena, then our reasonings are all false because none of them are sensuous." Bradley did not expect his readers to accept this conclusion without some squirming. In fact he had seen his readers squirming throughout his lengthy systematic destruction of logic. He has been from the first solicitous at their unease. At one point, when these readers appear finally to have found a way to preserve at least part of logic as valid, Bradley turned and said sadly, "We shall do well to prepare our minds for an unwelcome surprise." He did say it sadly, but could they help but think they saw the slightest flicker of a smile on his face?

It was perhaps with such a flickering smile that Bradley began the concluding subject of the *Principles*, "The Validity of Inference." The readers suddenly found themselves no longer in a logical treatise, but rather on a epic odyssey, their heroic journey almost over.

> The title of our chapter, welcome though it be, excites foreboding. We are glad when we see the harbour so near, but the approach brings with it an ultimate risk and a final anxiety. We have escaped some perils, but our safety has perhaps been dearly purchased. In the course which we have taken, the worst lies at the end, and that end is before us. We shall hardly sail in with vessel unscathed, and with colours flying: and, did fortune consent, we would gladly compromise. We would change all hope of a triumphant entry for the trust that our voyage might not end at sea. We are resigned to shipwreck, if only by any means something may be saved.

Alas, logic did not survive this final shipwreck. It went down with the ship. When the extent of the loss became clear, Bradley discreetly abstained from any further comparisons to epic journeys, and began to speak of "our logical disease" which, it seems, is terminal.

> This failure was symptom of our logical disease, a weakness not passing, nor logical in its area, but deep-rooted in the system. For

judgment and inference, if we are to have them at all, must both be *discursive*; they must work with ideas. But idesa do not exist, and they cannot exist, if existence means presence in the series of phenomena . . . . the idea does not happen, and it can not possess a place in the series. It is a mutilated content which, as such, can not claim to be more than an adjective. And the functions that work with these unrealities can not possibly reproduce the flow of events.

And, as the colours disappear beneath the waves, Bradley can put the matter more simply still. "To sum up the result—if reality consists in an actual sequence of sensuous phenomena, then our reasonings are all false." *If* reality consists in an actual sequence of sensuous phenomena. Bradley knows his readers will grasp at this last chance to save something. And, as always, he is there, sympathetic, helpful, to the last.

> We can not at the end of these toilsome marches accept the failure of our whole expedition. . . . And perhaps it is not our reasoning that will suffer a loss of dignity. Why should not that view which finds reality within the series of temporal events, be itself degraded to the rank of an illusion? Why should not the result of the deepest philosophies after all be the truth, and our sensuous presentment be misrepresentations that can not give fact?

Perhaps the sensuous itself is the mere appearance, the spiritual the reality.

But now Bradley asked a hard question. Would a spiritual reality be any more satisfying than its contrary? The "sensuous curtain" is certainly "a deception and a cheat, if it hides some colourless movement of atoms." But is it any less a deception and cheat if behind it is only "some spectral woof of impalpable abstractions, or unearthy ballet of bloodless categories."

> Though dragged to such conclusions, we can not embrace them. Our principles may be true, but they are not reality. They no more *make* that Whole which commands our devotion, than some shredded dissection of human tatters *is* that warm and breathing beauty of flesh which our hearts found delightful.

In the end, Bradley had repudiated the belief that the world formed a spiritual whole. In this sense, he had repudiated Green. However, he had not repudiated the search for "that Whole which commands our devotion." As if to give his ship-wreck readers one final hope, Bradley concluded *The Principles of Logic*:

> The desire to comprehend our Universe as the double outgrowth and revelation of a single principle, depends on a genuine impulse

of philosophy. It will hardly be fulfilled without patience and criticism, and never if we start with a blind acquiescence in the coarsest prejudices of popular thought.

Perhaps Green had failed to make his vision accessible because in his impatience he had acquiesced to popular prejudice. Perhaps it is a coarse prejudice that the world, if it is to be of a single principle, must be either material or spiritual. Perhaps there is possible a synthesis of these two contraries, a synthesis which would somehow transcend both. Perhaps we would return home at last.[1]

The work that was to realize, or dash, that final hope was *Appearance and Reality: a metaphysical essay*. It was published in 1893, the year after Nettleship's death on Mount Blanc.

The very subtitle Bradley chose for his culminating work must have been a source of apprehension for some of his readers. Ultimate philosophical syntheses are not often called essays. And Bradley's Preface to *Appearance and Reality* left no doubt that the subtitle had been chosen with care. Of the book as a whole, Bradley wrote, "Neither in form nor extent does it carry out the idea of a system." Rather the book is "a more or less desultory handling of perhaps the chief questions in metaphysics." The tentativeness of the book could scarcely be more emphasized. Bradley would not vouch that his questions were the chief questions; perhaps they were. He would not even be definite in his indefiniteness; he was desultory, more or less.

The book was intended to be a "critical discussion of first principles"; but it was not intended to discover those principles, but only to "stimulate inquiry and doubt." This was not to say that a complete rational system of first principles could not be reached in the Britain of his day. Bradley wrote, "I know no reason why the English mind . . . should not in our day produce a rational system of first principles." That such was now possible was, in Bradley's opinion, largely due "to men of a time shortly before my own, and who insisted well, if perhaps incautiously, on the great claims of Kant and Hegel."

No one was going to be able to claim that Bradley himself was incautious. He did not deny the influence the German writers had upon him, but he confessed "I do not know precisely" what that influence was. As for his book, it "does not design to be permanent, and will be satisfied to be negative, so long as that word implies an attitude of active questioning."

This attitude was, most of all, what Bradley was trying to convey in his preface. Bradley wished never again to enter "mere polemics." He only wished to "keep my natural place as a learner among learners." This was the attitude Bradley took toward his own essay which followed the preface. It was also the attitude he wished his reader to share. "I offer him a set of opinions and ideas in part certainly wrong, but where and how much I am unable to tell him. That is for him to find out, if he cares to and if he can."

In the Preface Bradley had humbled himself. This acted as but a preparation for the Introduction in which the humble Bradley humbled philosophy itself. At the beginning of this Introduction, metaphysics was defined in exalted terms—"an attempt to know reality as against mere appearance, or the study of first principles or ultimate truths, or again the effort to comprehend the universe, not simply piecemeal or by fragments, but somehow as a whole." Or rather it would have been exaltedly defined if words like "attempt" and "effort" had not been included. Metaphysics should be the knowledge of reality, first principles, the universe as a whole. But, no, it was rather an attempt, an effort; and, as such, it might succeed, or it might fail and remain forever an essay, a mere questioning.

Whether or not the attempt was to fail, Bradley would not allow it to be given up as futile before it was made. "To say reality is such that our knowledge cannot reach it, is a claim to know reality; to urge that our knowledge is of a kind which must fail to transcend appearance, itself implies that transcendence." To say such or urge such is to be "a brother metaphysician with a rival theory of first principles." Bradley himself was "so bold as to believe that we have a knowledge of the Absolute, certain and real, though I am sure that our comprehension is miserably incomplete." (The boldness affirmed in the sentence is negated by the trailing dependent clause; Bradley had a boldness of a very cautious type.)

At this point, Bradley heard an objection, the objection that he, while pretending to defend philosophy, was really conceding too much. If philosophy in its first principles can be at best miserably incomplete, then it is not worthwhile. Bradley responded to this objection, but not in terms designed to soothe the objector.

> I must suggest to the objector that he should open his eyes and should consider human nature. Is it possible to abstain from thought about the universe? I mean that, by various causes, even the average man is compelled to wonder and reflect. To him the world, and his

share in it, is a natural object of thought, and seems likely to remain one.

According to Bradley, this is the human root not only of metaphysics, but also of poetry, art, religion. You cannot deny that philosophy is worthwhile just because it is incomplete, anymore than you can deny poetry, art, and religion on the same grounds.

> And so, when poetry, art, and religion have ceased wholly to interest, or when they show no longer any tendency to struggle with ultimate problems and to come to an understanding with them; when the sense of mystery and enchantment no longer draws the mind to wander aimlessly and to love it knows not what; when, in short, twilight has no charm—then metaphysics will be worthless.

And to repudiate the twilight is to deny value to human life itself.

What of philosophy as the dispeller of mysteries, of the philosopher as the lover of only that which he knows? Of such a philosophy and such a philosopher, Bradley had little to say. Bradley insisted that philosophy is of value only "as a satisfaction of what may be called the mystical side of our nature—a satisfaction which, by certain persons, cannot be as well procured otherwise."

> All of us, I presume, more or less, are led beyond the region of ordinary facts. Some in one way and some in others, we seem to touch and have communion with what is beyond the visible world. In various manners we find something higher, which both supports and humbles, both chastens and transports us. And, with certain persons, the intellectual effort to understand the universe is a principal way of thus experiencing the Deity.

What of philosophy as the apex of human achievement, the final fulfillment of all that was good in religion, art, poetry? It is gone. Philosophy is only, for persons of a certain type, a principal way of experiencing that which most all other men also experience, each in his own way. The experience was the same, only the means were different. The way of reason did not leave the philosopher "initiated into something far higher than what the common herd possesses."

As by the end of the Preface Bradley had humbled himself, so by the end of his Introduction he had abased philosophy. The last sentence of the Introduction summed up both the Introduction and the Preface. "There is no sin, however prone to it the philosopher may be, which philosophy can justify so little as spiritual pride."

The pattern of Book I, "Appearance," of *Appearance and Reality* was familiar to any reader of *The Principles of Logic*. Here not a valid

logic, but a valid metaphysics was being sought. Nonetheless, the
result was the same, one failure leading but to another failure.

According to Bradley, metaphysics is supposed to solve "the
world's enigma." This enigma is that the world does not appear to be
rational, internally consistent. The philosopher endeavors to make
it so by taking something or other as reality—atoms in motion,
say—and then by deriving everything else from this reality, somehow
or other—much as the Cartesians had tried to derive all natural
phenomena from atoms in motion. That which is only derived from
reality, and hence is not the reality itself, is appearance—gravity, in
the Cartesian system, is reduced to being a mere appearance.

Bradley examined one after another of the schemes by which
philosophers had tried to separate appearance from reality. He began
with the Cartesian, the view that reality is constituted by "those
aspects of what we perceive or feel, which, in a word, are spatial."
One after another of these schemes he examined, and one after another
he found fraught with self-contradiction, and thereby condemned to
the world of mere appearance. And not just purely metaphysical
systems were found to be fraught with such self-contradiction, but
virtually all ideas whereby non-philosophers as much as philosophers
try to understand reality. Space, time, motion, change, thing, self,
one after another were found to be real only apparently.

By the time Bradley was beginning his attack upon the self, upon
his readers' very sense of their own identity, he anticipated these
readers to be on the verge of rebellion, much as over a century
earlier Hume had anticipated a similar reader rebellion when he had
begun to attack the notion of a cause. Much as Hume had done on
that occasion, Bradley turned to reassure his readers.

> You may say that we are each assured of our personal identity
> in a way we are not assured of the sameness of things, [the sameness
> of things was the most recent casualty] but this is, unfortunately,
> quite irrelevant to the question. That selves exist, and are identical
> in some sense, is indubitable. But the doubt is whether their sameness,
> as we apprehend it, is really intelligible, and whether it can be true
> in the character in which it comes to us.

Of course, this was faint assurance. Soon the self, like thing,
cause, and the rest, was found upon examination to be unintelligible.
Bradley, however, did not believe his readers would thereby lose their
assurance of the reality of the self. The self might not be comprehen-
sible to thought, but it was still real. This was exactly the reaction

Bradley wished his readers to have, not just to his examination of the
self, but of all the rest as well. Throughout the whole first book, his
readers, he assumed, were growing increasingly frustrated by the
failure of thought to comprehend their sense of reality. By the end of
Book I all that he could conclude was "Everything so far, which we
have seen, has turned out to be appearance.... But to deny its
existence or to divorce it from reality is out of the question."

The search of metaphysics was for means to remove contradictions;
but apparently all that had been achieved throughout Book I of
Appearance and Reality was the multiplication of contradictions. In
short, the readers had been led to the brink of philosophical despair.
Now, in Bradley's judgment, they were ready to experience the Deity,
the Absolute. Book II was entitled "Reality."

In it Bradley first had to counteract, at least partially, the despair.
He pointed out to his readers that throughout the first book, throughout all the failures, they had been experiencing an absolute, although
they might not have realized it at the time.

> Through the last Book the reader will remember we were for the
> most part criticizing. We were judging phenomena and were condemn-
> ing them, and throughout we proceeded as if the self-contradictory
> could not be the real. But this was surely to have and to apply an
> absolute criterion. For consider: you can scarcely propose to be
> quite passive when presented with statements about reality. You can
> hardly take the position of admitting any and every nonsense to be
> truth, truth absolute and entire, at least so far as you know. For, if
> you think at all so as to discriminate between truth and falsehood,
> you will find that you cannot accept open self-contradiction. Hence
> to think is to judge, and to judge is to criticize, and to criticize is
> to use a criterion of reality.

How can the readers deny this, when that is precisely what they had
been doing throughout the first book? They know it, as does Bradley.
And so he can challenge them. To deny their experiencing of the
absolute "would be mere blindness or confused self-deception."
Hence they have reached an absolute about reality. "Ultimate reality
is such that it does not contradict itself; here is an absolute criterion."

His readers, from their experience in Book I, had this absolute
criterion, but they also had something else. They not only knew that
reality was self-consistent, they also knew, from their own painful
experience, that thought about reality always led to self-contradiction,
all thought from the most abstruse speculations about the spatial
nature of the world to the more concrete talk about things. All this

thought, when examined, had been found to be self-contradictory.

So Bradley's readers really knew two things from their attempt at metaphysics. Reality as we seek it in philosophy does not ever contradict itself; thought eventually always does. The conclusion to be drawn was obvious. Thought was not part of reality; thought was but a mere appearance which had to be discarded if we were ever to experience reality as a consistent whole. In this conclusion, there was an irony. The readers had been led to it by thought itself. What his readers were seeing was, in Bradley's phrase, a "happy suicide," the happy suicide of thought.

Reality, the Absolute, is that self-consistent whole which is left after reflection dies. Thought which sought to divide one thing from another, one place from another, one time from another, the word from the thing, the subject from the object, appearance from reality, everything from everything else—thought has killed itself. What is left is the sentient whole from which thought has for so long separated us.

Now at last Bradley's readers knew why philosophy was to appeal to the mystical side of their nature, why its end could only be the *experiencing* of the Deity, why the net effect was to be humbling, chastening, transporting. The end was to be the end of philosophy, of thought, of reason, of any independent sense of oneself. The end was to be our absorption into the Deity, or Absolute, or Universe (as Bradley later termed it). It was to return to what Bradley called that "stage of existence which we suppose to come first in the development of the soul," the pristine stage before the soul had succumbed to the temptation of thought.[2]

The positive, even euphoric, terms in which the ordinarily ironic Bradley spoke concerning the Absolute obviously did not prevent the question whether or not this euphoria was justified. One could grant that thought or reason had committed suicide, and that this suicide was inevitable, without seeing it as a happy event. The death of reason did not necessarily have to the be birth of something new and satisfying, even to the mystical side of our nature. Why did Bradley think it was? Perhaps he simply was unable personally to face the unhappy truth that it was not. Such an attitude toward the Absolute was expressed in yet another of the Balliol rhymes. Since Bradley was not himself a fellow of Balliol, the rhyme was ostensibly about his brother, A. C. But there was only one philosopher at Oxford who was famous for having both suffered bad health and seen the Absolute.

My name is A.C. Bradley,
And when my liver's doing badly
I take refuge from the "Brute",
In the Blessed Absolute.

How could Bradley reply to the insinuation that only a failure of nerve prevented him from ending his final synthesis in despair rather than bliss?

In an essay written late in life, years after the publication of *Appearance and Reality*, Bradely appears to have faced the darkness that many found implicit in the work. He admitted that his reasoning could lead to intellectual despair, since his reasoning showed that the hopes of reason would never be fulfilled in this world. He admitted the inevitable result of his philosophizing was "the mere denial of any known satisfactory doctrine, together with the personal despair of any future attainment." Nonetheless, this despair, Bradley wished to insist, had its good side. It taught us that the only whole to command our devotion should be that which is within our reach.

> Our real world of fact may, for anything we know, be one of the least pieces of reality, and there may be an indefinite number of real worlds superior to our own. On the other hand, our world is the one place in which we are able to live and work. And we can live there in no way except by making our construction of facts in space and time, and by treating this construction as the one sphere in which our life is actual. *Cultiver notre jardin* is the beginning, and it is in a sense the end, of wisdom. No other place but here, no other time but now, no other world but this world of our own, can be our concern. . . . We must till our garden awake and in no dream to gain the fruits and flowers for which alone it is worth while to live, and which, if anything there are better, at least to us are everything. If this is not Heaven, it at least comes nearer to the reality of the Blessed Vision than does any stupid Utopia or flaming New Jerusalem adored by the visionary.

Till your gardens, and ignore the delusions of visionaries. In the three decades Bradley lived after the publication of *Appearance and Reality*, he followed his own advice. He tilled his own philosophical garden. (He wrote short essays clarifying points in his arguments, and he brought out new editions of his books.) And he tried no new major works of philosophy. There was, however, one final work which he directed to be published only after his own death. It was a collection of one hundred aphorisms, on which he had worked for decades.

The attraction of this form for him was explained by one of the aphorisms themselves. "An aphorism is true where it has fixed the impression of a genuine experience." In these aphorisms, the final fruits of his experience, Bradley tried to capture his impressions as he himself tried to live a delusionless life. Many of the aphorisms were intended to unmask pervasive delusions.

The delusion of a providence—

"*At Monte Carlo.* This is the Temple of Providence where disciples still hourly mark its ways and note the system of its mysteries. Here is the one God whose worshipers prove their faith by their works, and in their destruction still trust in Him."

The delusion of a world which cares about good and evil—

" '*Sidera cum tacet nox.*' The moral law and the starry Heaven; each according to Kant, overpowers us with reverence. We almost forget to wonder that the latter should even know how to smile in disregard for the former."

The delusion that we are immortal—

"Every sunset, were it conscious, must think itself immortal, because it is unique."

The delusion that we are loved for ourselves—

"Our pleasure in any one who in some way resembles those we love should warn us that no love is in its essence individual."

The delusion that we are worth being loved for ourselves—

"The soul's immutable core—if there is one—can hardly be amiable. And to love any one for himself perhaps in the end becomes unmeaning."

The delusion that we are even liked for ourselves—

"If any one is to remain pleased with you, he should be pleased with himself whenever he thinks of you."

The delusion that we really care about goodness—

"The deadliest foe to virtue would be complete self-knowledge."

The delusion that we have principles—

"A man may find, when he is in love, that in reality his principles were only other feelings."

The delusion that we can ever be happy—

"The secret of happiness is to admire without desiring. And that is not happiness."

The delusion of philosophy—

"The shades nowhere speak without blood, and the ghosts of Metaphysic accept no substitute. They reveal themselves only to that victim whose life they have drained, and, to converse with shadows, he himself must become a shade."

The delusion of civilization—

"A great library to one man is a temple of immortal spirits. On another it strikes as a most melancholy charnel-house of souls."

The delusion of a happy maturity—

"After a certain age every milestone on our road is a grave-stone. And the rest of life seems a continuance of our own funeral procession."

The delusion that love is ever really satisfied—

"To love unsatisfied the world is a mystery, a mystery which love satisfied seems to comprehend. The latter is wrong only because it cannot be content without thinking itself right."

The delusion that love is ever really satisfied—

"We may approve of what we love, but we cannot love because we approve. Approbation is for the type, for what is common and therefore uninteresting. But love is the passionate attempt to find oneself in another. And oneself is unique."

The delusion that we ever really wish to find ourselves in others, that we ever really wish to satisfy our love—

"Every mortal desires above all things to be unique."

The delusion that the desire to communicate is not selfish—

"The craving to be understood may in the end be the merest egoism."

The delusion that we can ever fully communicate—

" 'One never tells more than half', and in the end perhaps one cannot. In the end the heart is alone."

The delusion that we can ever really communicate—

"Our live experiences, fixed in aphorisms, stiffen into cold epigram. Our heart's blood, as we write with it, turns to mere dull ink."

We are really neither loved not loving, neither understood nor understanding, neither happy nor good. We are only alone in a world totally indifferent to us, and in this world we are as ephemeral as sunsets.

And we endure our lives through delusion—

> " 'Le soleil ne la mort ne se peuvent regarder fixement.' It is well, then, that our life should set in clouds."

We endure our lives through delusion—

> "One said of suicide, 'As long as one has brains one should not blow them out', And another answered, 'But, when one has ceased to have them, too often one cannot.' "

All of these aphorisms were but scholia to Bradley's first—

> " 'Everything comes to him who waits'—among other things death."

And the first was dry and barren.

In the end, Bradley's sensual Absolute did not command devotion, the garden itself seemed a delusion. And when that delusion was gone, all that was left was despair. Then, Green's immortal vision endured only as the grinning mummy of itself. Then, the twilight had finally lost its charm.[3]

PART IV

INDEFINABLES

CHAPTER THIRTEEN

G. E. MOORE AND BERTRAND RUSSELL
(to 1904)

Sometime near the beginning of our own century, G. E. Moore and Bertrand Russell, themselves both fellows of Newton's own college, Trinity College, Cambridge, discovered indefinables. The exact date, the circumstances, even the relative contributions of the two men are uncertain. Both Moore and Russell did leave autobiographical reminiscences—and Russell's, in particular, was lengthy. However, by the time they wrote these reminiscences, they had come to have serious misgivings about their discovery, if they still regarded it as a discovery at all. And so the details, at least as they recollected them, were left unrecorded.

Nevertheless, one of their students about the time of the discovery, John Maynard Keynes, did record the enthusiasm it evoked in those closest to them. "It was exciting, exhilarating, the beginning of a renaissance, the opening of a new heaven on a new earth, we were the forerunners of a dispensation, we were not afraid of anything."

The sense of being forerunners of a new dispensation was perhaps enhanced by Moore, Russell, Keynes, and a number of the others in their circle, all being members of a secret Cambridge society called The Apostles. Even the existence of the society was supposed to be kept a secret from the uninitiated. A member was to learn of the society only at the moment he was informed that he had become one of the elect. During their meetings an Apostle was free to discuss with his fellows any subject whatsoever. There were, of course, certain rules of protocol. One of these was that the Apostles must always refer to themselves as Reality, and to the larger but lesser world of non-Apostles as Appearance.

Moore and Russell were not afraid of anything. Most of all they were not afraid of Mr. F. H. Bradley. Whereas Bradley had led reason into the abyss, Moore and Russell were confident that they, using indefinables, could lead it back out again. Then reason would never again be so threatened. Then at last it would give to man the certainty he had so long sought. Then at last the perennial twilight would be dispelled.

As Keynes and his generation of Apostles had learned not to be afraid of anything from Moore and Russell, so Moore and Russell had learned not to be afraid of F. H. Bradley from fellow Apostle John Ellis McTaggart, their teacher of philosophy. McTaggart thought that Bradley had neglected the central part of Hegel's teaching, the dialectic, which showed precisely how contradictions build rather than destroy. Bradley had shown that the various categories of human thought were infected by contradictions, but he failed to show how these contradictions always point to the categories immediately above themselves—how the contradictions in mathematics point to physics for their resolution, how the contradictions in physics point to chemistry for their resolution, those in chemistry to biology, and those in biology finally to ethics. Hegel's dialectic demonstrated a logical hierarchy of categories. Through the ascent from the categories of mathematics to those of ethics, logic itself required that the true be the good, that the impersonal be but a partial manifestation of the personal, that the real be the ideal becoming conscious of itself. McTaggart put it as follows.

> [The Dialectic] demonstrates that the lower categories, in themselves, and to whatever matter of intuition they may be applied, involve the higher categories also .... Not only is it impossible to explain the phenomena of vegetable and animal life by the idea of mechanism, but the idea is inadequate even to explain the phenomena of physics. Not only can consciousness not be expressed merely in terms of life, but life is an inadequate category even for biological phenomena. With such a system we are able to admit without any danger whether to its consistency or to its practical corollaries, all that science can possibly claim as to the interrelation of all the phenomena of the universe, and as to the constant determination of mind by purely physical causes. For not only have we justified the categories of the spirit, but we have subjected the whole world of experience to their rule. We are entitled to assert, not only that spirit cannot be reduced to matter, but also that matter must be reduced to spirit. It is of no philosophical importance, therefore, that all things should, from the scientific standpoint, be determined by material causes. For all material determination is now known to be only spiritual determination in disguise.

The dialectic culminated for Mc Taggart in the proof not of God but of human immortality. The ultimate triumph of the personal over the impersonal was for McTaggart that of the individual over the grave. To demonstrate rationally the certainty of this triumph was the highest task of philosophy. As much as Hegel had contributed to it, he was far from finishing it. Finishing it McTaggart thought might take generations. Yet, inevitably, it would be finished. The achievement of Hegel made that certain.

While Hegel was one source of McTaggart's confidence in the future, another must have been his two young students, G. E. Moore and Bertrand Russell. At the same time McTaggart himself was systematically studying the relevant aspects of Hegel in preparation for his own attempt at synthesizing the ideal and the real, the ethical and the scientific, Moore was working on the categories of ethics, and Russell on those of mathematics and science. By 1898, Moore had already produced a paper arguing for the internal consistency of some of the categories of ethics. And by 1897 Russell had produced something even more impressive.

In 1897 Russell's *An Essay on the Foundations of Geometry* had appeared, dedicated "to John Ellis McTaggart to whose discourse and friendship is owing the existence of this book." In it Russell argued that the "contradictions arising out of the relativity and continuity of space" could only be resolved by reference to matter. In other words, geometry considered by itself was not quite rational. To be made consistent it would have to be subsumed under physics. Russell had taken the first step toward reducing all the categories to those of spirit. Moreover, at the end of *An Essay* he seemed already preparing for the second step; there he observed that the idea of matter, like that of space before it, was vexed by certain paradoxes.

McTaggart, for his part, had finished *Studies in Hegelian Dialectic* in 1896. And in 1901 he published his *Studies in Hegelian Cosmology* in which he began to discuss the implications of Hegelian dialectic for the question of immortality. However, by this time Moore and Russell had deserted McTaggart and his program, for one of their own.

To the attentive ear, this desertion was announced in a series of lectures on the seventeenth century German philosopher Gottlieb Leibniz which Russell delivered at Cambridge in 1899. Bertrand Russell was a substitute for McTaggart, the regular lecturer, who was visiting his family in New Zealand. McTaggart seems to have suggested his protegé Russell as his own substitute.

In the lectures Russell did not mention McTaggart by name. Ostensibly, he stuck to his subject. Yet the historical example of Leibniz, as Russell developed it, had a twentieth century parallel which the Cambridge audience could scarcely have missed. Russell had argued that Leibniz's philosophy was an attempt to save reason from its annihilation in the monism of Benedict Spinoza. Russell was sympathetic with what Leibniz had tried to do. Russell did not doubt that Leibniz's view of reality, particularly his insistence upon the reality of individual persons, was much closer to the truth than Spinoza's. Nonetheless, Leibniz had made a fatal mistake. He had accepted Spinoza's assumptions about logic. Having done this, Leibniz was doomed to failure. He could avoid Spinoza's unhappy conclusions only by inconsistency. And Russell was unmerciful in pointing out the fundamental inconsistencies in Leibniz's reasoning.

The Cambridge audience could scarcely have missed the remarkable parallels which existed between McTaggart and Leibniz, on the one hand, and Bradley and Spinoza, on the other. Equally clear was the message: what McTaggart was trying had been tried before, and had been a conclusive failure. When the lectures came to be published, Russell went further to make sure that his readers did not miss the contemporary implications of his analysis of the past. Perhaps, out of courtesy, he could not mention derogatorily the man who had allowed him to give the lectures in the first place. He could, however, add a few footnotes which pointed out certain similarities between Spinoza's assumptions about logic and those of a well known contemporary philosopher, Mr. F. H. Bradley.

The publication of McTaggart's *Studies in Hegelian Cosmology* provided G. E. Moore with the occasion to make his own rebellion against McTaggart public. He wrote two reviews of the book, one in 1902, the other in 1903. The first can be taken as representative. Moore praised McTaggart for explaining with "most unusual clearness both what his conclusion is and what are the premises and arguments by which he holds it to be proved." Unfortunately, McTaggart's arguments were unusual only in their clarity, and not in their force. His arguments, as Moore put it with respect to one of them, might "produce a feeling of probability in the minds of those who have the amiable disposition to accept any argument for which they can find no distinct refutation ... however, it is certain that no reasonable person can be blamed for entirely refusing assent to the conclusion." Moore did praise McTaggart, but only for stating his arguments so clearly that "their complete impotence may be easily exposed." To expose his teacher's impotence was the purpose of both Moore's reviews.

One of the younger Apostles, Lytton Strachey, put the matter even less politely.

> McTaggart's seen through God
> And put him on the shelf;
> Isn't it rather odd
> He doesn't see through himself.

McTaggart's impotence Moore, Russell, and the younger Apostles did not intend to inherit. They were not going to rely on the amiable dispositions of their readers. They wished conclusions which no reasonable person could deny without blame. They aspired beyond what previous generations of philosophers had achieved.[1]

G. E. Moore and Bertrand Russell were confident that they could fulfill these aspirations because they knew where they had to start. Logic, the very procedures of reason, had to be defined so that reason could never again turn against itself. Logic, in its very foundations, had to preclude the happy suicide of thought. Then, and only then, what was built would be built for all time. So logic had to be founded upon pristine ideas, ideas which reason itself could never violate, ideas which analysis could never defile. In short, the ideas themselves had to be indefinable.

Russell had mentioned the logical necessity of indefinable ideas in his lectures on Leibniz. As he put it, "Since one idea can only be defined by another, we should incur a vicious circle if we did not admit some indefinable ideas." It was just such a vicious circle which Bradley had used in his *Principles of Logic* to destroy logic. Bradley had, in effect, demanded a definition for every idea. Bradley had made logic appear to generate a whirlwind which destroyed all ideas and soon overwhelmed logic itself.

The whirlwind could be quieted by indefinable ideas. This much was clear to Moore and Russell. But the most difficult task remained, proving that such ideas were. So in the early years of this century, Moore and Russell were trying to perfect the analytic procedure by which they could reach the true indefinables. Perhaps the clearest general account of this procedure was given by Russell in 1903.

> This discussion of indefinables—which forms the chief part of philosophical logic—is the endeavor to see clearly, and to make others see clearly, the entities concerned, in order that the mind may have that kind of acquaintance with them which it has with redness or the taste of a pineapple. Where, as in the present case, the indefinables are obtained primarily as the necessary residue in a process of analysis, it is often easier to know that there must be such entities than actually to perceive them; there is a process analogous to that

which resulted in the discovery of Neptune, with the difference that
the final stage—the search with a mental telescope for the entity
which has been inferred—is often the most difficult part of the under-
undertaking.

Russell assumed his readers would recognize the discovery of
Neptune as one of the great triumphs of Newtonian astronomy. At
about the time John Stuart Mill was experiencing his mental crisis,
irregularities in the orbit of the outermost planet then known, Uranus,
had become disturbing for some astronomers. The irregularities
seemed to violate Newtonian physics. Finally, the hypothesis was
proposed that these irregularities were being caused by the gravitational pull of an unknown planet beyond the orbit of Uranus. Astronomers computed the mass and orbit of this hypothetical planet,
eventually to be called Neptune. The discovery of Neptune in 1846
was hailed by at least one contemporary as the "greatest verification"
of Newton's principle of gravity.

If Russell's readers did know about the discovery of Neptune,
they would have seen the comparison Russell was implying between
Newton's achievement and his own. Just as Newton had found the
key which unlocked the secrets of the world of nature, and thereby
made discoveries like that of Neptune possible, now Russell (and
Moore) had discovered the key to the world of reason itself.

The above comparison occurred in the preface to Russell's *The
Principles of Mathematics*. In this work Russell hoped to show to
exist some of the indefinables of logic. But this was not all. He wished
also to show that mathematics itself was but a deduction from these
indefinables. Mathematics and logic were one, and they were complete without any reference to the categories of physics. By establishing the indefinables of mathematics and logic, Russell hoped to
prevent even the first step of Hegel's dialectic, the very step that a
few years earlier Russell had tried to make unavoidable.

"The", "a", "and", "or", "some", "all", "every"—these are a few
of the logical terms which Russell sought to make for his readers as
distinctive and irreducible as the taste of a pineapple. He also tried
to make his audience see that certain propositions as well have an
irreducible logical form. In other words, just as when we analyze
concepts we find that certain concepts are indefinable, so too when we
analyze propositions we sooner or later come to propositions which
cannot be further analyzed without losing meaning. In perceiving this,
we are perceiving the indefinable logical form of a proposition.

Indefinable concepts and indefinable propositional forms were the reality toward which the philosopher worked. Their existence assured him that his labors would not lead him into the abyss Bradley euphemistically named the Absolute. All knowledge could now be given a firmer foundation. That included the knowledge given to men by Isaac Newton.

Near the end of *The Principles of Mathematics*, Russell applied his analytic techniques to Newton's ideas of absolute space and time. According to Russell, Newton, "not being a skilled philosopher," had failed to present an adequate logical foundation for absolute space and time. Over two centuries later, Russell did this for him. Now at last absolute space and time stood firm. The ideas themselves had all tinge of contradiction removed from them. And Newton's empirical arguments remained, according to Russell, "unrefuted, and so far as I know irrefutable."

While Russell was laying the foundations of mathematics and, by the by, giving the philosophically unskilled Newton a hand, Moore was laying the foundations of ethics. The very title Moore chose for his work invited comparison with Newton's: *Principia Ethica*.

"Everything is what it is and not another thing." This was the epigraph of the *Principia Ethica*. Bishop Butler had written it in his *Analogy of Religion* (first published in 1736). His remark epitomized the logical basis on which the good bishop had tried to preserve Christianity from attempts to absorb it into Newtonian natural philosophy. Christianity was what it was and not another thing.

This remark also epitomized the general struggle of Moore and Russell to preserve the true indefinables from being absorbed into some mystical absolute; it epitomized, in particular, what Moore wished to do in ethics. In his *Principia* Moore intended to make his readers realize that good is what it is and not another thing. Through careful analysis, Moore would convince his readers that good must be an indefinable; then he would encourage them to point their mental telescopes where they could see it. By the end of the *Principia Ethica*, the experience of good would be for Moore's readers as irreducibly real as the taste of pineapple. It would be as real for them as it already was for G. E. Moore. As Moore put it, " 'Good' . . . is one of those innumerable objects of thought which are themselves incapable of definition, because they are ultimate terms by reference to which whatever *is* capable of definition must be defined."

This is the point at which the analogies with pineapples and planets break down. The taste of pineapple, or even that of a mere apple, is an experience which some men have not had. And only a handful have actually seen Neptune. The experience of good, in contrast, is one that presumably all mature human beings have had, although they might not have realized it for what it was, the perception of an indefinable. Men might have to search the skies for Neptune, not being sure such a planet is there. But they can search their mental skies knowing that the idea of good has to be there somewhere. They worry not about never seeing it at all, but about never seeing it distinctly.

Not seeing the idea of good sufficiently distinctly is, according to Moore, the mistake of all previous ethics. Previous moral philosophers have had such a blurred vision that they have mistaken the idea of good for other ideas—for pleasure, duty, or something else. They have failed to see that good is what it is and not another thing. Nevertheless, the philosophers of the past, whether they recognized it or not, did have within their minds the real idea of good, an indefinable idea independent of all other ideas. (And so did Moore's readers.) In arguing that good was, say, pleasure they were trying to do the impossible. They were trying to make identical what was not in fact, even in their own minds, identical. Occasionally these philosophers admit they are wrong. Moore, for example, could quote John Stuart Mill admitting that "virtue is sometimes desired as well as pleasure." Like all other moral philosophers, John Stuart Mill occasionally was forced to admit that good was not the same as that to which he hoped to reduce it.

In such a way, Moore could refute earlier views on ethics. Each moral philosopher eventually drops his guard, and admits his error. However, unlike Bradley in his *Ethical Studies*, Moore wished somewhere to have his readers stop. He did not wish them to conclude that all our ideas are inadequate to our ethical aspirations. He wished his readers to be satisfied with the idea of good itself. To have them feel so satisfied, he had to make them experience the idea of good in all its distinctiveness. But how could he do this?

He could not do it directly. He could not describe good itself without contradicting his own central contention that good was unanalyzable. He could not describe it in terms of something other than itself. He could only try to do it indirectly. He could point to those wholes of which good always seemed to be a constituent part.

He could point to those things which were incontestably good, and trust that the audience would perceive good as a distinctive part of them.

But Moore did not write as facilely as Russell. Not surprisingly, therefore, it was Bertrand Russell who wrote the most accessible account of the procedure which Moore himself used.

> When people ask "What do you mean by 'good'?", the answer must consist not in a verbal definition such as could be given if one were asked "What do you mean by 'pentagon'?" but in such a characterization as calls up the appropriate idea to the mind of the questioner. This characterization may, and probably will, itself contain the idea of good, which would be a fault in a definition, but is harmless when our purpose is merely to stimulate the imagination to the production of the idea which is intended. It is in this way that children are taught the names of colours: they are shown (say) a red book, and told that that is red; and for fear they should think "red" means "book", they are shown also a red flower, a red ball, and so on, and told that these are all red. Thus the idea of redness is conveyed to their minds, although it is quite impossible to analyse redness or to find constituents.

Just as one might proceed with a child who did not have a distinct understanding of red, so did Moore near the end of the *Principia Ethica* proceed with his readers. He had to show his readers things which were intrinsically good. But what things are intrinsically good? This question he took to mean "what things are such that, if they existed *by themselves*, in absolute isolation, we should yet judge their existence to be good." This way of stating the question— Moore called it the method of absolute isolation—prevented the readers from making a mistake similar to that Russell's child might have made in confusing "red" and "ball." Moore's readers might have been inexperienced enough to mistake "intrinsically good" for "good as a means." Once he had gotten the readers to ask the question in the proper way, then he could point to those wholes which were obviously intrinsically good.

> If, now, we use this method of absolute isolation, and guard against these errors, it appears that the question we have to answer is far less difficult than the controversies of Ethics might have led us to expect. Indeed, once the meaning of the question is clearly understood, the answer to it, in its main outlines, appears to be so obvious, that it runs the risk of seeming a platitude. By far the most valuable things, which we know or can imagine, are certain states of consciousness, which may be roughly described as the pleasures of human

intercourse and the enjoyment of beautiful objects. No one, probably, who has asked himself the question, has ever doubted that personal affection and the appreciation of what is beautiful in Art or Nature, are good in themselves; nor if we consider strictly what things are worth having *purely for their own sakes*, does it appear probable that any one will think that anything else has *nearly* so great a value as the things which are included under these two heads.

Principia Ethica, much more than the esoteric *Principles of Mathematics*, convinced the younger Apostles that they were living at the beginning of a new dispensation. Lytton Strachey wrote to Moore, "The truth, there can be no doubt, is really now upon the march. I date from October 1903 the beginning of the Age of Reason." And to a fellow Apostle, himself also an admirer of Moore, Strachey exclaimed, "And the wreckage! That indiscriminate heap of shattered rubbish among which one spies the utterly mangled remains of Aristotle, Jesus, Mr. Bradley, Kant, Herbert Spencer, Sidgwick, and McTaggart! Plato seems the only person who comes out even tolerably well. Poor Mill has, simply, gone."

Plato might have come off tolerably well, but only compared to those consigned to the rubbish heap. G. E. Moore was quite simply, in Maynard Keynes' words, "better than Plato." And some of the Apostles had begun to describe Moore's mental powers in almost superhuman terms. "What a brain the fellow has! It dessicates mine! Dries up my lakes and seas and leaves me an arid tract of sand. Not that he is arid—anything but: he's merely the sun."[2]

In 1903 G. E. Moore announced what was perhaps the most important implication of his and Russell's discovery of indefinables. Idealism, which had dominated German philosophy for about a century and British philosophy for almost half that long, had been refuted. He announced this in a paper titled simply "The Refutation of Idealism."

The idealist hopes to prove that the universe is spiritual. This is a remarkable ambition because if the idealist is right, then the universe is quite different from what is commonly supposed. It means that the universe is, in some sense, intelligent, purposeful, and that it is not mechanical. Having thus described idealism, Moore was careful to profess humble reverence before so sublime a philosophical vision.

> For my own part I wish it to be clearly understood that I do not suppose that anything I shall say has the smallest tendency to prove

that reality is not spiritual: I do not believe it possible to refute a single one of the many important propositions contained in the assertion that it is so. Reality may be spiritual for all I know; and I devoutly hope it is.

Moore devoutly hoped it is, but the arguments used by idealists to prove it to be so, troubled him. In particular, one argument which "to the best of my belief is considered necessary to their position by all Idealists" troubled him. It in particular troubled him because it happened to be false.

No one, it seemed, had ever had any good reason for supposing that reality was spiritual. Nonetheless, Moore did not mean to suggest that men should refrain from supposing true so uplifting a vision of the universe. For all Moore knows "to suggest pleasant and plausible suppositions may be the proper function of philosophy." Moore could only regret that he had nothing of the kind to suggest.

> Even if I prove my point, I shall have proved nothing about the Universe in general. Upon the important question whether Reality is or is not spiritual my argument will not have the remotest bearing. I shall only attempt to arrive at the truth about a matter, which is in itself quite trivial and insignificant, and from which, so far as I can see and certainly so far as I shall say, no conclusions can be drawn about any of the subjects about which we most want to know.

The only importance Moore humbly claims for his subject—and he will not even insist upon this claim—is that if what he argues is correct, then "all the most striking results of philosophy—Sensationalism, Agnosticism, and Idealism alike—have, for all that has hitherto been urged in their favor, no more foundation than the supposition that a chimera lives in the moon." But, of course, as Moore said, his subject is trivial, insignificant, and uninteresting. It might seem to you remarkably ambitious. But compared to the ambition of the idealist, it is modest indeed.

The proposition on which any proof of idealism depended was "*Esse* is *percipi*"—or, as Moore translated it, "To be is to be experienced." The ways in which the spirituality of the universe is deduced from this proposition are, in Moore's words, "familiar enough."

> It is said that since whatever is, is experienced, and since some things are which are not experienced by the individual, these must at least form part of some experience. Or again that, since an object necessarily implies a subject, we must conceive it to belong to some subject or subjects, in the same sense in which whatever is the object of our

experience belongs to us. Or again, that, since thought enters into
the essence of all reality, we must conceive behind it, in it, or as its
essence, a spirit akin to ours, who thinks: that "spirit greets spirit"
in its object.

Moore did not question the validity of these deductions. Rather he
wished to question the proposition from which the deductions were
made. Although the deductions themselves were logically correct,
if to be is not to be experienced, then we are left as "far from a proof
that reality is spiritual, as if they were all false too."

In the *Principia Ethica*, Moore had refuted hedonism by making his
readers see that pleasant and good were distinct ideas. Good was what
it was and not another thing. Now Moore had to make his readers see
that to be and to be experienced were also distinct. The procedure was
similar. He carefully analyzed the question. The question whether
or not to be and to be experienced were the same was refined, after
much analysis, into the question whether or not a sensation and our
awareness of it were distinguishable. At this point Moore thought
he had reached indefinables. Awareness, or consciousness, Moore
insisted, was itself an indefinable which existed in an indefinable
relationship to the sensation. When we are aware of blue, this awareness is "itself something distinct and unique, utterly different from
blue."

To be sure, there had been those philosophers who have denied the
unique relationship of knowing—just as there were those philosophers
who denied the uniqueness of good by trying to reduce good to
pleasant. But, just as Moore could quote the hedonists testifying
against themselves, so now he could quote those philosophers who
denied this uniqueness doing the same. He could show his readers
that those philosophers as well have at times "recognized that
something distinct is meant by consciousness."

Even so, in the end Moore had to admit that consciousness was
something very difficult to perceive distinctly.

> The moment we try to fix our attention upon consciousness and
> to see *what*, distinctly, it is, it seems to vanish: it seems as if we had
> before us a mere emptiness. When we try to introspect the sensation
> of blue, all we can see is the blue: the other element is as if it were
> diaphonous. Yet it *can* be distinguished if we look attentively enough,
> and if we know that there is something to look for. My main object
> in this paragraph has been to try to make the reader *see* it; but I fear
> I shall have succeeded very ill.

If Moore had succeeded ill, it was because of his own inadequacies as a writer or perhaps because the readers had not been looking attentively enough. Or it might just be that awareness is exceedingly difficult to see. As Moore himself admitted, "awareness is and must be in all cases of such a nature that its object, when we are aware of it, is precisely what it would be if we were not aware." If Moore had failed to enlighten his readers, it might have been for all these reasons. However, there was one reason that he would not accept as an explanation. He would not even entertain the possibility that he might have failed because consciousness was not distinct. It *can* be distinguished. And when it is, then idealism is seen to be "as baseless as the grossest superstition."

G. E. Moore was content to announce his refutation of idealism in the professional journal of philosophy, *Mind*. Beyond his Cambridge students and associates Moore made little effort to attract followers for his and Russell's new philosophy. Bertrand Russell was not so shy. On the discovery of the *Principia Ethica* alone, Russell published no less than four separate essays including a review. (Moore, although he did write one long review of the *Principles of Mathematics*, never had it published.)

According to Russell, moral philosophers had always aspired to the certainty attained by the natural philosophers and mathematicians. This was, Russell insisted, a legitimate aspiration. "The object of ethics, by its own account, is to discover true propositions about virtuous and vicious conduct, and . . . these are just as much a part of truth as true propositions about oxygen or the multiplication table." Therefore, Russell concluded, ethics is, at least in aspiration, "merely one among the sciences." Moreover, now that the true principles of ethics were understood, now that it was known that ethics had to be based upon "notions of intrinsic good and evil," a truly scientific ethics was within reach.

Russell was also prepared to explain the implications of Moore's refutation of idealism. Reality was not spiritual, the universe was not personal. Moore might not have proven this, but he had come so close to doing it that no reasonable man would believe the contrary. Moore had shown that the central argument of idealism was false, just as Russell had shown that its dialectic would never progress beyond mathematics if mathematics was properly understood. So all that was left was the world of our senses, and the world science tells us is behind them. This world, so similar to that described by

Lucretius centuries earlier, Russell described for his readers in an essay, "A Free Man's Worship." The following is his summing up.

> Such in outline, but even more purposeless, more void of meaning, is the world which Science presents for our belief. Amid such a world, if anywhere, our ideals henceforth must find a home. That Man is the product of causes which had no prevision of the end they were achieving; that his origin, his growth, his hopes and fears, his loves and his beliefs, are but the outcome of accidental collocations of atoms; that no fire, no heroism, no intensity of thought and feeling, can preserve an individual life beyond the grave; that all the labours of the ages, all the devotion, all the inspiration, all the noonday brightness of human genius, are destined to extinction in the vast death of the solar system, and that the whole temple of Man's achievement must inevitably be buried beneath the debris of a universe in ruins—all these things, if not quite beyond dispute, are yet so nearly certain, that no philosophy which rejects them can hope to stand.

Russell himself hoped to build a philosophy on these foundations, a philosophy which would stand as long as the Temple of Man, and would perhaps even be the inmost altar of that Temple. It was not too much to hope. After all, Moore had proven that ethics was but a part of the world of science, and that there was no reason for believing in another world beyond that one. And Russell had shown that this world of science was rationally self-sufficient. Or rather he had begun to show it.[3]

CHAPTER FOURTEEN

BERTRAND RUSSELL AND ALFRED NORTH WHITEHEAD
(1904-1914)

The Principles of Mathematics was the first step towards Bertrand Russell's ultimate goal. Establish the rational self-sufficiency of mathematics, and then do the same for physics. And so on, until the whole of man's intellectual achievement has been given foundation in indefinables. This achievement might eventually be buried beneath the debris of his universe, but at least it would no longer be in danger of collapsing from within.

It was an ultimate goal which would take at least a lifetime to complete. Not even the first step had been completed with the publication of *The Principles of Mathematics*. This work itself needed a second volume in which the body of mathematics was in fact logically deduced from the logical indefinables.

In this labor, G. E. Moore would be of no help. After 1903 he was no longer at Cambridge. The term of his fellowship at Trinity College had expired, and, although he was financially independent, he did not wish to stay at Cambridge without a formal position. When a friend moved to Edinburgh, Moore went with him. (Russell's fellowship had also expired, but he, likewise financially independent, chose to stay on at Cambridge.)

Moreover, even if Moore had stayed, he could have been of little help. Moore had come to philosophy from classics. He did know some mathematics, but not enough to help on the monumental labor which Russell now wished to begin. As early as 1900 Russell had urged Moore to take special tutoring in mathematics, but Moore never had.

While working on *The Principles of Mathematics*, Russell had been influenced by many continental philosophers of mathematics. For instance, Russell found so much of his own work anticipated in that of his Austrian contemporary Gottlieb Frege he devoted an appendix of *The Principles* to it. But Russell needed more than just correspondence and an occasional meeting; he needed close collaboration. Deducing the body of mathematics would be no small task even for two men. So Russell turned to Alfred North Whitehead.

A family connection existed between the Whiteheads and the

Russells. Whitehead's father had actually been pastor of the Russell family church. (There was an earldom in the Russell family, for which Bertrand was second in line.) This connection appears to have passed on to a second generation. Before Bertrand Russell had matriculated at Cambridge, Alfred Whitehead the son, himself eleven years older and already a fellow of Trinity College, had begun to take an almost pastoral interest in his progress. Whitehead served on the committee which decided whether prospective undergraduate Bertrand Russell should be awarded a scholarship. When another boy did better than Russell in the scholarship examination, Whitehead, who happened to be the committee member entrusted with the examinations, destroyed the other boy's to ensure Russell's selection. As an undergraduate, Russell was tutored for his mathematical tripos by Whitehead himself. (Whitehead felt his handling of the scholarship matter justified when Russell did better on his tripos than the other boy.) And when Russell became an Apostle, he discovered that Whitehead was one as well. And when, after graduation, Russell submitted *An Essay on the Foundations of Geometry* in competition for a postgraduate fellowship, Whitehead was one of the two-man committee which awarded it to him.

So it was perhaps as natural that Russell should turn to Whitehead for collaboration on his major work as it was for Whitehead to agree. At the time he agreed, Whitehead had published but a fraction of what Russell had. While their views on the foundations of mathematics were quite similar, Whitehead had published no philosophy.

The work on the second volume of *The Principles* proved more difficult than had been anticipated. Soon they came to realize that the first volume was itself, in Russell's words, "a crude and rather immature draft." The new version of the work would have to be written over from the very beginning. This time a title was chosen more in keeping with the tradition of Newton (and Moore). The new work was to be *Principia Mathematica*, the Latin suggesting the eternal and unchanging character of the principles developed on its pages.

However appropriate the new title, the work still did not go well. Since he was starting again from the beginning, Russell felt he should resolve some paradoxes he had left unresolved in *The Principles of Mathematics*. The most difficult of these paradoxes were all of a similar type. One had been famous from ancient times, from the time of the very first efforts to discover the first principles of logic. When

Epimenides the Cretan says that all Cretans always lie, is he telling the truth? No logical answer seemed possible to most ancient logicians. If Epimenides is telling the truth, then he himself must be lying; and if he is lying, then he could be telling the truth. No logical answer seemed possible to Bertrand Russell either, although he knew there had to be one. All Russell could do was discover more examples of the same kind of paradox. He even found the most general form of the paradox. Is the class of all classes which are not members of themselves, itself a member of itself? If it is, then it is not; if it is not, then it is. This was to be known as Russell's Paradox. It was not, however, the kind of immortality Russell sought.

He wanted solutions, not paradoxes. He had important work to get on to, and here he was stopped by some childish paradoxes. "It seemed unworthy of a grown man to spend his time on such trivialities, but what was I to do?" He had to solve them, but he could not. "Every morning I would sit down before a blank sheet of pages. Throughout the day, with a brief interval for lunch, I would stare at the blank sheet. Often when evening came it was still empty." This went on for months. Not until 1905 did Russell begin to see a solution, but the solution required him to give up much of what he had earlier held to be certain.

In *The Principles* Bertrand Russell had discovered many of the indefinables which would make logic and mathematics rationally self-sufficient. Among those indefinables that he had discovered were "all," "a," "some," "any," "every," and "the." Had he not seen them with his mind's eye? Were they not as distinctive as the taste of pineapple? As potentially perceptible as the planet Neptune?

There had been an unfortunate aspect to this analogy with the discovery of the planet Neptune. One of the chief predictors of Neptune had been the French astronomer Urbain Leverrier. Once the discovery was made, some thought Leverrier the greatest French astronomer since Laplace. A few years after his triumph, Leverrier became interested in the irregularities observed in the orbit of Mercury, irregularities which seemed to challenge Newtonian principles in much the same way those of Uranus had. Using the same methods he had developed earlier, Leverrier postulated the existence of an unknown planet between Mercury and the sun. So confident was he of its discovery that Leverrier named it beforehand, Vulcan. Vulcan was never found. (And by the time Russell was writing his *Principles of Mathematics* the irregularities of Mercury still defied

15

absorption into the Newtonian system). Russell was now to decide that some indefinables he had discovered in *The Principles of Mathematics* were Vulcans, not Neptunes.

Russell found the beginning of his answer while dealing with a lower level paradox than either Epimenides or Russell's own. "The present King of France is not bald." Is this proposition true or false, given that there is now no king of France? The difficulty we have answering that question comes from the fact that this proposition can mean two quite different things. It can mean, "There is an entity which is now King of France and is not bald." Or it can mean, "It is false that there is an entity which is now King of France and is bald." When the proposition is thus re-written, its truth or falsity becomes obvious. If the first meaning is intended, the proposition is obviously false; if the second, it is true. The ambiguity in the original proposition came from the phrase "the present King of France." Once that phrase was re-written as "there is an entity which is now King of France" the solution was almost at hand. Here, however, Russell paid his price.

The important difference between the two expressions is that in the second the "the" has been omitted—the indefinable "the" has been analyzed away. Russell could resolve his paradoxes, but to do so he had to give up some of his logical indefinables. By 1905, only two years after the publication of *Principles of Mathematics*, Russell had decided that his mental telescope had not discovered quite so many indefinables as he had thought.

Russell, as always, put the matter in its most positive light. He had, after all, discovered the correct logical interpretation of such denoting phrases as "a man," "the man," and the like. He announced this discovery in his 1905 paper "On Denoting." Denoting phrases should, for logical purposes, be re-written so that articles like "the" and "a" were excluded. Russell had, in effect, discovered the definitions for these articles.

The definitions of these tiny words were, alas, far from tiny. Russell, for instance, suggested that the proposition "The father of Charles II was executed" be interpreted as really meaning "It is not always false of x that x begat Charles II and that x was executed and that 'if y begat Charles II, y is identical with x' is always true of y." Russell admitted that this "may seem a somewhat incredible interpretation." It certainly seemed so to the editor of *Mind*, the philosophy journal to which Russell submitted "On Denoting" for publication.

This editor urged Russell, for the sake of his reputation, to withdraw the article. Russell, undaunted, insisted it be published.

Nevertheless, Russell had anticipated the logical philistinism of his readers; he knew that to them his suggestion would seem somewhat incredible. Throughout the essay he bore this philistinism with a confident good humor. He patiently pointed out that if some such interpretation were not accepted, then when George the fourth asked if Scott was the author of *Waverly*, one would be logically justified in replying "Scott is Scott." This, Russell added, would not be an acceptable answer, for "an interest in the law of identity can hardly be attributed to the first gentleman of Europe."

With a similar nobility of mood, Russell then discussed whether the present King of France was bald. There was, of course, no present King of France. On the other hand, the most recent one that comes to mind, did lose his hair, albeit with his head still attached.

> By the law of excluded middle, either "A is B" or "A is not B" must be true. Hence either the present King of France is bald or the present King of France is not bald must be true. Yet if we enumerated the things that are bald, and then the things that are not bald, we should not find the present King of France in either list. Hegelians who love synthesis will probable conclude that he wears a wig.

To show how his own method could save his readers from such paradoxes Russell chose as his central example the statement "The first line of Gray's Elegy states a proposition." He even gave his readers the first line: "The curfew tolls the knell of parting day." Was it the curfew that tolled the knell of parting day for the readers, or was it Russell's paper? Was he really implying that, if they did not understand what he was doing, they should follow the example of the lowing herd and plowman, simply homeward plod and leave "the world to darkness and to me."

Could Bertrand Russell, the brother of an earl, really be suggesting such an ungentlemanly thing? Why, of course not. And yet, if readers did jump to such conclusions, it was partly Russell's own fault. He used what were supposedly simple examples. Yet, somehow they all seemed to relate to one another in ways allusive but real. There standing together were Charles II, in mourning for his beheaded father; the King of France, missing at least his hair; Sir Walter Scott, reliving an unsuccessful Jacobite uprising; and George the fourth, poor, ineffective George the fourth, least kingly of all recent British monarchs (pity he did not have more sense of his royal identity).

And in the midst of this boneyard of royal failures, there sat Thomas
Gray observing that:

> The beast of heraldry, the pomp of power,
> And all that beauty, all that wealth e'er gave,
> Awaits alike the inevitable hour.
> The paths of glory lead but to the grave.

No one could doubt that the author of "On Denoting" fully
appreciated the delights of allusive connotations; but at the same time
Russell was showing his readers this, he was also arguing that they
should, on occasion, for certain purposes, engage in the most unwitty,
crabbed kind of literalism imaginable. And who were they to deny
this, except on logical grounds? Who were they to deny this after
Russell has been so witty, so charming, so utterly disarming?

At the end of "On Denoting" Russell said that he would remain
silent in this paper about many of the important implications of his
interpretation of denoting phrases. "I will only beg the reader not to
make up his mind against the view." Bertrand Russell never remained
silent for long, however. And there was much to be done. Once a
few of those indefinables had been defined, then more could be if it
proved convenient. They suddenly had lost their inviolable status.

This was extremely important for the resolution of paradoxes like
that named after Russell himself. In 1906, and then again in a more
complete form in 1908, Russell announced the resolution of these
paradoxes. The latter paper appeared in the *American Journal of
Mathematics*, and was entitled "Mathematical Logic as Based on the
Theory of Type."

In this paper the readers were first introduced to seven of the
paradoxes which had most troubled him in his early work on *Principia
Mathematica*, including naturally the Epimenides paradox and Russell's
own paradox. Common to all these paradoxes, Russell observed,
was a peculiar use of the word "all."

> In all the above contradictions (which are merely selections from an
> indefinite number) there is a common characteristic, which we may
> describe as self-reference or reflexiveness. The remark of Epimenides
> must include itself in its own scope. If all classess, provided they
> are not members of themselves, are members of *w* [the class of all
> classes which are not members of themselves], this must also apply
> to *w* . . . . In each contradiction something is said about all cases of
> some kind, and from what is said a new case seems to be generated,
> which both is and is not of the same kind as the cases of which all
> were concerned in what was said.

Once the problem is put this way, *and* once "all" is seen to be a word like any other, then the way to avoid this type of paradox is obvious. "All" will no longer be used in that way, however natural it might seem to common sense. "All" can never again be used reflexively. Russell put the restriction more elegantly: "Whatever involves *all* of a collection must not be one of the collection." As he summed it up, the whole matter was simply one of how we decided to use "all."

But it was not quite as simple as that. This can be seen from a proposition of Russell's own choosing, "All propositions are either true or false." This proposition, by Russell's restriction, cannot refer to itself. Therefore, the proposition is not really about all propositions, however much it might appear to be. Rather it was only about propositions of a certain logical type, of which this particular proposition was not one.

So in resolving the paradoxes, Russell had really made two discoveries. Not only had he discovered that "all" could not be used in a certain way, but he also, in following out the implications of this discovery, had discovered a logical hierarchy of propositions. Those propositions which were not about other propositions Russell called first order propositions. Propositions about first order propositions are logically of a different type; they are second order propositions. When one interprets propositions in terms of their position on the hierarchy of logical types, the paradoxes like that of Epimenides disappear.

> If Epimenides asserts "all first order propositions affirmed by me are false", he asserts a second order proposition; he may assert this truly, without asserting truly any first order proposition, and thus no contradiction arises.

If Epimenides guilefully tries to include his second order propositions among his lies, the logician can guilefully promote his assertion to the third order, and the paradox will again be avoided. The earl *ex post facto* becomes a duke. Poor Epimenides will soon realize that the logician has as unlimited a number of titles in his hierarchy as Epimenides has paradoxical statements. The ignoble cretan has been vanquished by the noble don.

Or rather the cretan had been almost vanquished. Russell admitted that there remained a few loose ends to be tied up. These he left unspecified, except to say that they were philosophical difficulties, not suitable to be raised in a journal of mathematics. And, anyway, it was clear that the correct resolution of these paradoxes, after millennia of trying, had at least been approximated. What little difficulties remained were dwarfed by the magnitude of the triumph. Now only time separated Russell and Whitehead from the completion of their *Principia*.[1]

A sign of Bertrand Russell's renewed confidence was the publication of a little essay, "The Study of Mathematics." Russell had actually first written this in 1902, when he had just submitted *The Principles of Mathematics* to press, and had yet to realize how much trouble those few little paradoxes he had uncovered were going to cause him.

Mathematics should be taught "to awaken the learner's belief in reason, his confidence in the truth of what has been demonstrated, and in the values of demonstration." The learner will see how the intellect had conquered subjects which only a little time ago "had been given over to Chaos and old Night." The learner will be taught to see "whatever is most general in its purity, without any irrelevant trappings." This vision itself was intrinsically good.

> Real life is, to most men, a long second best, a perpetual compromise between the ideal and the possible, but the world of pure reason knows no compromise, no practical limitations, no barrier to the creative activity embodying in splendid edifices the passionate aspiration after the perfect from which all great work springs. Remote from human passions, remote even from the pitiful facts of nature, the generations have gradually created an ordered cosmos, where pure thought can dwell as in its natural home, and where one, at least, of our nobler impulses can escape from the dreary exile of the actual world.

No sooner had he written these words in 1902, than mathematics, thanks to those dreary little paradoxes whose difficulty he had under-estimated, ceased to be a refuge, a natural home, and became merely another vexation of the spirit. Now, in 1907, Russell, having made only a few compromises, and having but a few small barriers before him, could once again feel about mathematics as he had in 1902. And so in 1907 he published "The Study of Mathematics" for the first time.

G. E. Moore was experiencing no comparable euphoria. He too had begun to compromise his indefinables. But he did not have the consolation that in doing so he was solving perennial philosophical problems. So there was less to distract him from what he had lost.

In the six years he spent in Edinburgh, 1903-9, Moore wrote little, a few papers and a number of reviews. Moore's reviews could be quite harsh. He would first make the author's central contention as clear as possible, and then determine whether he had offered any reasons which would convince an unamiable reader that the contention was true. One work he dismissed as "so wanting in clearness of thought that I doubt whether it can be of much use to anyone." Another was dismissed in the second stage of evaluation.

> So much for Mr. Gibson's meaning. By way of argument for this extraordinary proposition, I cannot find that he offers anything whatever. It only remains then to consider whether the mere statement of it is sufficient to advocate it successsfully. Surely it must be plain that, on the contrary, it refutes itself.

Moore was a demanding reviewer, but he was at this time as demanding of himself, and he was finding himself wanting. The most extended of Moore's efforts during this period was a sixty-page essay on "The Nature and Reality of Objects of Perception" which was published in 1906. Moore began this essay with the common sense conviction that something exists other than ourselves and our immediate sense perceptions. The philosopher's task was to clarify the exact meaning of this conviction and then to find good reasons for it. (Hume would have agreed that this was the job of philosophy, and he would have added that the philosopher's failure to perform even this task is proof of philosophy's impotence.)

> How do we know that anything exists except our own perceptions and what we directly perceive? How do we know that there are any other people who have perceptions in some respects similar to our own?

The bulk of Moore's paper was spent trying to clarify what was meant by these questions. As in his "Refutation of Idealism," Moore was apologetic for being so tiresome with his lengthy analysis. As in his "Refutation of Idealism," there was also an edge to the apologies. If his readers need apologies, it is only because they do not sufficiently understand what constitutes importance in philosophy.

> I am sorry to say that I have not yet reached the end of my explanations as to what my meaning is. I am afraid that the subject may seem tedious. I can assure you that I have found it excessively tedious to try to make my meaning clear to myself. I have constantly found that I was confusing one question with another, and that, where I had thought I had a good reason for some assertion, I had in reality no good reason. But I may perhaps remind you that this question, "How do we know so and so?" "What reason have we for believing

it?" is one of which philosophy is full; and one to which the most various answers have been given. Philosophy largely consists in giving reasons; and the question what are good reasons for a particular conclusion and what are bad is one upon which philosophers have disagreed as much as on any other question.

Moore was not bearing the philistinism of his audience with a confident good humor. What he anticipated was to be his readers' complaint against his paper he turned into a general complaint against philosophy, a complaint in which Moore could join. And he had ample cause to join in the complaint. After his excessively tedious analyses, after he had decided exactly what he meant by the questions, he could find no good reason for the answer he wished to give.

Only three years earlier, there were indefinables to which he could appeal. Now, it seems, he no longer saw them, or at least he no longer saw any indefinables which could help him with the case at hand. "Philosophy largely consists in giving reasons," Moore had written. (Bradley had written that it largely consists in "finding bad reasons for what we believe by instinct.") After his excessively tedious analysis, Moore found that all he could do was to reassert his instinctive belief in the reality of objects of perception.

> The more I look at objects round me, the more I am unable to resist the conviction that what I see does exist as truly, and as really, as my perception of it. The conviction is overwhelming.

But presumably the conviction was overwhelming before Moore's readers began his essay. What then had been achieved? The readers might have been impressed with both the difficulty of the question, and the care with which this difficulty was made clear. They might in short have been impressed by Moore, by how methodical he was, how willing he was to risk tedium for the sake of philosophy. Although they had reached no answer to the question, perhaps they had reached the answer to another question. How should philosophers proceed? They should proceed as G. E. Moore does. This was an emphasis of which Moore himself approved. As he concluded his essay, he admitted he had only found "grounds for suspense of judgment as to whether what I see does not really exist." But he insisted he had found "grounds, too, for renewed enquiry, more careful than such enquiry has sometimes been in the past."[2]

By 1910, *Principia Mathematica* was finished, except for an important fourth volume Whitehead was supposed to add later. (The three large volumes were published over the next three years.) In the final version the indefinables were second to the method. The analysis itself, and the deductions based upon its result, were the test of the truth or falsity of *Principia Mathematica*. The result of the analysis, of course, was what would have earlier been described as the discovery of indefinables. Now the matter would be put in another way, one not quite so ambitious.

After following their analysis so far, Russell and Whitehead settled on certain indefinables. Whether these indefinables were really indefinables was now a matter of indifference to them. No mental telescope here. Perhaps these "indefinables" could actually be defined in terms of a smaller set. That did not trouble Russell and Whitehead. They did not claim for them ultimate status. They only claimed that the main features of mathematics could be deduced from them.

If Russell and Whitehead had been interested in having their readers see certain indefinables as really indefinable—something that was central to both *The Principles of Mathematics* and *Principia Ethica*—they would have prominently displayed the analysis which led them to select these indefinables. Far from being prominently displayed, the analysis was completely omitted from *Principia Mathematica*.

> The preliminary labour of analysis does not appear in the final presentation, which merely sets forth the outcome of the analysis in certain undefined ideas and undemonstrated propositions. It is not claimed that the analysis could not have been carried farther: we have no reason to suppose that it is impossible to find simpler ideas and axioms by means of which those with which we start could be defined and demonstrated. All that is affirmed is that the ideas and axioms with which we start are sufficient, not that they are necessary.

Not suprisingly, the theory of logical types, fundamental as it was to the resolution of the paradoxes, occupied a prominent position in the final version of *Principia Mathematica*. So important was this theory as it was developed in the first volume, that the second volume began with a "prefatory statement" which was included to "bring together in one discussion various explanations which are required in applying the theory of types to cardinal arithmetic." (Arithmetic was the main subject of volume two.) Moreover, the introduction to the *Principia* as a whole had a chapter devoted exclusively to the theory.

This chapter, "The Theory of Logical Types," was essentially just a revision of Russell's earlier paper "Mathematical Logic as Based on the Theory of Type." The changes made, on the whole, were not substantive. They were rather changes in tone.

"Mathematical Logic as Based on the Theory of Type" was just a paper for a mathematical periodical. It was an outstanding paper, perhaps; but it was not in itself an enduring monument to the human intellect. The massive edifice of *Principia Mathematica* was to be such a monument. *Principia Mathematica* was to be for all time. As a monument, it was to tower over history much as did Newton's *Philosophiae Naturalis Principia Mathematica*. Every part of it should convey a sense of the occasion.

Therefore, parts of "Mathematical Logic" had to be revised. For instance, Russell had written in the paper:

> But the theory in question seems not wholly dependent on this indirect recommendation; it has also, if I am not mistaken, a certain consonance with common sense which makes it inherently credible. This, however, is not a merit upon which much stress should be laid; for common sense is far more fallible than it likes to believe.

This now had to be revised to read:

> But the theory in question is not wholly dependent upon this indirect recommendation: it has also a certain consonance with common sense which makes it inherently credible.

In an enduring monument to the human intellect, ploys of feigned humility—"if I am not mistaken"—have no place, nor do sententious observations about common sense fallibility. (Principias are written to show that such fallibility can be transcended.) Moreover, the indefinite relation denoted by the semi-colon can be replaced by the exact equivalence of the colon. And, in any enduring monument to the human intellect, "seems" must become "is."

And it was not just the wording that had to be changed; the very structure of the essay itself had to be revised. In his "Mathematical Logic," Russell had taken a natural method of development. First he had made his readers aware of the problem of the paradoxes. Then the common feature of the paradoxes was elucidated. A way to avoid this feature— excluding the reflexive use of "all"—is then proposed. This proposal is finally perfected in the theory of types. The readers have been taken through a step by step procedure which leads them to the theory of types.

Such a structure, effective as it might be for an essay, was too personal for a Principia. Russell had in one of his other essays tried to describe the impersonal beauty of mathematics. He had said that mathematics was of value precisely because it satisfied us impersonally.

> Mathematics takes us still further from what is human, into the region of absolute necessity, to which not only the actual world, but every possible world, must conform; and even here it builds a habitation, or rather finds a habitation eternally standing, where our ideals are fully satisfied and our best hopes are not thwarted.

This was Russell coming down from the mountain, describing what he had seen. In *Principia Mathematica* Russell and Whitehead were on the mountain itself. And *Principa Mathematica* was to be what they saw there. No personal needs of the readers, no matter how easily met, were to be allowed to mar the structure of impersonal necessity.

So the order of discussion in "The Logical Theory of Types" is almost exactly the reverse of what it had been in "Mathematical Logic." The theory of types came first, the discussion of the paradoxes last. Even though the first sentence of "The Logical Theory of Types" read "An analysis of the paradoxes to be avoided shows that they all result from a certain kind of vicious circle," the paradoxes to be avoided are not described until the conclusion of the paper. The order of presentation is to follow the order of logical priorities. This will insure that the readers will see this work not as a persuasive process, but as a necessary whole.

Five years after the three volumes of *Principia Mathematica* were published, Russell wrote a popularization of it. In *An Introduction to Mathematical Philosophy*, as it was called, Russell made a remarkable admission. Despite the fundamental importance of the theory of types, and all the time he and Whitehead has spent on it, Russell admitted the theory "does not belong to the finished part of our subject: much of this theory is still inchoate, confused, and obscure."[3]

"In its chase after idols this age has not wholly forgotten the gods, and reason and faith in reason are not left without advocates." The author of this observation was George Santayana, and the advocates of reason and faith in reason to whom he was alluding were Bertrand Russell and G. E. Moore.

Santayana was a Spaniard by birth who has been educated at Harvard and had risen to the position of professor of philosophy there. His own philosophical position was idiosyncratic, a description he probably would have taken as a compliment. He was opposed to the notion of philosophy as a profession, something done by groups or movements. He wrote in his work of 1905, *The Life of Reason*:

> The true philosopher, who is not one chiefly by profession, must be prepared to tread the wine press alone. He may indeed flourish, like a bay-tree in a grateful environment, but more often he will rather resemble a reed shaken by the wind. Whether starved or fed by the accidents of fortune he must find his essential life in his own ideal.

So fragile a view of the philosopher himself paralleled an equally unexalted view of reason itself. "Reason, with the order which in every region it imposes on life, is grounded on an animal nature and has not any function other than to serve the same."

This was a view far from the impersonal philosophical principles after which Moore and Russell had sought. And Moore, for one, found Santayana virtually unintelligible. Santayana's *Life of Reason* was the book Moore had attacked as "so lacking in clearness that I doubt it would be any use for anyone." Moore did admit that Santayana could write well, but writing well and philosophising clearly were quite different. As Moore put it, "Mere confused suggestions may, no doubt, have a great aesthetic value; for confusion of thought does not seem to be inconsistent with very high literary merit."

Santayana would scarcely have approved of Moore's division of the philosophical from the aesthetic. At about the same time Moore was writing his review, Santayana was delivering a series of lectures intended to undermine any such division. In these lectures, entitled in their published form *Three Philosophical Poets*, Santayana argued that philosophy, in its highest form, is poetry.

> In philosophy itself investigation and reasoning are only preparatory and servile parts, means to an end. They terminate in insight ... a steady contemplation of all things in their order and worth. Such contemplation is imaginative. No one can reach it who has not enlarged his mind and tamed his heart. A philosopher who attains it is, for the moment, a poet.

But it was in prose, in his *Winds of Doctrine* (first published in 1912), that Santayana tried to show Bertrand Russell and G. E. Moore to be philosophical reeds. In his critique Santayana chose to focus on the writings of Russell. Not regarding tediousness as a merit of any kind, he found Moore's writing uncongenial. Even so, Santayana conceded, to be tedious was perhaps inevitable of a man who sought to refute idealism.

A man with such a mission requires a certain narrowness and concentration of mind; he has to be intolerant and to pound a good deal on the same notes. We need not wonder if Mr. Moore has written rather meagrely and with a certain vehemence.

Fortunately, the writings of the expansive Russell provided ample evidence of the "archaic dogmatism" which they both espoused. Santayana found it charming that over two millennia after Plato's death philosophers still could be found who believed they directly perceived the world of reason. Santayana characterized this belief as follows.

> This ideal world is knowable by separable mental consideration, a consideration which is, however, empirical in spirit, since the ideal world of ethics, logic, and mathematics has a special and surprising constitution which we do not make but must attentively discover.

Such an archaic belief existing in the twentieth century was charming, but was it true? Santayana, himself no mathematician, could not challenge Russell on mathematics. And yet there was something about the way in which Russell eulogized mathematics that interested him. When Russell wrote something like—"The true spirit of delight, the exaltation, the sense of being more than man, which is the touchstone of the highest excellence, is to be found in mathematics as surely as poetry"—he was not writing mathematics, immune to the criticism of all but initiated mathematicians. He was rather making an assertion about values.

> Mr. Russell . . . speaks explicitly of the value of mathematical study, a point of ethics and not directly in logic; yet his moral philosophy is itself so much assimilated to logic that the distinction between the two becomes somewhat dubious; and as Mr. Russell will never succeed in convincing us that moral values are independent of life, he may, quite against his will, lead us to question the independence of essence, with that blind gregarious drift of all ideas, in this direction or in that, which is characteristic of human philosophising.

Santayana had maneuvered Russell onto grounds where he and his readers could begin to raise doubts. If Russell was mistaken in, as Santayana put it, "hypostatising" good, then he could have been just as mistaken when he assured his readers that he perceived a world of essence behind the more esoteric appearances of mathematics. Santayana and his readers might not be familiar with these esoteric appearances, but they are sufficiently familiar with those more common appearances behind which Russell claims to perceive "good" in all its essence.

Santayana conceded to Russell that "good" was indefinable—or at least he was not prepared to supply a definition for it. But, having made this concession, Santayana claimed that he still did not see "good." Santayana's understanding of logic, he admitted, might not be "very accurate or subtle." However, he did not think he was required to admit the existence of something imperceptible to him, just because he could not define the word which was supposed to denote it.

> For the human system whiskey is truly more intoxicating than coffee, and the contrary opinion would be error; but what a strange way of vindicating this real, though relative distinction, to insist that whiskey is more intoxicating in itself, without reference to any animal; that is it pervaded, as it were, by inherent intoxication, and stands dead drunk in its bottle! Yet just in this way Mr. Russell and Mr. Moore conceive things to be dead good and dead bad.[4]

In March and April 1914 Bertrand Russell delivered the Lowell Lectures in Cambridge, Massachusetts. Santayana had been instrumental in getting Russell invited. And although Santayana was not there—he had resigned his Harvard professorship to return to Europe—his criticisms were a real presence.

What Russell hoped to do in these lectures was to give "a rough preliminary account of the more precise results [Whitehead] is giving in the fourth volume of our *Principia Mathematica*." This final volume was to demonstrate that the principles laid down in the first three volumes were adequate to account for "the relation between crude data of sense and the space, time, and matter of mathematical physics." Moore had been trying, without complete success, to prove the reality of the objects of our perceptions; now Whitehead, using the methods of the *Principia*, was going to show what exactly we can know. Hence Russell chose to entitle his lectures simply *Our Knowlegde of the External World*.

In general, Russell's confidence had not been shaken by the criticism of Santayana. The lectures began with a declaration of this confidence.

> Philosophy, from the earliest times, has made greater claims and achieved fewer results, than any other branch of learning. Ever since Thales said that all is water, philosophers have been ready with glib assertions about the sum-total of things; and equally glib denials have come from other philosophers ever since Thales was contra-

dicted by Anaximander. I believe that the time has now arrived when this unsatisfactory state of things can be brought to an end.

Nonetheless, Santayana had had his effect. Russell later admitted that after reading Santayana he lost his belief "in the objectivity of good and evil." "Santayana's criticism, in a book called *Winds of Doctrine*, caused me to abandon this view, though I have never been as bland and comfortable without it as he was." The pineapple in the end tasted like just another apple.

This concession was there in his first lecture, even though it was not named as such. In that first lecture Russell was at pains to emphasize that his and Whitehead's revolutionary philosophy had nothing whatsoever to do with ethics. In fact, its indifference to ethics was an integral part of its revolutionary character. Philosophy, like science, had to be ethically neutral if it was ever to be more than "a set of pleasing dreams."

So Moore and his *Principia* were consigned to the blind gregarious drift, lest they drag Russell and his *Principia* into it with them. And Santayana is never mentioned by name. But he is there as Russell labors to preserve logic, mathematics, and physics from the drift. In fact, for a time Russell speaks to his audience in Santayana's voice, the man of common sense debunking the pretensions of philosophers.

Russell was no longer the spokesman for esoteric mental operations—no longer will he say with glee, as he had written just two years earlier, "Anyone who wishes to be a philosopher must become accustomed to believing much that appears absurd to common sense." Or at least he will no longer say that approvingly. Now he will pose against the philosophers, philosophers who with "their naive faith . . . in the omnipotence of reason" have continually questioned our knowledge, even our knowledge of the external world. Russell will defend our knowledge for us; he will use reason not "to defeat common sense and thus leave the field clear for mysticism," but as a "harmonizing, controlling force" over our thoughts. His logic would be used to reinforce our knowledge, not to destroy it. Thus Russell began to teach his listeners about this new logic.

> In every proposition and in every inference there is, besides the particular subject matter concerned, a certain form, a way in which the constituents of the proposition or inference are put together. If I say, "Socrates is mortal," "Jones is angry," "The sun is hot," there is something in common in these three cases, something indicated by the word "is." What is in common is the form of the proposition, not an actual constituent.

Here Russell was pointing to a logical indefinable. He was, however, not pointing to it as an esoteric object like Neptune or the taste of pineapple, as an object of a special mental experience or intuition; rather he is pointing to it as an object we already know implicity.

> Thus some kind of knowledge of logical forms, though with most people it is not explicit, is involved in all understanding of discourse. It is the business of philosophical logic to extract this knowledge from its concrete integuments, and to render it explicit and pure.

Of course, knowledge of logical forms, even when explicit and pure, is not knowledge of the external world. Logic alone will not give knowledge of chairs, tables, mountains, and trees, to use Russell's own instances of the things of this world. Needed, according to Russell, is another kind of knowledge which, when combined with that of logical forms, will yield the external world. This other kind of knowledge is that provided by sensation. When knowledge of logical form is removed from a statement about the external world, there still remains a knowledge of sensation. These two are the two ultimate, pristine ways of knowing, each indubitable in itself. Russell summed up his contention:

> The hardest of hard data are of two sorts: the particular facts of sense, and the general truths of logic. The more we reflect upon these, the more we realize exactly what they are, and the more luminously certain do they become .... Real doubt, in these two cases, would, I think, be pathological. At any rate, to me they seem quite certain, and I shall assume that you agree with me in this.

We believe in the existence of trees and mountains, trees and mountains which exist even when no one is observing them. These enduring things are obviously not themselves sense facts. This is the point where logic, a logic provided by those competent in philosophy, saves our knowledge of the external world. The philosopher can show the man of common sense how his enduring thing is a logical hypothesis which is consistent with the hard data of senses. After some effort Russell arrived at the following tentative definition.

> We can now define the momentary common-sense "thing", as opposed to its momentary appearances. By the similarity of neighbouring perspectives, many objects in the one can be correlated with objects in the other, namely with the similar objects. Given an object correlated with it in all perspectives that system may be identified

with the momentary common sense "thing." Thus an aspect of a "thing" is a member of the system of aspects which is the "thing" at the moment.... All the aspects of a thing are real, whereas the thing is a merely logical construction. It has, however, the merit of being neutral as between different points of view, and of being visible to more than one person, in the only sense in which it can ever be visible, namely, in the sense that each sees one of its aspects.

Common sense has been saved from mysticism, but in the process has lost its integrity. The things of common sense are real only as fleeting hypotheses to be changed in light of new sensual truths. The existence of a tree can never be proven with absolute certainty. Its postulation can only be approved as consistent with the hard data of logic and sensation. In itself, it is hopelessly soft and vulnerable.

Common sense had served Russell well. It had provided a common ground between himself and his listeners. In defense of "our" knowledge Russell gained assent to his principles. But now he had gained this assent, and he needed our knowledge no longer. Now he could speak of our knowledge as but an inferior version of his own; he could speak of common sense as but a primitive form of science.

> Physics started from the common sense belief in fairly rigid bodies —tables, chairs, stones, mountains, the earth, and moon, and sun. This common sense belief, it should be noticed, is a piece of audacious, metaphysical theorizing; objects are not continually present to sensation, and it may be doubted whether they are there when they are not seen or felt. . . . We have here a first departure from the immediate data of sensation, though it is a departure merely be way of extension, and was probably made by our savage ancestors in some very remote prehistoric period.

Now he could criticize common sense almost as severely as he had earlier criticized the pretensions of the mystical philosopher. Now common sense had become an audacious piece of metaphysical theorizing, audacious and immature. Mature theorizing would be found in physics, at least physics as it would be purified in the fourth volume of *Principia Mathematica*.

Governing the progress from primitive common sense to sophisticated modern physics were immutable principles. These principles determine superior-inferior, better-worse, the good and the bad of our constructions of the world. Now finally these principles are being understood in themselves. Once understood, they need only be applied to the accumulated body of scientific theories, and men will for the first time know that they really do know about the world.

> The one and only condition, I believe, which is necessary in order
> to secure for philosophy in the near future an achievement surpassing
> all that has hitherto been accomplished by philosophers, is the crea-
> tion of a school of men with scientific training and philosophical
> interests, unhampered by traditions of the past, and not misled by
> the literary methods of those who copy the ancients in all except
> their merits.

That the natural leaders of such a school, or at least some of them,
already existed, Bertrand Russell's listeners did not need to be told.
Nor did they need to be told that the days of philosophers who had
been misled by literary methods were numbered. The future was
Russell's, not Santayana's.

Santayana himself took the news in good spirits. He had actually
discussed with Russell the substance of his lectures before they were
delivered. Russell's attempt to extend his philosophy beyond mathematics by grounding it in sensation Santayana thought a mistake
in judgment. He wrote to a correspondent at this time about Russell:

> His philosophy seems to have taken a new turn—to construct the
> universe out of sense data . . . it is a substitution of means for ends
> and of an analysis of knowledge for the object of it. Since I dis-
> covered this I have largely lost interest in Russell as a thinker; but
> he is a very amusing person.

Years later Santayana had not changed his mind. He repeated his
regret to the same correspondent. "Of course I read what Bertie
Russell writes although, as you know, I think he has relapsed into
the British original sin of empiricism, and all his intelligence and
keenness will not help him out of the consequent impotence and
sterility."[5]

CHAPTER FIFTEEN

ALFRED NORTH WHITEHEAD (1914-1922)

By 1914, Bertrand Russell, G. E. Moore, Alfred North Whitehead were no longer young men. Moore and Russell were in their forties, Whitehead well into his fifties. Both Russell and Moore once again had positions at Cambridge. Russell held a lectureship specially created for him in the principles of mathematics; Moore was lecturer in moral science. Whitehead had resigned his lectureship in mathematics (which he had held since before the turn of the century) to move to London; soon he was given an administrative position at the University of London commensurate with his eminence. So in 1914 they all were apparently settled in their middle age, their reputations established in their chosen fields, their positions secure in their chosen university, and, most importantly, their chosen faith in reason almost unshaken.

This chosen faith was shared with them, learned from them, by John Maynard Keynes. It was a faith, as Keynes later thought about it, based upon an "a priori view of what human nature is like, both other people's and our own, which was disastrously mistaken."

> We were the last of the Utopians, or meliorists as they are sometimes called, who believed in continuing moral progress by virtue of which the human race already consists of reliable, rational, decent people, influenced by truth and objective standards. . . . In short, we repudiated all versions of the doctrine of original sin, of there being insane and irrational springs of wickedness in most men. We were not aware that civilization was a thin, precarious crust erected by the personality and the will of the few, and only maintained by rules and conventions skillfully put across and guilefully preserved.

Keynes believed that "this religion of ours was a very good one to grow up under." But he also insisted that "as the years wore on towards 1914, the thinness and superficiality, as well as the falsity, of our view of man's heart became, as it now seems to me, obvious."

In referring to the date 1914, Keynes was, of course, alluding to the beginning of the Great War which killed and maimed so many of his generation. In its four year duration over a million were counted dead, and over five million wounded. Keynes would almost certainly

have agreed with those who saw this as so uncompensated a human
loss that they compared the Great War to the great plagues of old,
this one a plague visited upon men by themselves.

The ferocity of the war itself was perhaps evidence enough that
civilization was only a thin, precarious crust. If it was not, however,
the enthusiasm with which the bulk of intellectuals supported their
own nations' aspirations would have been. These intellectuals helped
their countrymen see the hand of God in this Great War, or rather
helped them to envisage themselves as His Hand. Each side was
fighting to triumph over evil; each side, through its victory, was
going to make the world safe and just. All this helped convince
Keynes of original sin.

Bertrand Russell was from the first opposed to the war, and from
the first he spoke out against it in the name of reason, and from the
first he was unheeded. Russell had long been active in political causes.
His first published book, published even before his *Essay on the Foundations of Geometry*, was a series of lectures on the development of
the German socialist movement. This book is less memorable for
its conclusion—the German ruling class ought, if only in pursuit
of their own self-interest, be more humane to the working classes
—than for its portrayal of Lassalle, an early leader of the German
socialists.

> It is almost impossible on first reading the history of Lassalle's
> agitation not to wonder in what its great importance consists. Barely
> a dozen great speeches, three or four brilliant defenses in Court,
> a few pamphlets and a very few followers—that, at first sight, seems
> to sum up Lassalle's achievements. What he really did, however,
> lay not in the immediate results, but in his emotional effect on men's
> minds, in the forcible attention which his supremely dramatic appear-
> ance demanded and obtained from the whole nation. He forced men,
> even against their will, to reflect on their political circumstances,
> and see them as they were.

To force men, even against their will, to reflect on their political
circumstances—this was the role Russell chose for himself during
the Great War. He pointed out over and over again that war was no
longer rational. For instance, he wrote in the essay "Is Permanent
Peace Possible?":

> In the uncivilized past it was in the self-interest of one tribe to
> attack and subdue another. But through the growth of commerce
> and manufactories it has come about that nine-tenths of the interests

of one civilised nation coincide with nine-tenths of the interests of any other.

This was the role he chose for himself, and the role he expected other men of reason to choose. Russell expected the other men of reason, the other philosophers, scientists, mathematicians, and the like, to make the same point until it could no longer be ignored. But in this expectation Russell was bitterly disappointed. The men of reason, who were supposed to be above the common herd, did not act as if they were. From the beginning they behaved, as a group, no better than the rest. As early as 1915 Russell was led to write "An Appeal to Intellectuals" in which he castigated them for perverting their vocation.

"The guardians of the temple of truth have betrayed it to idolators, and have been the first to promote the idolatrous worship." What was the cause of this priestly sacrilege? Russell admitted, if only temporarily, that knowledge alone was not enough. "Knowledge with elevation of mind is the chief instrument of human progress; knowledge without elevation of mind easily becomes devilish and increases the wounds which man inflicts on man."

Russell did not specify exactly what this "elevation of mind" was. He did not, however, have to look far for a "devilish" turn of mind. He quickly found it among his own philosophical associates. In 1916, his old friend and teacher John Ellis McTaggart was at the forefront of a successful movement at Cambridge to have Russell removed from his lectureship for unpatriotic activity.

Alfred Whitehead, now living in London, had no part of this movement. However, he, like McTaggart, was a fervent supporter of the war. And the war marked the end of any philosophical collaboration between himself and Russell.[1]

Before the war, Alfred Whitehead, always slow to publish, had been content to let Russell appear the spokesman for them both. Whitehead contented himself with speaking and writing about the technical aspects of their subject. His mathematics could completely absorb him, and the stories told about his capacity for concentration during the writing of *Principia Mathematica* verge on the legendary.

Whitehead would remain silent for days, so long that his wife would worry that he was going insane. Russell told of once coming with a friend to visit Whitehead in his garden. He was sitting at a table working on his mathematics. "Davies and I stood in front of him at a distance of no more than a yard and watched him covering page after page with symbols. He never saw us, and after a time we went away with a feeling of awe."

Whitehead was the awesome mathematician of *Principia Mathematica*, but just its mathematician; Bertrand Russell was its philosopher. That was the impression. So when a popular publishing enterprise contracted both Russell and Whitehead to write books for its Home Library, Russell did *Problems of Philosophy* while Whitehead was assigned *An Introduction to Mathematics*.

With the war, this changed. Whitehead had become president of the Mathematical Association. The beginning of his presidential address of 1916 shows how the war, combined with Whitehead's prominence, forced him to speak beyond the confines of his specialty.

> When I had the honour of being made President of the Mathematical Association, I did not foresee the unusual responsibility which it entailed. It was my intention to take as the theme of a presidential address the consideration of some aspect of those special subjects to which my own special researches have principally been directed. Events have forced me to abandon that intention. It is useless to discuss abstract questions in the midst of dominant practical preoccupation. We cannot disregard the present crisis in European civilization.

Whitehead turned his mathematical prowess to the war effort. And by 1918, two years after his presidential address, he had produced a new method for "the calculation of the path of a shell in high-angle fire." The importance of this discovery was that it simplified artillery calculation "such as to make very moderate demand on a skilled draftsman." Perhaps now more British shells would find their targets. (At about the same time Whitehead was discovering his new method, enemy shells were destroying some of the places he associated with his childhood; decades later, in 1936, when another great war threatened Europe, Whitehead recollected that during the first one "a bomb fell on the house where I was born, another in the garden where I played.")

Whitehead contributed to the war effort more than just through technical skills. He could also, when called upon, give a rousing patriotic address to youths. The following is from a speech he made while awarding prizes at a Polytechnic Institute in 1917.

> What our fighting men have done for us, for the world in general, and for the future of England, is so overwhelming that words cannot

praise them enough. I will just say one thing to you: when you read of great deeds done in past times, of perils encountered, of adventures, of undaunted courage, of patriotism, of self-sacrifice, of suffering endured for noble cause, you each can say—I, too, have known such heroes; they are among my countrymen, they are among my fellow students and companions, they are among the dear intimates of my home. And for those who have fallen, it is for us to erect a monument sufficient to transmit to future ages the memory of their sacrifice. For this purpose there is only one memorial which can suffice, namely, the cause for which they died. The greatness of England, the future of England, has been left by them to our keeping. Guard it well.

A little more than a year later, shortly before the Great War itself had run its course, one of the dear intimates of Whitehead's home, his eighteen year old son Eric, was numbered among the fallen.

While Russell and Whitehead had been working on *Principia Mathematica*, Russell had not worried about Whitehead's long silences. He had worried about Mrs. Whitehead's health. (She suffered periodic heart seizures.) Beyond concern for Mrs. Whitehead herself, Russell was also convinced that, if she did die, Whitehead would be so struck with grief as to be rendered permanently incapable of creative work. Now Whitehead had to face death, the death of a son in a war he, the father, had advocated. And he had to face it in metropolitan London, far away from the private gardens, for fellows only, of Trinity College, Cambridge. Lucien Price, a journalist who first knew the Whitehead's decades after the war, wrote, "Only as one came to know them gradually year after year did one even remotely understand how Eric's loss was felt." He also recorded Whitehead in 1944 saying "absently" of Eric, "He was the most fascinating human being I have ever known."

Whitehead never did finish the fourth volume of *Principia Mathematica*. (Like *The Principles of Mathematics*, it remains forever incomplete.) His work took a different turn. So much so, when Russell after the war asked to see some of Whitehead's new work in manuscript to help him bring together some of his own ideas, Whitehead politely refused.

Earlier Whitehead had been content to let Russell act as spokesman; now he was not. Earlier Russell had claimed completeness for the world of reason, and Whitehead tacitly agreed. Earlier Russell had claimed that reason made almost certain the ultimate futility of the human world; and Whitehead had not demurred. But now he would. That completeness of reason which Whitehead had so long sought he would now try to show to be a delusion. He would show that life was not ultimately futile; the idea of immortality had a meaning logic could not deny.

In this new work, Whitehead had the assistance of a new development in physics. Newton was wrong. His principle, the immortal principle, was dead. Among the phenomena that killed it were the miniscule but persistent irregularities in the orbit of the planet Mercury. Absolute space and time which for centuries had assured the rationality of natural processes had been proven to be chimeras.

In Britain this revolution was fully appreciated only after 1919 when a British expedition provided a crucial experimental confirmation that Relativity and not Absolute Space and Time ruled the world. Whitehead had suspected as much since before the war. Now he himself wrote an account of the announcement of this confirmation for a weekly news magazine. In it he was careful not to blame those physicists who had mistakenly resisted Einstein's theory.

> No one who knows the theory [of relativity] will feel inclined to blame the physicists for shying at it. Fantastic consequences flowed from it, consequences quite inconsistent with the traditional philosophy of science, which is in the main the legacy of the Aristotelian domination of the Middle Ages. In those times men took refuge from a disorganized world in a certain trim tidiness of thought. Accordingly when modern science started on its career in the seventeenth century it took over the concept of a material universe adventuring through a space and time which would be otherwise empty and eventless. Science had persistently endeavored to explain any observed happening in terms of the fact that at a certain time certain material is in one place and is going somewhere else.

This tidy world had now been replaced by a different one, one of relativity. With respect to space, this meant that "there cannot be first space and then the things to put in it, any more than there can be first the grin and then the cat to fit on to it. This doctrine of the relativity of space reduces all statements about configurations and motions of matter in space to statements about relations and changes of relations between various bits of stuff."

The same year of Whitehead's account of relativity Albert Einstein himself wrote to a British periodical to express his gratitude for the expedition and his hope that this signified a return to international cooperation on non-political subjects. "After the lamentable breakdown of the old active intercourse between men of learning, I welcome this opportunity of expressing my feelings of joy and gratitude toward the astronomers and physicists of England." Einstein, however, was not as optimistic as this letter sounded. In the same year, in a continental publication, he had written of a unified European intellectual community that seemed lost forever. It had died long before the Great War. It had been epitomized by the universal use of the Latin language. It was in its decline in Newton's own time. (Newton's *Principia* was, in fact, the last British book of major significance written in Latin.)

> As late as the seventeenth century the savants and artists of all Europe were so closely united by the bond of a common ideal that cooperation between them was scarcely affected by political events. This unity was further strengthened by the general use of the Latin language. Today we look back at this state of affairs as at a lost paradise. The passions of nationalism have destroyed this community of the intellect, and the Latin language which once united the whole world is dead. The men of learning have become representatives of the most extreme national traditions and lost their sense of an intellectual commonwealth.

Whitehead, too, sensed the loss of a philosophical paradise. But for Whitehead the philosophical paradise that was lost, was the one Einstein had ended. There could be only one Newton, and there could never be another one. In his later years, Whitehead would repeat over and over the profound effect the fall of Newton had had upon him. Now, in retrospect, he could see that the fall was unavoidable before Einstein had written on relativity. (Whitehead would date the fall 1900, a suitable date for the beginning of a new age.) Time and again, his remarks on Newton's fall were recorded.

> Let me speak personally for a moment. I had a good classical education, and when I went up to Cambridge early in the 1880's my mathematical training was continued under good teachers. Now nearly everything was supposed to be known about physics that could be known—except for a few spots, such as electromagnetic phenomena, which remained (or so it was thought) to be co-ordinated with the Newtonian principles. But, for the rest, physics was supposed to be nearly a closed subject. Those investigations to co-ordinate went on through the next dozen years. By the middle of the 1890's there were a few tremors, a slight shiver as of all not being quite secure, but no one sensed what was coming. By 1900 the Newtonian physics were demolished, done for! Still speaking personally, it had a profound effect on me; I have been fooled once, and I'll be damned if I'll be fooled again! Einstein is supposed to have made an epochal discovery. I am respectful and interested, but also sceptical. There

is no more reason to suppose Einstein's relativity is anything more final than Newton's *Principia*.

Other times he spoke more impersonally:

> We supposed that nearly everything of importance about physics was known. Yes, there were a few obscure spots, strange anomalies having to do with the phenomena of radiation which physicists expected to be cleared up by 1900. They were, but in so being, the whole science blew up, and the Newtonian physics, which had been supposed to be fixed as the Everlasting Seat, were gone. Oh, they were and still are useful as a way of looking at things, but regarded as a final description of reality, no longer valid. Certitude was gone.

He would often try to convey how "fantastic" was the world before the Great War.

> I was taught science and mathematics by brilliant men and I did well in them; since the turn of the century I have lived to see every one of the basic assumptions of both set aside; not, indeed, discarded, but of use as qualifying clauses, instead of as major propositions; and all this in one life-span—the most fundamental assumptions of supposedly exact sciences set aside. And yet in the face of that, the discoveries of the new hypotheses in science are declaring, "*Now, at last, we have certitude*"—when some of the assumptions which we have seen upset had endured for more than twenty centuries.

But, always, the point of Whitehead's recollection was the same:

> There is not a single concept of the Newtonian physics which was taught as a whole truth, that has not now been displaced. The Newtonian ideas are still useful, as useful as they ever were. But they are no longer true in the sense in which I was taught that they were true. This experience has profoundly affected my thinking. To have supposed you had certitude once, and certitude about the solidest-looking thing in the universe, and then to have had it blown up in your hands into inconceivable infinities has affected everything else in the universe for me.[2]

In his first book published after the Great War, Alfred North Whitehead tried to assess the philosophical implications of the recent revolution in science. The book was entitled *An Enquiry Concerning the Principles of Natural Knowledge*. This title might seem to suggest that it was a further development of the position Russell had defended in *Our Knowledge of the External World*. Rather the book was more striking in its differences from the earlier one. Gone were the predictions of final resolutions to philosophical problems. These predictions were replaced by what appeared to be denials that we will ever achieve such final resolutions. Now, after the war, Whitehead seemed to think that the best philosophy could do was reconcile us to the twilight.

> This book is merely an enquiry. It raises more difficulties than those which it professes to settle. This is inevitable in any philosophical work, however complete. All that one can hope to do is to settle the right sort of difficulties and to raise the right sort of ulterior questions, and thus to accomplish one short step further into the unfathomable mystery.

Whitehead himself made clear why a world of mystery was attractive. His book was begun amidst the anxiety of the Great War as "a refuge from immediate fact." It was finished amidst what Whitehead termed "the anguish which is the price of victory." The book bore the dedication:

> To
> ERIC ALFRED WHITEHEAD
> Royal Flying Corps
> November 27, 1898 to March 1, 1918
> Killed in action over the Forêt de Gobain
> giving himself that the city of his vision
> may not perish
> The music of his life was without discord
> perfect in its beauty.

Is the world such that the cities of vision and the music of lost lives endure beyond failing memories? In the noonday brightness of Russell's world, no. But in a world of unfathomable mystery, perhaps. And it was to just such a world that Whitehead saw relativity pointing.

Whitehead realized that Einstein did not espouse such a world. Einstein, as much as Russell and Newton before him, wanted a tidy world, even though it was now clear (as it had not been to Newton) that a tidy world was one in which persons have no lasting place. Despite the authority of Einstein, Whitehead was convinced that relativity pointed to an untidy world.

Only the philosopher could properly understand the implications of relativity. The philosopher tried to see nature as a whole, and avoided being focused on a few particular phenomena or technical reasonings. The philosopher could see that the "scientific concepts of space and time are the first outcome of the simplest generalizations from experience, and that they are not to be looked for at the tail end of a welter of differential equations."

With much of Whitehead's analysis of the implications of relativity, Russell would have had no quarrel. For Whitehead the principle of relativity denies the existence of a perfectly rational world lying outside our own, against which our own is to be measured. Relativity denies the existence of the world of absolute space and time, of points and instants. Relativity recognizes that we never measure our world against this perfect one. We always measure within the world, one thing relative to another. We measure with things, with sticks and clocks, not space and time. And the things with which we measure are never perfect. They never give us points and instants. Our supposed points, if looked at closely enough, always have length and breadth; our instants are never quite instantaneous. If we speak as if they are, we will only be led into philosophical perplexities.

> The way out of the perplexities, as to the ultimate data of science in terms of which physical explanation is ultimately to be expressed, is to express the essential scientific meaning of time, space, and material as issuing from fundamental relations between events and from recognition of the characters of events. These relations between events are those immediate deliverances of observation which are referred to when we say that events are spread through space and time.

With this analysis Russell would probably not have disagreed. Much of it was foreshadowed in *Our Knowledge of the External World.* Both Russell and Whitehead by 1914 appear to have agreed that any philosophical account of science would have to construct entities of science out of "events," perceptions of a temporal and a spatial extent. Whitehead was, in effect, just applying the kind of analysis he had taught Russell before the war to the important new development of relativity. To this Russell would not have objected.

What he would have found objectionable was the context within which Whitehead placed this analysis, a context much more compatible with McTaggart's philosophy than Russell's own. In Whitehead's hands, relativity was being used to absorb physics into biology, to make the organism central to an understanding of nature. Whitehead realized that most of his readers, like Russell, would have been appalled by this effort. So he only developed it gradually, and for the most part by insinuation.

Early in the book, while defining the concept of organism, he had pointed out its incompatibility with traditional physics.

> The essence of an organism is that it is one thing which functions and is spread through space. Now functioning takes time. Thus a biological organism is a unity with a spatio-temporal extension which is of the essence of its being. This biological conception is obviously incompatible with the traditional ideas.

Having said this, Whitehead quickly added, lest his readers think that he was arguing for a vital principle, "The argument does not in any way depend on the assumption that biological phenomena belong to a different category from other physical phenomena."

So the readers were reassured. The obvious inference was that biological phenomena are to be reduced to physical phenomena; the biological was just another form of the physical. What Whitehead did not mention at this point was that the biological would become physical only when the physical had become organic. Having gained his readers' assent to an apparently minor point—the essence of an organism is that it is a spatio-temporal extension—Whitehead could then turn to assess the implications of the principle of relativity. Relativity has done away with points and instants. They are illusions, metaphysical monstrosities which, upon analysis, disappear, leaving us with a world of events, of entities with spatio-temporal extensions. Then it becomes clear. The physical and the biological are, after all, of the same category, the organic.

Whitehead never asserted this most important implication of his reasoning. He was careful to keep within his self-appointed limit, "to illustrate the principles of natural knowledge by an examination of the data and experiential laws fundamental for physical science." The statements about organisms were merely asides, as inessential to the main argument of the book as was the dedication to his dead son. His readers were to draw their own inferences.

Whitehead sustained this stance throughout the book, until the last chapter. There it is as if, like Newton in his General Scholium, Whitehead could not bear the possibility that his readers would think his work humanly dry and barren. In this last chapter he decided that a short excursion on life would not be amiss since some of the ideas have a "bearing on biological conceptions as to the sense in which life can thus be included."

The chapter is entitled "Rhythms." With the departure of points and instants, physical objects could no longer be seen as exactly conforming to physical laws. (They could only do that if they were at particular points at particular instants.) Rather what was observed were recurring patterns of behavior, such patterns being aptly termed rhythms. A law of nature was a rhythm within this natural world. The physical world exhibits rhythm, and yet is not rhythm the essence of life itself? Are not the rhythms of the physical but an inferior version of the higher rhythms of the vital?

> Life preserves its expression of rhythm and its sensitiveness to rhythm. Life is the rhythm as such, whereas a physical object is an average of rhythms which build no rhythm in their aggregation; and thus matter is in itself lifeless. . . . The rhythm is then the life, in the sense in which it can be said to be included within nature.

But is life entirely included within nature? If the world is alive, might death and discord not really rule it? Whitehead had led his readers toward the unfathomable mystery of such a world. Having led his readers in this direction, he could, however indirectly, however hestitantly, begin to suggest the possibility of immortality. He could point out, "So far as direct observation is concerned all that we know of the essential relation of life in nature is stated in two short poetic phrases."

The first poetic phrase was from Tennyson:

> Blow, bugle, blow, set the wild echoes flying,
> And answer, echoes, answer, dying, dying, dying.

This, Whitehead believed, was the more obvious, the apparent relation of life to nature; it was a description of "its relapse into matter." For Whitehead the second poetic fragment, however, saw more deeply into the true relation of life to nature. It was Wordsworth's:

> The music in my heart I bore
> Long after it was heard no more.

With this phrase Whitehead ended his book, dedicated as it was to the music of his son's life, seeking as it seemed to be an easing of the discord of his death.[3]

During the first five years after the war, Whitehead used every occasion to emphasize what in one paper he called the "bombshell" of relativity. It had forced us to realize the relatedness of things.

This was Whitehead before the Royal Society of Edinburgh:

> There is no such entity as mere A in isolation. A requires something other than itself . . . . When we perceive green, it is not green in iso-

lation, it is green somewhere at some time. The green may or may not have the relationship to some other object, such as a blade of grass. Such a relation would be contingent. But it is essential that we see it somewhere in space related to our eyes at a certain epoch of our bodily life ... there can be no knowledge of green without apprehension of times and places. Green presupposes here and there, and now and then. In other words, green presupposes the passage of nature in the form of a structure of events.

This was Whitehead addressing the Chemical Society of the Imperial College, London:

> Nature is known to us in our experience as a complex of passing events. In this complex we discern definite mutual relations between component events, which we may call their relative positions, and these positions we express partly in terms of time.

This was Whitehead addressing an audience at Trinity College, Cambridge:

> Our knowledge of nature is an experience of activity (or passage). The things previously observed are active entities, the "events". They are chunks in the life of nature. These events have to each other relations which in our knowledge differentiate themselves into space-relations and time-relations. But this differentiation between space and time, though inherent in nature, is comparatively superficial; and space and time are each partial expressions of one fundamental relation between events which is neither spatial nor temporal. This relation I call "extension."

This was Whitehead addressing the Aristotelian Society of London:

> On the absolute theory, bare space and bare time are such very odd existences, half something, half nothing. They always remind me of Milton's account of the Creation with the forepaws of the lions already created and their hinder quarters still unfinished.
> "The tawny lion, pawing to get free
> His hinder parts ..."
> It seems so much simpler to sweep all this odd assortment of existences into the mind; and then all their contents have to follow them into the same dust-bin as being nothing else than the outcome of the diseased mentality of existence. The point I am endeavouring to make is that relativity lends a uniformity to the type of existence as disclosed in sense awareness.

That all four of these statements originated in lectures is no mere coincidence. After the *Enquiry*, Whitehead no longer wrote books. He rather delivered lectures which were then collected into books. This choice was a consistent deduction from his commitment to relativity.

There is no such entity as mere A in isolation. Whitehead had said this in many different ways. We must not try to see A in itself—located at a certain point, at a certain instant—we must see it in its relations to other things. "A" in this formula could be something simple like the color green, or it could be something much more complex like Whitehead's own ideas. Whitehead had to make his readers see that relativity applied as much to his ideas as it did to everything else. He had to make his readers conscious of the fact that they were not seeing his thought in itself, but rather in a certain relation.

When philosophers from the time of Plato on have wished, for whatever reason, to achieve this effect, they usually have written in dialogue form. This Whitehead himself believed he should do also, but he found himself unable.

> The custom of modern presentations of science, and my own diffidence of success in the art of managing a dialogue, have led me to adopt the modified form of lecturing in which the audiences—real audiences, either in America, Edinburgh, or South Kensington—are to be regarded as silent interlocutors demanding explanations of the various aspects of the theory.

So Whitehead always presented his ideas in relation to a group. A Royal Society, a Chemical Society, a Cambridge audience; and always Whitehead is careful to specify the occasion. Here he is accepting the James-Scott Prize for the encouragement of the philosophy of science; there he is speaking "on the occasion of a festival promoted by the former pupils and colleagues of Professor Charlotte Angus Scott." Always in their proper relations, never by themselves.

At times he would go to extremes to make certain that his readers did not think a given perspective to be the only one. In the middle of the published version of a series of lectures given at Cambridge, Whitehead intruded the lecture he had given to the London Chemical Society. There it was, breaking up the continuity achieved by the others, a continuity which might have induced his readers to forget about dialogue. So Whitehead broke the continuity, without even bothering to remove from the intruder remarks like: "I remember that I am lecturing to the members of a chemical society who are not for the most part versed in advanced mathematics." To have smoothed the transition would have been to have spoiled the effect.

This intrusion occurred in one of two collections of lectures Whitehead published in the early twenties. At the beginning of the other, Whitehead placed a preface suggesting that the ideal order in which the lectures should be read was relative to the readers' interests. If you were interested in philosophy you should probably read them in the order in which they were published. If you were interested in mathematics, you should read them in the opposite order. And if you were interested primarily in physics, you should start in the middle and work from there.

In all these lectures, Whitehead did not speak of the broader cosmological subjects he had broached at the conclusion of the *Enquiry*, the organic rhythm of the universe and the immortality of the spirit. Perhaps it was the occasions on which he was invited to speak, or perhaps it was simply his position as a philosopher of science and mathematics that restrained him. Perhaps he felt that this was the proper domain of others; a McTaggart, for example, should publically probe these metaphysical depths, but not a Whitehead.[4]

In the years since Russell and Moore had turned away from him, John Ellis McTaggart had been trying to finish his system. As time went on, he felt that Hegel had achieved much less than McTaggart or Hegel had thought he had; and McTaggart began to write his own philosophical synthesis, *The Nature of Existence.** In *The Nature of Existence*, McTaggart would demonstrate that the universe was good, all its evils being dwarfed into insignificance by the final good towards which it was inexorably moving. This universe was of its essence spiritual, and such that every man survives the grave, eventually to taste the final good, a "love so direct, so intimate, and so powerful that even the deepest mystic rapture gives us but the slightest foretaste of its perfection."

The first volume of *The Nature of Existence* was published in 1921. McTaggart was in the midst of revising the second and final volume when he unexpectedly died. (The diagnosis was the same as had been for Green, blood poisoning.) The manuscript for the second volume was turned over to another Cambridge philosopher, C. D. Broad.

Broad was the closest to a disciple that McTaggart still had. He lectured in philosophy at Cambridge and was a fellow of Trinity College. While Broad had never been selected an Apostle, a sign of the

---

* The title itself evidenced his changed attitude toward Hegel. Originally McTaggart had intended to entitle his synthesis *The Dialectic of Existence*. But by the time he wrote it he had abandoned Hegel's dialectic for the deductive method of *Principia Mathematica*—hence the change in title.

respect in which he was held at Trinity College was that he lived in the
same rooms Newton had while a fellow. (Broad would only justify
his selection by citing Horace: "Our fathers, themselves worse than
our grandfathers, begot us, worse than both and soon to curse the
world with offspring viler still.")

The second volume of *The Nature of Existence*, edited by C. D.
Broad, finally appeared in 1928. Broad seems to have been
disappointed at the indifference with which McTaggart's masterpiece
was received. To counteract this, Broad produced *An Examination
of McTaggart's Philosophy*, a three volume, twelve hundred page
analysis of *The Nature of Existence*, section by section. It took him
ten years to complete. The last volume Broad began with a quotation
from *Paradise Lost* which ended:

> Greatly instructed I shall hence depart;
>   Greatly in peace of thought; and have my fill
> Of knowledge, what this vessel can contain:
>   Beyond which was my folly to aspire!

A reader of Broad's *Examination* is, in the end, more impressed by
the folly than by the knowledge. Broad did praise McTaggart for the
ingenuity of his argumentation—"In this respect Leibniz is the only
philosopher that I know who can be compared with McTaggart"—
and for his clarity. (Shades of Russell and Moore.) The clarity, however, revealed that the ingenuity was misplaced. According to
Broad's analysis, McTaggart's most important proofs were virtually
all fallacious, and hence his conclusions did not hold. There was no
glee, only sadness in Broad as he reached the end of his *Examination*.
When he finished it, he was in his fifties, and not looking forward to
any new syntheses of his own. He made clear at the conclusion of
the last volume that in looking into the grave of McTaggart's philosophy, he was looking into that of his own.

> I have now completed my task of building a mausoleum and com-
> posing an epitaph for McTaggart's philosophy. It is somewhat de-
> pressing to stand by the grave of such high hopes and such eager
> intellectual effort. Successive generations of philosophers are like
> "the Priest who slew the slayer and shall himself be slain." It is a
> sobering thought that inevitably this *Examination* must soon follow
> *McTaggart's Philiosophy* into the common grave of all human activities,
> and that the two will thenceforth rest together under the lines
>   *Hi motus animorum, atque haec certamina tanta,*
>   *Pulveris exigui iactu compressa quiescunt.*

The epitaph, although Broad did not cite the source, was from Virgil's discussion of bees in the *Georgics*. Virgil had described, in epic terms, a battle between two swarms of bees, and then with these two lines he brought the battle back into perspective.

> These upheavals of the spirit, these prodigious contests
> Are quieted by a meager handful of thrown dust.

These were perhaps fitting lines for McTaggart or Broad or any of the other slain priests themselves ordained by murder, fitting lines for a time when all these philosophers together seem but a swarm or two or three, a time when all their cherished hostile buzzing has lost its human meaning.

Nonetheless, these lines were not an adequate expression of how Broad himself felt as he realized that the life work of both his teacher and himself would soon be lost in the swarm, his feelings of sadness and regret as he stood by the grave of such high lost hopes, such eager futile effort. This was better expressed by the epigraph he chose for the final section of his *Examination*, or "Retrospect" as he called it. The epigraph was from the concluding lines of *Paradise Lost*.

> In either hand the hastening angel caught
> Our lingering parents; and to th' eastern gate
> Led them direct; and down the cliff as fast
> To the subjected plain; then disappeared.
> They looking back, all th' eastern side beheld
> Of Paradise, so late their happy seat!
> Waved over by that flaming brand; the gate
> With dreadful faces thronged and fiery arms.[5]

CHAPTER SIXTEEN

ALFRED NORTH WHITEHEAD AND G. E. MOORE
(from 1920)

In 1925 Alfred North Whitehead was offered a professorship of philosophy at Harvard University. It was not a professorship of mathematics or of the philosophy of science—it was a professorship of philosophy, pure and simple. Now he could have a situation that would allow him to develop the most fundamental implications of relativity. He knew that others would expect him to reject the offer, but his own reaction, as he later reported it, was immediate. "There is nothing in the world I would rather do."

The initial book of his Harvard professorship, *Science and the Modern World*, was the Lowell Lectures of 1925, the same endowed lecture series at which Russell had delivered *Our Knowledge of the External World*. Here Whitehead began to describe in broadest terms his new vision.

To get this vision accepted he had first to refute the very view of nature which Russell had defended in "A Free Man's Worship," a view which denies the organic, purposeful character of the universe, a view which can only see in the ultimate future of mankind a faint echo dying, dying, dying. Russell's view was simply an expression of the general scientific cosmology that Whitehead believed had dominated Western Science after the time of Newton. Individual theories might come and go, but persisting was this general cosmology "which presupposes the ultimate fact of an irreducible brute matter, or material spread throughout space in a flux of configurations."

> In itself such a material is senseless, valueless, purposeless. It just does what it does do, following a fixed routine imposed by external relations which do not spring from the nature of its being. It is this assumption that I call "scientific materialism". Also it is an assumption which I shall challenge as being entirely unsuited to the scientific situation at which we have now arrived.

The scientific situation at which we have now arrived was, of course, that dominated by relativity, a theory which supported organicism rather than materialism. However, Whitehead realized that this situation, even if it was just as he thought it was, did not quite carry the day for his philosophy. Whitehead was couching his analysis in historical terms, and history is no docile tool for the defender of system.

If our scientific situation has changed now, who is to say it will not change back again? Who is to say that Einstein's theory, or a successor, or a successor to a successor, might not in a decade, or a century, or three, support materialism as strongly as Newton's ever did? What does history show but that there are no everlasting seats? To what more can history lead than to a suspense of judgement on the claims of materialism and organicism?

Whitehead was aware of this difficulty, but he still wished to provoke a choice in favor of his organic philosophy. Whitehead realized that relativity alone was not sufficient to carry the day. He needed more to convince his audience that Wordsworth's "The music in my heart I bore/Long after it was heard no more" was more profound than Tennyson's "echoes answering dying, dying, dying." For the argument to show that materialism was false, he went to poetry.

In the pivotal lecture of *Science and the Modern World*, Whitehead described how the confidence of Milton's "Just are the ways of God/And justifiable to man" had become the despair of Tennyson's age, a despair which Whitehead found typified in Matthew Arnold's "And we are here as on a darkling plain/Swept with confused alarms of struggle and flight,/Where ignorant armies clash by night." This destruction of confidence was the result of the mechanistic scientific cosmology which dominated European thought after Newton. As Whitehead put it, "The discrepancy between the materialistic mechanism of science and moral intuitions, which are presupposed in the concrete affairs of life, only gradually assumes its true importance as the centuries advance." By the late nineteenth century, the time of Tennyson, the discrepancy had become complete; man's moral aspirations were seen as totally opposed to the order of nature. The poets of this age had acceded to the inhuman demands of scientific materialism.

Their immediate predecessors, however, had not been so cowed. These were the poets of what Whitehead called the "Romantic Reaction." Coleridge, Wordsworth, Keats, Shelley—all of them, in defiance of scientific materialism, celebrated the organic unity of man with the world. Their world was one in which man's moral aspirations were at home. These poets, in particular, Whitehead

quoted at length, far greater length than the others. Especially he
quoted the childlike Shelley:

> The everlasting universe of Things
> Flows through the Mind, and rolls its rapid waves,
> Now dark—now glittering—reflecting gloom—
> Now lending splendour, where from secret springs
> The source of human thought its tribute brings
> Of waters, —with a sound but half its own
> Such as a feeble brook will oft assume
> In wild woods, among the Mountains lone,
> Where waterfalls around it leap for ever,
> Where woods and winds contend, and a vast river
> Over its rocks ceaselessly bursts and raves.

And, of course, Wordsworth:

> Ye Presences of Nature in the sky
> And on the earth! Ye Visions of the Hills!
> And souls of lonely places! can I think
> A vulgar hope was yours when ye employed
> Such ministry, when ye through many a year
> Haunting me thus among my boyish sports,
> On caves and trees upon the woods and hills,
> Impressed upon all forms the characters
> Of danger or desire; and thus did make
> The surface of the universal earth,
> With triumph and delight, with hope and fear,
> Work like a sea?

He had to quote these poets often, and he had to quote them at length,
because he had to make his readers feel how natural, how comfortable
this organic view of things was, how consonant it was with their
immediate experience before it was distorted by abstractions. He
had to make them feel how natural it was, and, in contrast, "how
strained and paradoxical is the view of nature which modern science
imposes on our thought." In short, he had to make them feel how
intrinsically preferable is the organic over the materialistic cosmology.
If he succeeded, then when he explained to his readers that modern
science no longer imposed the materialistic view on their thoughts,
but rather seems to impose the organic, they would be grateful
and not inclined to look beyond.[1]

Science and the Modern World, couched as it was in historical terms,
was not Alfred North Whitehead's fullest exposition of his metaphysical vision. That he saved for the Gifford lectures of 1927-28.

Process and Reality, as he called them, bore in its structure some significant similarities with *Principia Mathematica*.

Whitehead characterized *Process and Reality* as itself a four-staged process. First the cosmology was to be stated in summary form; then "the power of the scheme to put various elements of our experience into a consistent relation" was to be shown. At this point the reader would presumably have been convinced at least of the probability of the cosmology; so in the third stage Whitehead would formulate the cosmology in a more finished form, this in preparation for the fourth stage where he would draw the implications and answer his question "What does it all come to?"

The first two stages do bear a resemblance to the structure of the *Principia Mathematica*. In that work first came the postulation of certain fundamental logical notions, in particular the indefinables; then came the demonstration of the power of that scheme to put the various elements of mathematics into a consistent relation. *Principia Mathematica* had not claimed that these indefinables were themselves ultimate, but rather only that any future attempt to put the various elements of mathematics into a consistent relation would have to begin with the postulation of indefinables of the same kind—that is, indefinables of logic. In *Process and Reality* Whitehead was hoping to achieve a similar end. His fundamental postulates were organistic. He did not claim these to be the ultimate ones, but he did wish to convince his readers that any future attempt to put the elements of human experience into a consistent relation would have to be organistic.

Much of what Whitehead meant by an organic philosophy was implicit in his very definition of speculative philosophy: "the endeavor to frame a coherent, logical, necessary system of general ideas in terms of which every element of our experience can be interpreted." The key term was "coherence."

> "Coherence," as here employed, means that the fundamental ideas, in terms of which the scheme is developed, presuppose each other so that in isolation they are meaningless. This requirement does not mean that they are definable in terms of each other; it means that what is indefinable in one such notion cannot be abstracted from its relevance to the other notions. It is the ideal of speculative philosophy that its fundamental notions shall not seem capable of abstraction from each other. In other words, it is presupposed that no entity can be conceived in complete abstraction from the system of the universe, and that it is the business of speculative philosophy to exhibit this truth. This character is its coherence.

Gone are indefinables as individual as the taste of pineapple, as distinct as the planet Neptune. Whitehead's indefinables, the indefinables of all speculative philosophy, cohere—that is, they can no more be understood in isolation from the whole than an organ can be understood in isolation from the organism of which it is a part. Whitehead's indefinables are cells, not atoms; and, as such, they reflect the ultimate organic nature of the world.

This was not the only important contrast between *Process and Reality* and *Principia Mathematica*. In *Principia Mathematica*, it was implied that an ultimate set of indefinables could perhaps be found. In *Process and Reality*, Whitehead explicitly denied that such an ultimate set will ever be found. Philosophers, Whitehead believed, had been deluded by the finality of mathematics, a finality which is, in fact, only apparent. As he put it, "Philosophy has been misled by the example of mathematics; and even in mathematics the statement of the ultimate logical principles is beset with difficulties." Whitehead could at times profess a righteous indignation at the hubris of past philosophers, an indignation understandable coming from one who had seen the Everlasting Seat of science lost.

> How shallow, puny, and imperfect are efforts to sound the depths in the nature of things. In philosophical discussion, the merest hint of dogmatic certainty as to finality is an exhibition of folly.

Unlike Russell's condemnation of the hubris of all past philosophy, Whitehead's appears to leave no opening for himself to make his own personal claim to understand the ultimate nature of reality. And yet it was just such a claim to which Whitehead was leading his readers. He wished to assert that the world was certainly organic, to do so without giving the merest hint of dogmatic certainty.

Whitehead seems to have believed that the very nature of the organic philosophy saved this task from being impossible. The only real alternative to the organic philosophy conceived the world to be essentially static: unchanging atoms in unchanging space and time, their ordinarily unchanging states of inertia being changed only by unchanging forces. The single alternative to the organic philosophy was a world in which dogmatic finality would not be folly.

Once one has admitted that dogmatic finality is folly, then one has, in effect, assented to the organic philosophy. An organic philosophy alone accepts change, development, as real. It alone has completely abandoned "the notion of an actual entity as the unchanging subject of change." It alone sees time as a "perpetual perishing."

The history of Western thought does not present an emerging dogmatic finality such as the Newtonians thought had already been achieved. Rather it presents a perpetual perishing, an apparent chaos of conflicting opinions, philosophical principles coming to be and passing away. An organic philosophy does not attempt to explain away this fact, but accepts it as a primary given. It seeks reality within the process, just as the biologist finds the reality of life in the process of development.

No wonder, therefore, that the organic philosophy has been the perennial philosophy. The various pretenders to dogmatic finality have come and gone, but organicism has endured. The Newtonian theory of space and time, for instance, was a doctrine "philosophers have never accepted, though at times some have acquiesced." The organic philosophy, in contrast, is "the oldest of European doctrines." It was, after all, given its best formulation by Plato himself, and what safer generalization about the European philosophical tradition than that "it consists of a series of footnotes to Plato"? The organic philosophy was, in short, the original philosophy. It, of all the philosophies, accepts the "ultimate, integral experience" of man, his pristine experience "unwarped by the sophistications of theory."

> That "all things flow" is the first vague generalization which the unsystematized, barely analyzed, intuition of men has produced. It is the theme of some of the best Hebrew poetry in the Psalms; it appears as one of the first generalizations of Greek philosophy in the form of the saying of Heraclitus; amid the later barbarisms of Anglo-Saxon thought it reappears in the story of the sparrow flitting through the banqueting hall of the Northumbrian king; and in all stages of civilization its recollection lends its pathos to poetry. Without doubt, if we are to go back to that ultimate, integral experience, unwarped by the sophistications of theory, that experience whose elucidation is the final aim of philosophy, the flux of things is one ultimate generalization around which we must weave our philosophic system.

Whitehead cannot directly prove this last contention; rather he must make his readers feel it. He must appeal to his readers to abandon all the abstractions which cushion the primitive experience of the passing of things, this experience with its attendant pathos. And if he is successful in his appeal, then Whitehead's readers will begin to think of those passings which have touched them most deeply, so deeply that they thought they had gotten a glimpse into the nature of things.

Flux is in the nature of things; but, if this flux were all, if the nature of things were chaos, then there would be no point to speculative philosophy, no point to the search for a system of ideas with which to interpret our experience, no point because such a search would by its very nature be futile. Yet in an organism there is a pattern being realized through its development, a pattern which seems preordained, almost eternal. And if we do look at our primordial experience carefully enough, or rather if we look to other men's expression of their experience, we do not find the notion of transience there alone. We find with it a contrary notion, a notion which "dwells on permanences of things—the solid earth, the mountains, the stones, the Egyptian Pyramids, the spirit of man, God." It is this search for the permanences within the flux, the search to find a way to see the flux as actualizing permanences, that constitutes the core of metaphysics. Or so Whitehead thought.

> That we fail to find in experience any elements intrinsically incapable of exhibition as examples of general theory is the hope of rationalism. This hope is not a metaphysical premise. It is the faith which forms the motive for the pursuit of all sciences alike, including metaphysics .... The preservation of such faith must depend on an ultimate moral intuition into the nature of intellectual action—that it should embody the adventure of hope. Such an intuition marks the point where metaphysics—and indeed every science—gains assurance from religion and passes over into religion. But in itself the faith does not embody a premise from which the theory starts; it is an ideal which is seeking satisfaction.

Now Whitehead's readers could begin to see "what it all comes to." The hope of rationalism is, for Whitehead, a faith in an immanent God, an emerging order to which all the apparent chaos somehow contributes—all the conflicting principles of all the conflicting philosophies, all the dead sons of all the dead wars. To believe in God is to believe "this incredible fact—that what cannot be yet is."

When we come to believe in such a God—or rather, when we come to see such a God being realized through the processes of the world, then we will see that there is an objective immortality, a process "whereby what is divested of its own living immediacy becomes a real component in other living immediacies of becoming." We will see into "the multifariousness of the world—the fairies dance and Christ is nailed to the cross." We will see how the music of a man's life does not itself die with him, but becomes part of the dance of the world. And we we will see that "the immediacy of sorrow and pain is transformed into an element of triumph . . . the notion of redemption." And we will see that "the insistent craving is justified—the insistent craving, that zest for existence be refreshed by the ever present, unfading importance of our immediate actions, which perish and live evermore."[2]

Alfred North Whitehead saw. G. E. Moore did not. Moore's only published evaluation of Whitehead's mature philosophy was a review of a lecture series Whitehead gave shortly before he embarked on those to be entitled *Process and Reality*. These lectures, *Religion in the Making*, were the complement to *Science and the Modern World*, historically arguing as they did that religion found its final fulfillment in an organic philosophy.

In emphasizing this same point in *Process and Reality*, Whitehead was to quote from a vision of the Prophet Ezekiel. The Lord God gave Ezekiel this vision because the Hebrew people were in despair of ever being delivered. In the vision Ezekiel was transported to a valley filled with dry bones. When Ezekiel prophesied over these dry bones in the words the Lord God commanded him, "there was a noise and behold a shaking, and the bones came together, bone to his bone. And when I beheld, lo the sinews and the flesh came up upon them and the skin covered them above . . . and the breath came into them, and they lived, and stood up upon their feet, an exceedingly great army."

This was what the organic philosophy would do for the dry bones of the old philosophy and religion; it would, in Whitehead's words, "clothe the dry bones with the flesh of a real being, emotional, purposive, appreciative." It would not, however, clothe the dry bones of G. E. Moore, as his summarizing evaluation of *Religion in the Making* made clear.

> In considering these doctrines, it is important to remember that, according to Professor Whitehead, what "men call God—the supreme God of rationalized religion" is "*the actual but non-temporal entity whereby the indetermination of mere creativity is transmuted into a determinate freedom*" (p. 90). Apparently, therefore, he is asserting, in each case, not only that there is one and only one actual but non-temporal entity whereby etc., but also that this entity as a purpose, has knowledge, is wise, etc., as the case may be. What evidence does he suppose himself to have for these propositions? It seems quite clear that they could not follow from "the ultimate religious evidence," even if we include in it the dogma about "rightness," without the help of

some *other* truths. But *what* truths? One such, no doubt, in his view, is the dogma: "There is one and only one actual but non-temporal entity whereby, etc." But what is the evidence for this itself? Even if we grant that the alleged transmutation does take place, why should we suppose that it is effected *by* any entity whatever—why should it not simply happen? Or if there must be an entity which effects it, why should there not be several? Or if there must be only one, why should it be one which is not "actual," or which is "temporal"? And, even if these and other questions could be satisfactorily answered, what can be the evidence that the entity in question also has a purpose, has knowledge, is wise, etc., etc?. Professor Whitehead seems to leave us completely in the dark.

It is unlikely that Moore would have found good reasons for Whitehead's doctrines in *Process and Reality* any more than he had found them in *Religion in the Making*. By the end of the Great War, Moore was finding very few good reasons whatsoever. He found no good reasons for Alfred Whitehead's assertions, and he also found no good reasons for Bertrand Russell's denials.

After the war, Russell devoted less and less time to philosophy. But, in 1921, he did find time to apply the reasonings of *Our Knowledge of the External World* to our knowledge of ourselves. The result, published as *The Analysis of Mind*, was much the same. Our belief in the existence of ourselves turned out to be much like our belief in the existence of trees and tables, an audacious piece of metaphysical theorizing which, upon careful analysis, was unjustifiable.

Russell, as Moore put it in a review of *The Analysis of Mind*, "advocates the view that, though it is true that I do perceive and remember and desire and feel, etc., yet nothing whatever exists which does perceive or remember or believe or desire or feel, nor anything whatever which is an act of perception or remembrance or belief." In favor of this position, Russell in his book had presented, in Moore's opinion, "one very strong argument"—namely that we never directly observe the subject of acts of perception, remembrance, or belief. "Mr. Russell, however, does not discuss at all the perhaps equally strong arguments in favour of the view that, though it is not obvious that we observe such things yet in fact we really do." Russell, in short, had never seriously entertained the possibility that he might be wrong. Moreover, Russell had based what arguments he did present upon a particular philosophical theory —a theory Moore carefully described—to which "there seem to be very serious objections." These objections "Mr. Russell does not discuss . . .;

and he does not appear to offer a single argument in favour of his theory."

Moore no longer found Whitehead or Russell convincing. Neither did he find convincing his own younger self. For instance, he could no longer see the indefinable good which he had spent so many of his younger days contemplating. In a discussion of a relatively insignificant book on ethics, one by a Mr. Joseph, Moore wrote the following tortured assessment of his own earlier position.

> In the *Principia* I proposed to prove that "good" (and I think I sometimes, though not always, was using this word to mean the same as "worth having for its own sake") was indefinable. But all the supposed proofs were certainly fallacious; they entirely failed to prove that "worth having for its own sake" is indefinable. And I think perhaps it is definable: I do not know. But I also still think that very likely it *is* indefinable.

Faced with the old question, "Is 'good' definable?", a question he had thought about for a quarter century, Moore could only vacillate. Perhaps it is; I do not know. Likely it is not. Within the space of two sentences, Moore had assented to all three possible answers, and had thereby assented to none.

Moore wrote very little in his later years. Most of what he did publish were contributions to symposia of the Aristotelian Society of London. Whenever a member of the society thought he had a good reason for a proposition, G. E. Moore would politely point out that it was not as good a reason as he thought. Professor Stout's views on the nature of universals and propositions, Mr. Ryle's and Mr. Braithwaite's on imaginary objects, Mr. Kneale's on existence as a predicate—Moore pointed out, in turn, how the reasons these men offered for their views were really not very good.

These refutations, together with the reviews of Russell, and Whitehead, were almost all that Moore published in the two decades after the war. He did write an obituary for McTaggart in which McTaggart was praised as a philosopher who tried to be clear and who tried to find good reasons; Moore only regretted that McTaggart had not been clearer and had not found better reasons.

After the war, G. E. Moore, considered by his associates to be at the height of his philosophical powers, wrote no more books. One who knew him well then—the Mr. Braithwaite whose views on imaginary objects Moore had found unsatisfactory—explained this inability to produce sustained work as follows: "He saw the reasons against any view so clearly he could never make up his mind which was on the whole the most defensible, especially since he was ingenious in recasting every theory into its least objectionable form." Defend a theory—Whitehead on God—and Moore would attack it. Attack a theory—Russell on consciousness—and Moore would defend it.

In all this, the net effect was to undermine commitment to everything except to the quality of philosophical argumentation. Even if the philosophical argumentation was to lead nowhere, it should do so as competently as possible. With his commitment to philosophical standards, with his professionalism, Moore was a logical choice in 1921 to assume the editorship of the journal *Mind*. This editorship, his lectures at Cambridge (completely re-written every year), and the meetings of the Aristotelian Society took most of his energies.

Nevertheless, there was one positive philosophical task that Moore still pursued throughout the rest of his life. He wished, it seemed, to find just one undeniable philosophical argument, just one, just to show that there were such. The nature of good, on which he had tried to write a Principia, was obviously too complicated a question to hope for finality. Something simpler was needed, so simple as to be obvious to those who had not been corrupted by the taste of philosophy.

He settled on re-writing his refutation of idealism. We know that the world exists, and that in this world there are others like ourselves. In 1903 he had defended this belief against the preposterous philosophical contention that the material world does not really exist. Looking back upon that defense, Moore did not find it satisfactory. When he included it in a collection of his papers published in 1922, he insisted that the paper seemed to him "to be very confused, as well as to embody a good many downright mistakes." He would not even have consented to its reprinting if he had not been "told that, for some readers at all events, it would be a convenience that it should be reprinted along with the rest, if only for the sake of reference."

He had perhaps failed in 1903. Over twenty years later he would try again. The paper was entitled "A Defense of Common Sense," and in it Moore tried to defend common beliefs against the doubts of philosophers. The tone is self-assured. He began with a list of propositions "every one of which (in my own opinion) I *know*, with certainty, to be true."

> There exists at present a living human body, which is *my* body. This body was born at a certain time in the past, and has existed continuously ever since, though not without undergoing changes; it was, for instance, much smaller when it was born, and for some time afterwards, than it is now. Ever since it was born, it has been either in contact with or not far from the surface of the earth.

And so Moore continued for more than a page asserting, with what had become uncharacteristic vigor, proposition after proposition: the existence of a world which ante-dated his own existence, the existence of other human beings who had lived and died before he had been born, who had had many of the same experiences he had had, and who had also had beliefs both true and false, and who had also had hopes both realized and disappointed.

This long list of propositions might seem to his readers, Moore realized, but a list of truisms. However, they were all propositions the truth of which, at least as far as Moore could tell, many philosophers have denied. And they were all propositions for which Moore could show, if he was not mistaken, there is no good reason to deny.

He could show this by having his readers try to assume the contrary. Let them assume that some philosopher has had a good reason for denying these propositions. To assume this is to assume the existence of that philosopher. It is, in fact, to assume all the propositions which Moore had carefully listed, "for when I speak of 'philosphoers' I mean, of course (as we all do), exclusively philosophers who have been human beings, with human bodies that have lived upon the earth, and who have at different times had many different experiences." To know that philosophers have denied these propositions is to know that they are wrong in making this denial. As for these philosophers themselves, do they not continually allude to other philosophers? Do they not also continually allude to the existence of their readers?

At this point some of Moore's readers might have thought that he was about to claim to have proven the truth of those propositions he had so carefully listed. But it was at precisely this point that Moore introduced the distinction between the claim to be able to defend a group of propositions and the claim to be able to prove them. To defend, one only has to defend from attack; that is all Moore has done. All Moore has done has been to show that all philosophers who have attacked these propositions have been inconsistent. That is different from proving the propositions; it is also different from proving that inconsistency is a bad thing.

The strange thing is that philosophers should have been able to hold sincerely, as part of their philosophical creed, propositions inconsistent with what they themselves *knew* to be true; and yet, so far as I can make out, this has really frequently happened.

In 1939, fifteen years later (he had written no paper in between), Moore tried again. This time the paper was entitled "A Proof of an External World." After almost a lifetime of trying, he had finally settled on what he thought to be "a perfectly rigorous proof" of the existence of the external world.

I can prove now, for instance, that two human hands exist. How? By holding up my two hands, and saying, as I make a certain gesture with the right hand, "Here is one hand," and adding, as I make a certain gesture with the left, "and here is another." And if, by doing this, I have proved *ipso facto* the existence of external things, you will all see that I can also do it now in numbers of other ways: there is no need to multiply examples.

It seemed that Moore had finally found the proof for which he had looked for almost a lifetime; he had finally found it in a simple gesture.

And yet, as Moore was about to leave to deliver this proof, he looked distraught. "Cheer up," he was told, "I'm sure they will like it." He replied only, "If they do, they'll be wrong."[3]

In the 1940's, Whitehead turned eighty; Moore and Russell, seventy. They were all old men, and their youthful confidence had proven unjustified. This they all admitted, each in his own way.

Whitehead would cheerfully insist upon it, for he saw the failure of reason as pointing to a higher truth. So he conluded one of his last lectures, a lecture entitled "Immortality" and delivered to the Harvard Divinity School in 1941, in the following words.

What I am objecting to is the absurd trust in the adequacy of our knowledge. The self-confidence of learned people is the comic tragedy of civilization. . . . The conclusion is that Logic, conceived as an adequate analysis of the advance of thought, is a fake. It is a superb instrument, but requires a background of common sense. . . . My point is that the final outlook of Philosophic thought cannot be based upon the exact statements which form the basis of special sciences. The exactness is a fake.

G. E. Moore, characteristically, gave the driest assessment. When Moore was described by a critic as a great questioner, but an "extremely weak and unsatisfying answerer," an admirer tried a rebuttal.

Moore would have none of it. He wrote in response in 1942, "I did want to answer questions, to give solutions to problems, and I think it is a just charge against me that I have been able to solve so few of the problems I wished to solve."

As for Bertrand Russell, the philosopher ever glib, he remained undaunted even in defeat. Russell made one final attempt at philosophical synthesis in 1948 in his *Human Knowledge: Its Scope and Limits*. There he admitted that his own attempt to give a rational account of human knowledge was, like all the others, a failure. He admitted that in this sense "we know nothing whatever, and knowledge in this sense is a delusive vision." He admitted that "the perplexities of philosophers are due, in large measure, to their unwillingness to awaken from this blissful sleep." Russell admitted all this, yet he still managed to conclude in a confident tone. His own philosophy at least had been inspired by the doctrine "that all human knowledge is uncertain, inexact, partial." And so Russell could conclude triumphantly, "To this doctrine we have not found any limitation whatever."[4]

EPILOGUE

The confidence of the Cambridge philosophers had run its course, much as earlier confidences had run theirs, much as later confidences seem destined to run theirs.

This is not to say that nothing will ever be new under the sun. After all, the time of the end, if such there be, will abound in novelty. In particular, then, if the prophet Daniel's vision was true, many shall run to and fro, and knowledge shall be increased.

In the meantime, whoever persists in the pursuit of first principles appears fated to run to and fro merely.

SOURCES

PREFACE

[1] Paul Fussell, *The Rhetorical World of Augustan Humanism* (Oxford, 1965), p. 7; Lord Acton, *Essays in the Liberal Interpretation of History*, ed. William H. McNeill (Chicago, 1967), p. 398; Arnold Toynbee, *A Study of History*, v. 1 (Oxford, 1934), p. 4; Wayne Booth, *The Rhetoric of Fiction* (Chicago, 1961), pp. 141-2.

[2] Wallace Stevens, *The Palm at the End of the Mind*, ed. Holly Stevens (New York, 1971), pp. 164-5.

INTRODUCTION

[1] John Milton, *Paradise Lost* (London, 1667). Also, C. A. Patrides, *Milton and the Christian Tradition* (Oxford, 1966), Chapter 4; Stanley Fish, *Surprised by Sin* (New York, 1967).

[2] William Stukeley, *Memoirs of Sir Isaac Newton's Life*, ed. A. N. White (London, 1936). Also, *The Poems of Alexander Pope*, ed. J. Butt, v. 9 (London, 1951), p. 317.

[3] Douglas McKie and Gavin de Beer, "Newton's Apple," *Notes and Records of the Royal Society of London* (henceforth to be cited as *Notes and Records*), v. 9 (1952), pp. 46-54, 333-5,

Leonard Huxley, *Life and Letters of Thomas Henry Huxley* (New York, 1901), v. 1, p. 234; Albert Einstein, "Forword," Isaac Newton's *Opticks* (New York, 1952). Also, Roger Hahn, *Laplace as a Newtonian Scientist* (Los Angeles, 1967).

PART I

CHAPTER ONE

[1] John Tulloch, *Rational Theology and Christian Philosophy in the Seventeenth Century* (Edinburgh, 1872), v. 2; Ernst Cassirer, *The Platonic Renaissance in England*, trans. J. P. Pettegrove (Edinburgh, 1953); Rosalie L. Colie, *Light and Enlightenment* (Cambridge, 1957).

Simon Patrick ("S. P."), *A Brief Account of the New Sect of Latitudemen* (London, 1662), reprinted in *The Phenix*, v. 2 (1708), pp. 499-518.

[2] Benjamin Whichcote, *Moral and Religious Aphorisms ... to Which are Added Eight Letters ... between Dr. Whichcote ... and Dr. Tuckney* (London, 1753). Also, "Sir Walter Mildmay," *Dictionary of National Biography*, ed. Leslie Stephen and Sidney Lee (London, 1917), v. 13, p. 375; Howard Schutz, *Milton and Forbidden Knowledge* (New York, 1955), Chapter 1.

[3] *Conway Letters: The Correspondence of Anne, Viscontess Conway, Henry More, and their Friends*, 1642-1684, ed. M. H. Nicholoson (New Haven, 1930); Aharon Lichtenstein, *Henry More: The Rational Theology of a Cambridge Platonist* (Cambridge, Mass., 1962).

Joseph Mede, *Clavis Apocalyptica* (London, 1627); Francis Potter, *An Interpretation of the Number 666* (Oxford, 1647); Henry More, *The Apology of Dr. Henry More* (London, 1664); *Synopsis Prophetica* (London, 1664). Ernest Tuveson, *Millenium and Utopia* (Berkeley, 1949); C. A. Patrides, *The Phoenix and the Ladder* (Berkeley, 1964).

Thomas Hobbes, *Leviathan* (London, 1651). Charles T. Harrison, "The Ancient Atomists and English Literature of the Seventeenth Century," *Harvard Studies in Classical Philology*, v. 45 (1934), pp. 1-56; Samuel Mintz, *The Hunting of Leviathan* (Cambridge, 1962), Chapter 5. Also, Thomas Hobbes, trans., *Iliad* (London, 1677), Book VI, lines 135-6.

Henry More, *Philosophical Poems* (London, 1647); *An Antidote against Atheisme, or, An Appeal to the Naturall Faculties of the Minde of Man, whether there be not a God* (London, 1652); *The Immortality of the Soul, So farre forth as it is demonstrable from the Knowledge of Nature and the Light of Reason* (London, 1659); *Divine Dialogues, Containing Sundry Disquisitions and Instructions Concerning the Attributes of God and His Providence in the World* (London, 1668); *Enchiridion Metaphysicum: sive, De Rebus In corporeis Succincta et Luculenta Dissertatio* (London, 1671). Also, John Worthington, "Introduction" to John Smith, *Select Discourses* (London, 1660).

Michel de Montaigne, *Essays*, trans. John Florio (London, 1603). Also, Philip Hallie, *The Scar of Montaigne* (Middleton, 1966).

[4] Ralph Cudworth, *Discourse Concerning the True Notion of the Lord's Supper* (London, 1642); Henry More, *Conjectura Cabbalistica, or, A Conjectural Essay of Interpreting the minde of Moses according to a Threefold Caballa: Viz. Literal, Philosophical, Mystical, or, Divinely Moral* (London, 1653). Also, Anne Conway, *The Principles of the Most Ancient and Modern Philosophy* (Amsterdam, 1690).

Francis Yates, *Giordano Bruno and the Hermetic Tradition* (London, 1964); J. E. McGuire and P. M. Ratansi, "Newton and the 'Pipes of Pan'," *Notes and Records of the Royal Society of London*, v. 21 (1966), pp. 126-34; D. P. Walker, *The Ancient Theology* (London, 1972). Also, Danton Sailor, "Moses and Atomism," *Journal of the History of Ideas*, v. 25 (1964), pp. 3-16.

CHAPTER TWO

[1] A. R. Hall, "Sir Isaac Newton's Notebook, 1661-5," *Cambridge Historical Journal*, v. 9 (1948), pp. 239-50.

René Descartes, *A Discourse of a Method*, trans. Thomas Newcombe (London, 1649). Richard Popkin, *History of Scepticism* (New York, 1964), Chapters 9-10.

Marjorie Nicholson, "The Early Stage of Cartesianism in England," *Studies in Philology*, v. 26 (1929), pp. 356-74; Sterling Lamprecht, "The Role of Descartes in Seventeenth-Century England," *Studies in the History of Ideas*, v. 3 (1935), pp. 181-243; Arrigo Pacchi, *Cartesio in Inghilterra* (Bari, 1973), Chapters 1-2, 4. Also, Henry More, "The Preface General," *A Collection of Several Philosophical Writings of Dr. Henry More* (London, 1662), pp. iii-xxviii.

John Tull Baker, *An Historical and Critical Examination of English Space and Time Theories* (Bronxville, 1930), Chapters 1-3; E. A. Burtt, *Metaphysical Foundations of Modern Science* (New York, 1932), pp. 135-61; Alexandre Koyré, *From Closed World to Infinite Universe* (Baltimore, 1957), Chapters 5-6.

[2] Isaac Newton, "De Gravitatione et Aequipondo Fluidorum," *Unpublished Scientific Papers of Isaac Newton* (henceforth to be cited as *Unpublished Papers*), eds. A. R. and M. B. Hall (Cambridge, 1962), pp. 90-156.

Percy Osmond, *Isaac Barrow* (London, 1944), Chapters 3, 5-6; Edward Strong, "Barrow and Newton," *Journal of the History of Philosophy*, v. 8 (1970), pp. 155-72. Also, "Isaac Barrow," *Dictionary of National Biography*, v. 1, p. 1221.

[3] Ralph Cudworth, *The True Intellectual System of the World*, Part 1 (London, 1676). Also, Thomas Birch, "An Account of the Life and Writings of R. Cudworth, D. D.," prefixed to the second edition of *The True Intellectual System* (London, 1743).

[4] Nancy Pulver, *The Royal Society: Concept and Creation* (London, 1967).

Isaac Newton, "Optical Papers," reprinted from *Philosophical Transactions* (1672-76) in *Isaac Newton's Papers and Letters on Natural Philosophy* (henceforth to be cited as *Newton's Papers*), ed. I. B. Cohen (Cambridge, Mass., 1958), pp. 47-176. Also, *The Correspondence of Isaac Newton* (Cambridge, 1959-67), eds. H. W. Turnbull and J. F. Scott, 4 vols.; A. I Sabra, *Theories of Light from Descartes to Newton* (London, 1967), pp. 231-97.

Henry More, "Prefatio," *Opera Omnia* (London, 1675-79), v. 1, translated into English as "Preface" to *The Theological Works of the Most Pious and Learned Henry More, D. D.* (London, 1708); *A Plain and Continued Exposition of the Prophecies or Divine Visions* (London, 1681). (Newton's copy is at present at the Bancroft Library of the University of California at Berkeley.)

Isaac Newton, *Observations upon the Prophecies of Daniel and the Apocalypse of St. John*, ed. B. Smith (London, 1733); "The Language of the Prophets," *Theological Manuscripts*, ed. M. McLachlan (Liverpool, 1950). Also, Frank Manuel, *Isaac Newton Historian* (Cambridge, Mass., 1963), pp. 139-56.

⁵ W. W. Rouse Ball, *An Essay on Newton's Principia* (London, 1893), Chapters 2-5; Florian Cajori, "Newton's Twenty Years' Delay in Announcing the Law of Gravitation," *Sir Isaac Newton, 1727-1927*, ed. F. E. Brasch (Baltimore, 1928), pp. 127-88; R. S. Westfall, "Hooke and the Law of Universal Gravitation," *British Journal for the History of Science*, v. 3 (1967), pp. 245-61; Derek T. Whiteside, "Before the *Principia*: The Maturing of Newton's Thought on Dynamical Astronomy, 1664-84," *Journal of the History of Astronomy*, v. 1 (1970), pp. 5-19; Richard Westfall, *Force in Newton's Physics* (London, 1971), pp. 323-467. Also, Henry Pemberton, *A View of Sir Isaac Newton's Philosophy* (London, 1728).

Stephen P. Rigaud, *Historical Essay on the First Publication of Sir Isaac Newton's Principia* (Oxford, 1838), pp. 63-77; Robert Schofield, "Halley and the *Principia*," *Newton's Papers*, pp. 397-404; John Herivel, "Halley's First Visit to Newton," *Archives internationales d'Histoire des Sciences*, v. 13 (1960), pp. 63-6; I. Bernard Cohen, *Introduction to Newton's Principia* (Cambridge, Mass., 1971), Chapter 6.

CHAPTER THREE

¹ Isaac Newton, *Philosophiae Naturalis Principia Mathematica* (London, 1687); *Mathematical Principles of Natural Philosophy*, trans. Andrew Motte (London, 1729). Also, I. Bernard Cohen, "Newton's Use of 'Force,' or Cajori versus Newton: A Note of Translations of the *Principia*," *Isis*, v. 58 (1967), pp. 226-30.

"The Ode Dedicated to Newton by Edmund Halley," trans. Leon Richardson, published in Florian Cajori's revision of Motte's translation of Newton (Berkeley, 1934), pp. xiii-xv; Alexander Weinstein, "Ode on Newton's Theory of Gravitation by Edmund Halley," *Science*, v. 97 (1943), pp. 69-70. Also, Stephen Rigaud, *Historical Essay*, pp. 85-6.

² E. A. Burtt, *Metaphysical Foundations*, pp. 207-64; Stephen Toulmin, "Criticism in the History of Science," *Philosophical Review*, v. 68 (1959), pp. 1-29, 203-27; Richard Westfall, "Newton and Absolute Space," *Archives internationales d'Histoire des Sciences*, v. 17 (1964), pp. 121-32; Alexandre Koyré, *Newtonian Studies* (Cambridge, Mass., 1965), pp. 53-114.

³ Richard Westfall, *Force in Newton's Physics*, pp. 467-512.

⁴ Isaac Newton, *A Treatise of the System of the World demonstrated in an Easy Popular Manner* (London, 1728); I. B. Cohen, "Introduction," Newton's *A Treatise* (London, 1969), pp. vii-xxii.

CHAPTER FOUR

¹ *Journal des Scavans of 1688*, pp. 237-8; Christiaan Huygens' letter, Huygens' *Œuvres Completes*, v. 9 (1909), p. 190; Christiaan Huygens, *Un traité de la Lumière*

... *avec un Discourse de la Cause de la Pesanteur* (Leyden, 1690); Alexandre Koyré, *Newtonian Studies*, pp. 115-24.

Fatio de Duiller—Huygens' letters, *Newton's Correspondence*, v.3, pp. 193-7; J. E. McGuire and P. M. Rattansi, "Newton and the 'Pipes of Pan'," pp. 108-43.

Frank Manuel, *A Portrait of Newton* (Cambridge, Mass., 1968), Chapters 9-10; Charles Domson, *Nicholas Fatio de Duiller and the Prophets of London* (unpubl. diss., Yale univ., 1972); I. Bernard Cohen, *Introduction to Newton's "Principia"*, Chapter 7.

[2] Frank Manuel, *A Portrait of Newton*, Chapter 13.

David Gregory, *Astronimæ physicæ & geometricæ elementa* (Oxford, 1702), English trans. 1715; John Keill, *Introductio ad veram physicam* (Oxford, 1701), English trans. 1720; *Introductio ad veram astronomiam* (Oxford, 1718), English trans. 1721.

Richard Bentley, *Four Letters from Sir Isaac Newton to Doctor Bentley containing Some Arguments in Proof of a Deity* (London, 1756), reprinted in *Newton's Papers*, pp. 279-312; *The Folly and Unreasonableness of Atheism* (London, 1693), selection relevant to Newtonian philosophy reprinted in *Newton's Papers*, pp. 313-94; William Whiston, *A New Theory of the Earth* (Lndon, 1696). Also, Paolo Casini, *L'Univero-Machina* (Bari, 1969), Chapters 3-4.

Jacques Rohault, *Physica* (London, 1697, 1702), trans. Samuel Clarke. Also, Michael Hoskins, "'Mining All Within': Clarke's Notes to Rohault's Traité du Physique," *The Thomist*, v.24 (1962), pp. 353-62; Alexandre Koyré, *Newtonian Studies*, pp. 170-2; Paolo Casini, *L'Universo-Machina*, pp. 109-25.

John Keill, *An Examination of Dr. Burnet's Theory of the Earth Together with Some Remarks on Mr. Whiston's New Theory of the Earth* (London, 1698); William Whiston, *A Vindication of the New Theory of the Earth* (London, 1698); John Keill, *An Examination of the Reflections on the Theory of the Earth, Together with a Defence of the Remarks on Mr. Whiston's New Theory* (Oxford, 1699); William Whiston, *A Second Defense of the New Theory of the Earth from the exceptions of Mr. John Keill* (London, 1700). Also, David Kubrin, *Providence and the Mechanical Philosophy* (unpubl. diss., Cornell Univ., 1968), pp. 259-338.

William Whiston, *Memoirs of the Life and Writings of Mr. Whiston* (London, 1753).

[3] I. Bernard Cohen, *Introduction to Newton's "Principia"*, Chapter 9.

Edward Strong, "Newton and God," *Journal of the History of Ideas*, v. 13 (1952), pp. 147-67; J. E. McGuire, "Force, Active Principles, and Newton's Invisible Realm," *Ambix*, v. 15 (1968), pp. 187-208.

[4] Isaac Newton, "Conclusio," *Unpublished Scientific Papers*, pp. 321-47; *Opticks; or a Treatise of the Reflextions, Refractions, Inflections and Colours of Light* (London, 1704). Also, Isaac Newton, *Lectiones Opticæ annis 1669, 1670, et 1671* (London, 1729).

Alexandre Koyré, "Les Queries de l'*Optique*," *Archives internationales d'Histoire des Sciences*, v. 13 (1960), pp. 15-29; J. E. McGuire, "Force, Active Principles and Newton's Invisible Realm," pp. 154-208.

CHAPTER FIVE

[1] Hélène Metzger, *Newton, Stahl, Boerhaave et la Doctrine Chimique* (Paris, 1930), Part I; A. R. and M. B. Hall, "Newton's Theory of Matter," *Isis*, v.51 (1960), pp. 131-44; Robert E. Schofield, *Mechanism and Materialism* (Princeton, 1970), Chapter 1; Arnold Thackray, *Atoms and Powers* (Cambridge, Mass., 1970), Chapter 2.

[2] Robert Schofield, *Mechanism and Materialism*, Chapters 2-4; Arnold Thackray, *Atoms and Powers*, Chapter 3.

Benjamin Woorster, *A Compendious and Methodical Account of the Principles of Natural Philosophy* (London, 1722); Roger Cotes, *Hydrostatical Lectures* (London, 1738), p. 126. Also, John Keill, "In qua Leges Attractionis aliaque Physices Principia traduntur," *Philosophical Transactions*, v.26 (1708), pp. 97-110.

Stephen Hales, *Vegetable Staticks . . . Also a Specimen of an Attempt to Analyze Air* (London, 1727). Also, A. E. Clark-Kennedy, *Stephen Hales* (Cambridge, 1929); Henry Guerlac, "Stephen Hales," *Dictionary of Scientific Biography*, ed. Charles C. Gillispie, v.6 (New York, 1972), pp. 35-46.

³ Henry Guerlac, "The Continental Reputation of Stephen Hales," *Archives internationales d'Histoires des Sciences*, v.4 (1951), pp. 393-404.

Leslie Stephen, *English Thought in the 18th Century* (London, 1902), v.1, Chapters 2-6; Hélène Metzger, *Attraction universelle et Religion naturelle . . .* (Paris, 1938); Robert Hurblutt, *Hume, Newton, and the Design Argument* (Lincoln, Nebraska, 1965); John Herman Randall, "The Religious Consequences of Newton's Thought," *The Annus Mirabilis*, ed. R. Palter (Cambridge, Mass., 1970), pp. 333-43.

John Freind, *Prælectiones Chymicæ* (London, 1709; Amsterdam, 1710); "Praelectionum Chymicarum Vindiciae," *Philosophical Transactions*, v.27 (1712), pp. 330-42; Marie Boas Hall, "John Freind," *Dictionary of Scientific Biography*, v.5 (1972), pp. 157-7.

Stephen Hales, *Hæmastaticks* (London, 1733); *Philosophical Experiments* (London, 1739).

⁴ John T. Desaguliers, *Physico-mechanical Lectures* (London, 1717). Also, A. R. Hall, "John Theophilus Desaguliers," *Dictionary of Scientific Biography*, v.4 (1971), pp. 43-6.

The Constitution . . . of Accepted Free Masons (London, 1723); D. C. Lee, *Desaguliers of No. 4 and his Services to Freemasonary* (London, 1932); Douglas Knoop, *A Short History of Freemasonry to 1730* (Manchester, 1940).

John T. Desaguliers, "An Account of a Book entitul'd *Vegetable Staticks*," *Philosophical Transactions*, v.34 (1728), pp. 264-91, 323-31; *The Newtonian System of the Word, the best model of Government* (London, 1728); "An Attempt to Solve the Phenomenon of the Rise of Vapours . . .," *Philosophical Transactions*, v.35 (1729), pp. 16-22; Benjamin Martin, *Philosophical Grammar* (London, 1738); *A Supplement* (Bath, 1746). Also, Martyn Clare, *The Motion of Fluids* (London, 1735), pp. 127-8; John Rowning, *A Compendious System of Natural Philosophy* (London, 1735, 1738), Part II, Dissertation VII; W. E. Knowles Middleton, *A History of the Theories of Rain* (London, 1965), Chapters 2, 5.

Henry Guerlac, "Francis Hauksbee: experimenteur au profit de Newton," *Archives internationales d'Histoire des Sciences*, v.16 (1963), pp. 113-28; P. M. Heineman and J. E. McGuire, "Newtonian Forces and Lockean Powers," *Historical Studies in the Physical Sciences*, v.3 (1971), pp. 237-46; John Heilbron, *History of Electricity in the 17th and 18th Centuries* (Berkeley, forthcoming), Part III.

John T. Desaguliers, "Some Thoughts Concerning the Cause of Electricity," *Philosophical Transactions*, v.41 (1739), pp. 175-85; "Some Conjectures Concerning Electricity and the Rise of Vapours," *Philosophical Transactions*, v.42 (1742), pp. 140-3; *A Course of Experimental Philosophy* (London, 1734-4), 2 vols., including "A Dissertation on the Cause of the Rise of Vapours and Exhalations in the Air," v. 2, pp. 342-3.

PART II

CHAPTER SIX

¹ John Bowring, "Memoirs of Bentham; including autobiographical conversations and correspondence," *The Works of Jeremy Bentham* (London, 1843), vols.

10-11 (henceforth cited as *Bentham's Works*); Leslie Stephen, *The English Utilitarians* (London, 1900), v.1.; Elie Halevy, *La Formation du Radicalisme Philosophique* (Paris, 1901), v.1; Shirley Letwin, *The Pursuit of Certainty* (Cambridge, 1965), Part 2. Also, Thomas Southwood Smith, *A Lecture Delivered over the Remains of Jeremy Bentham, Esq., . . .* (London, 1832), reprinted in *Bentham's Works*, v.11, pp. 83-95.

Charles Everett, *The Education of Jeremy Bentham* (New York, 1931), Chapter 3; Mary Mack, *Jeremy Bentham: an Odyssey of Ideas* (New York, 1963), Chapters 2-3.

² Jeremy Bentham, *An Introduction to the Principles of Morals and Legislation* (London, 1789), reprinted in *Bentham's Works*, v.1, pp. 1-154. Everett W. Hall, "The 'Proof' of Utility in Bentham and Mill," *Ethics*, v.60 (1949), pp. 1-18; John Plamenatz, *The English Utilitarians* (Oxford, 1958), pp. 70-82; David Lyons, *In the Interest of the Governed* (Oxford, 1973), Chapters 2-5.

³ Jeremy Bentham, *A Fragment on Government* (1776), reprinted in *Bentham's Works*, v.1, pp. 221-295; Jeremy Bentham, *Traités de legislation civile et pénale* (Paris, 1802), ed. and trans. Étienne Dumont, 3 vols.; "Bentham's *Principles de Legislation* par Dumont," *Edinburgh Review*, v.4 (1816), pp. 1-27. G. C. L. de Sismondi, "Sketch of the Life and Character of Stephen Dumont," printed in John Neal's edition of Bentham's *Introduction* (Boston, 1830); Bernard Gagnebin, "Jeremy Bentham et Étienne Dumont." *Jeremy Bentham Bicentenary Celebrations* (London, 1948); David Baumgardt, *Bentham and the Ethics of Today* (Princeton, 1952), pp. 323-69.

⁴ Jeremy Bentham, *Panopticon; or, Inspection-House* (London, 1791), 3 vols., reprinted in *Bentham's Works*, v.4, pp. 37-172; Bentham, "Panopticon versus New South Wales," *Bentham's Works*, pp. 173-248; Bentham, "Selections from Bentham's Narrative regarding the Penopticon Penitentiary Project," *Bentham's Works*, v.10, pp. 96-170. Gertrude Himmelfarb, "The Haunted House of Jeremy Bentham," *Victorian Minds* (New York, 1968), pp. 32-82.

CHAPTER SEVEN

¹ Alexander Bain, *James Mill* (London, 1882); Leslie Stephen, *The English Utilitarians* (London, 1900), v.2; David Ricardo, *Works*, ed. P. Straffa, vols. 6-9 (Cambridge, 1952). Also, Donald Winch, "Bibliography," *James Mill: Selected Economics Writings* (Edinburgh, 1966), pp. 444-8.

"Prefatory Address," *Anti-Jacobin Review and Magazine*, v.1 (1798), pp. i-vii; "Politics," *The Literary Journal or Universal Review of Literature Domestic and Foreign*, v.1 (1803), pp. 323-330.

James Mill, "Bentham on Scotch Reform," *Annual Review and History of Literature*, v.7 (1808), pp. 198-203; "Bexon's Code de la Législation Pénale'," *Edinburgh Review*, v.14 (1809), pp. 88-109; "C. J. Fox's *History of James II*," *Annual Review and History of Literature*, v.7 (1808), pp. 99-101. Also, Charles James Fox, *History of the Early Part of the Reign of James the Second* (London, 1808).

² Jeremy Bentham, "The Influence of Time and Place on Legislation," *Bentham's Works*, v.1, pp. 169-94.

³ Eric Stokes, *The English Utilitarians and India* (Oxford, 1959), Chapter 1; George D. Bearce, *British Attitudes Toward India 1784-1858* (Oxford, 1961). James Mill, *History of British India* (London, 1817), 3 vols. Duncan Forbes, "James Mill and India," *The Cambridge Journal*, v.5 (1951), pp. 19-33.

⁴ James Mill, "Affairs of India," *Edinburgh Review*, v.16 (1810), pp. 155-56. Eric Stokes, *The English Utilitarians and India*, Chapters 2-4; Chittaranjan Sinha, "Doctrinal Influences on the Judicial Policy of the East India Company's Administration in Bengal, 1772-1833," *The Historical Journal*, v.12 (1969), pp. 240-8.

James Mill, "Government," in *Supplement to the . . . Encyclopedia Britannica* (Edinburgh, 1824); and also in *Essays on Government Jurisprudence, Liberty of the Press and Law of Nations* (London, 1825); and also in *The Traveller*, April, 1821. James Hamburger, "James Mill on 'Universal Suffrage'," *Journal of Politics*, v.24 (1962), pp. 167-90; William Thomas, "James Mill's 'Essay' and Reform," *Historical Journal*, v.12 (1969), pp. 249-84; Wendell Robert Carr, "James Mill's Politics Reconsidered: Parliamentary Reform and the Triumph of Truth," *Historical Journal*, v. 14 (1971), pp. 553-80.

⁵ Thomas Macaulay, "Mill on Government," *Edinburgh Review*, v.49 (1829), pp. 159-89.

⁶ Graham Wallas, *The Life of Francis Place* (London, 1918); Harriet Grote, *The Personal Life of George Grote* (London, 1873); George Grote, "The Essentials of Parliamentary Reform," *The Minor Works of George Grote*, ed. Alexander Bain (London, 1873), pp. 1-55; "Philip Beauchamp," *An Analysis of the Influence of Natural Religion on the Temporal Happiness of Mankind* (London, 1822); "Gamaliel Smith," *Not Paul but Jesus* (London, 1823).

John Austin, "Primogeniture," *Westminster Review*, v.2 (1824), pp. 503-58; James Mill, "Edinburgh Review," v.1 (1824), pp. 205-49; James Mill, "Quarterly Review," v.2 (1824), pp. 463-503; George Grote, "Institutions of Ancient Greece," v.5 (1826), pp. 269-331; Harriet Grote, "Memoirs of the Countess of Genlis," v.6 (1828), pp. 134-57; John Bowring, "Coleridge and Poetry," v.12 (1830), pp. 1-31. George L. Nesbitt, *Benthamite Reviewing: The First Twelve Years of the Westminster Review* (New York, 1934).

"The Greatest Happiness Principle," *Westminster Review*, v.11 (1829), pp. 526-36; Thomas Macaulay, "Utilitarian System of Philosophy," *Edinburgh Review*, v.49 (1829), pp. 273-99.

⁷ Joseph Hamburger, *James Mill and the Art of Revolution* (New Haven, 1963). James Mill, "The Ballot," *Westminster Review*, v.18 (1830), pp. 1-37.

"Memoirs of Jeremy Bentham," *Edinburgh Review*, v.78 (1834), p. 461.

John Hill Burton, "Introduction to the Study of Bentham's Works," *Bentham's Works*, v.1, pp. 5-93; *Benthamiana; or, Select extracts from the works of Jeremy Bentham* (Edinburgh, 1843).

John Flowerdew Colls, *Utilitarianism Unmasked* (London, 1844); Elmer Louis Kaysen, *The Grand Social Enterprise* (New York, 1932), pp. 35-6.

CHAPTER EIGHT

¹ James Mill, *The Elements of Political Economy* (London, 1821); *Analysis of the Phenomena of the Human Mind* (London, 1829); "Education," *Supplement to the . . . Encyclopedia Britannica*. Also, John Plamenatz, *The English Utilitarians*, pp. 99-105.

² Leslie Stephen, *The English Utilitarians*, v.3; Michael St. John Parke, *The Life of John Stuart Mill* (London, 1954); Shirley Letwin, *The Pursuit of Certainty*, Part 3; James Hamburger, *Intellectuals in Politics* (New Haven, 1965). Also, John Stuart Mill, *Autobiography*, first edited by Helen Taylor (London, 1873).

Jeremy Bentham, *Chrestomathia* (London, 1815), reprinted in *Bentham's Works*, v.8., pp. 1-191; *Rationale of Judicial Evidence, specially applied to English Practice*, ed. J. S. Mill (London, 1827), 5 vols.

J. S. Mill, "On the Utility of Knowledge," first published as an appendix to Harold Laski's edition of Mill's *Autobiography* (London, 1924), pp. 267-74.

³ John Stuart Mill, "What is Poetry?" and "The Two Kinds of Poetry," *Monthly Repository*, v.7 (1833), pp. 60-70, 714-24—both essays reprinted in *Dissertations and Discussions* (London, 1859). M. H. Abrams, *The Mirror and the Lamp* (New York, 1953), Chapter 11; Thomas Wood, *Poetry and Philosophy: a study in the thought of John Stuart Mill* (London, 1961).

"Moore's *Fables for the Holy Alliance*," *Westminster Review*, v.1 (1825). p. 19; Thomas Love Peacock, "The Four Ages of Poetry," first printed in *Ollier's Literary Miscellany*, v.1 (1820), pp. 183-200.

John Stuart Mill, "Remarks on Bentham's Philosophy" and "Remarks on the Philosophy of James Mill," first appeared in Edward Lytton Bulwer's *England and the English* (London, 1833).

⁴ James Anthony Froude, *Thomas Carlyle: A History of his Life in London, 1834-1881* (New York, 1910), v.1, p. 64; Gertrude Himmelfarb, "The Other John Stuart Mill," *Victorian Minds*, pp. 113-54.

Samuel Coleridge, *Statesman's Manual* (London, 1816); *Specimens of the Table Talk of the late Samuel Taylor Coleridge* (London, 1835), July 4, 1833; *Biographia Literaria* (London, 1817), Chapter 6.

John Stuart Mill, "Bentham," *London and Westminster Review*, v.29 (1838), pp. 467-506; "Coleridge," *London and Westminster Review*, v.33 (1840), pp. 257-302. Also, F. R. Leavis, "Introduction," *Mill on Bentham and Coleridge* (London, 1950).

CHAPTER NINE

¹ John Stuart Mill, "Blakey's History of Moral Science," *Monthly Repository*, v.7 (1833), pp. 661-9.

² John Stuart Mill, *System of Logic* (London, 1843). Oskar Alfred Kubitz, *Development of John Stuart Mill's System of Logic* (Urbana, 1932); Alburey Castell, *Mill's Logic of the Moral Sciences* (Chicago, 1936); Richard William Thurn, *The Rhetorical Character of Philosophic Discourse: A study of J. S. Mill and T. H. Green* (unpubl. diss., Univ. Calif., Berkeley, 1973), Chapter 2.

³ John Stuart Mill, *On Liberty* (London, 1859). John Plamenatz, *The English Utilitarians*, pp. 124-34; Isaiah Berlin, *John Stuart Mill and the Ends of Life* (London, 1961).

⁴ Robert Leader, *Life and Letters of John Arthur Roebuck* (London, 1897), p.39; F. A. Hayek, *John Stuart Mill and Harriet Taylor* (Chicago, 1951).

PART III

CHAPTER TEN

¹ John H. Muirhead, *The Platonic Tradition in Anglo-Saxon Philosophy* (London, 1931), pp. 147-218; John Passmore, *A Hundred Years of Philosophy* (London, 1957), Chapters 3-4; A. J. M. Milne, *The Social Philosophy of English Idealism* (London, 1962), Chapters 1, 6.

Edward Caird, *Essays on Literature* (Glasgow, 1902). Also, Henry Jones and John H. Muirhead, *The Life and Philosophy of Edward Caird* (Glasgow, 1921).

² Benjamin Jowett, "Interpretations of Scripture," *The Interpretation of Scripture and Other Essays* (London, 1906); *Dialogues of Plato* (London, 1868), 4 vols.; *Sermons Biographical and Miscellaneous* (London, 1899), ed. W. H. Freemantle, p. 142.

Edward Caird, "Professor Jowett," *International Journal of Ethics*, v.8 (1897), pp. 40-7; E. A. Abbot and L. Campbell, *The Life and Letters of Benjamin Jowett* (London, 1897); Geoffrey Faber, *Jowett: a portrait with background* (London, 1957). Also, W. G. Hiscock, *The Balliol Rhymes* (Oxford, 1955).

³ J. Bryce, *Studies in Contemporary Biography* (London, 1904), pp. 85-99; John MacCunn, *Six Radical Thinkers* (London, 1907), Chapter 6; Melvin Richter, *The Politics of Conscience* (Cambridge, 1964). Also, Mary Augusta Ward, *Robert Elsmere* (London, 1888), 3 vols.

Thomas Hill Green, "An Essay on Christian Dogma," *The Works of T. H. Green*, ed. R. L. Nettleship (London, 1885-8), v.3, pp. 161-85 (henceforth to be

cited as *Green's Works*); "Force of Circumstances," *Green's Works*, v.3, pp. 3-10.
Also, T. H. Green, "Life and Immortality Brought to Light by Gospel," first
printed in Jean Pucelle, *La Nature et l'Esprit dans la Philosophie de T. H. Green*
v.2. (Louvain, 1965), pp. 268-81.

Gerard Manley Hopkins, "The Position of Plato to the Greek World," *The
Journal and Papers of Gerard Manley Hopkins*, ed. Humphrey House (London,
1959), pp. 116-7; *Further Letters of Gerard Manley Hopkins*, ed. Claude Abbet
(London, 1938), pp. 83 & 249; "Thou Art Indeed Just, Lord, if I Contend,"
Poems of Gerard Manley Hopkins (fourth edition, London, 1967), p. 106. Also,
Stephen Paget, *Henry Scott Holland* (London, 1921), p. 29.

⁴ T. H. Green, "Lectures on the English Revolution," *Green's Works*, v.3,
pp. 277-364. Also, John Milton, "Samson Agonisthes," first published in *Paradise
Regain'd . . . to Which is Added Samson Agonisthes* (London, 1671).

CHAPTER ELEVEN

¹ David Hume, *A Treatise of Human Nature* (London, 1739); *Enquiry Concerning
Human Understanding*, first published as *Philosophical Essays* (London, 1748);
History of England (London, 1762), Chapter 71; *The Letters of David Hume*, ed.
J. Y. T. Grieg (Oxford, 1932), v.1, p. 187. Richard Popkin, "David Hume: his
Pyrrhonism and his Critique of Pyrrhonism," *Philosophical Quarterly*, v. 1 (1951),
pp. 385-407; John Passmore, *Hume's Intentions* (New York, 1951), Chapter 7;
Anthony Flew, *Hume's Philosophy of Belief* (London, 1961), Chapter 1; Richard
Kuhns, "Hume's Republic and the Universe of Newton," *Eighteenth Century
Studies*, ed. Peter Gay (Hanover, N.H., 1972), pp. 75-95.

T. H. Green, "Introduction," *Hume's Philosophical Works*, ed. T. H. Green &
T. H. Grose (London, 1874), v. 1, pp. 1-372, reprinted in *Green's Works*, v. 1,
pp. 1-371. Also, Ramon M. Lemos, "Introduction" to Thomas Hill Green,
Hume and Locke (New York, 1968), pp. xi-xvi.

T. H. Green, "J. Caird's 'Introduction to the Philosophy of Religion',"
Green's Works, v. 3, pp. 138-46; Benjamin Jowett, *Sermons Biographical and Miscellaneous*, pp. 207-24.

² T. H. Green, "Can There be a Science of Man," *Mind*, v. 7 (1882), pp. 1-29,
161-85, 321-48; *Prolegomena to Ethics* (Oxford, 1883), ed. A. C. Bradley. G. Watts
Cuningham, *The Idealistic Argument in Recent British and American Philosophy*
(New York, 1933), Chapter 2.

R. L. Nettleship, "Memoir," *Green's Works*, v. 3, pp. xi-clxi.

Edward Caird, *A Critical Account of the Philosophy of Kant* (Glasgow, 1877);
Hegel (Edinburgh, 1883); James Caird, *An Introduction to the Philosophy of Religion*
(Glasgow, 1880); William Wallace, trans., *The Logic of Hegel* (London, 1874);
Hegel's Philosophy of Mind . . . with five introductory essays (London, 1894); T. H.
Green, *The Witness of God and Faith*, ed. Arnold Toynbee, (London, 1883);
A. C. Bradley, *Shakespearean Tragedy* (London, 1904).

R. L. Nettleship, *The Philosophical Remains of Richard Lewis Nettleship* (London,
1901), pp. 51-4; A. C. Bradley, "Biographical Sketch," prefixed to the above.

³ A. E. Taylor, "Francis Herbert Bradley, 1846-1924," *Proceedings of the British
Academy*, vol. 11 (1924-5), pp. 458-68; T. S. Eliot, "F. H. Bradley," *Essays
Ancient & Modern* (London, 1936).

F. H. Bradley, *Ethical Studies* (London, 1876). Jordan Maurice Churchill,
Moral Judgement and Self-Knowledge (unpubl. doctoral diss., Columbia Univ., 1956),
Chapter 4.

CHAPTER TWELVE

¹ F. H. Bradley, *Principles of Logic* (London, 1883). Richard Woolheim, *F. H.
Bradley* (London, 1959), Chapter 1.

[2] F. H. Bradley, *Appearance and Reality* (Oxford, 1893). Robert D. Mack, *The Appeal to Immediate Experience* (New York, 1945), pp. 9-26; Richard Woolheim, *F. H. Bradley*, "Epilogue"; S. K. Saxena, *Studies in the Metaphysics of Bradley* (London, 1966), Chapters 1-3; Garrett Vander Veer, *Bradley's Metaphysics and the Self* (New Haven, 1972), Chapters 6-9.

[3] F. H. Bradley, "On my Real World," *Essays on Truth and Reality* (Oxford, 1914), pp. 460-9; *Aphorisms* (Oxford, 1930). John Muirhead, *The Platonic Tradition in Anglo-Saxon Philosophy*, pp. 279-304.

PART IV

CHAPTER THIRTEEN

[1] G. E. Moore, "An Autobiography," *The Philosophy of G. E. Moore*, ed. P. A. Schlipp (New York, 1942), pp. 3-39; Bertrand Russell, *My Philosophical Development* (London, 1956); *Autobiography of Bertrand Russell*, v. 1 (London, 1967).

John Maynard Keynes, "My Early Beliefs," *Two Memoirs* (London, 1949); Michael Holroyd, *Lytton Strachey* (New York, 1967), v. 1, Chapters 4-5. Also, Frances M. Brookfield, *The Cambridge "Apostles"* (New York, 1907), Chapter 1; R. F. Harrod, *Life of John Maynard Keynes* (London, 1951), pp. 69-75.

John Ellis McTaggart, *Studies in the Hegelian Dialectic* (Cambridge, 1896); *Studies in Hegelian Cosmology* (Cambridge, 1901). Also, John Ellis McTaggart, *The Further Determination of the Absolute* (Cambridge, 1893), reprinted in *Philosophical Studies* (London, 1934), pp. 210-73; G. Lowes Dickinson, *John Ellis McTaggart* (Cambridge, 1931).

G. E. Moore, "Freedom," *Mind*, v. 7 (1895), pp. 179-204; Bertrand Russell, *An Essay on the Foundations of Geometry* (Cambridge, 1897). Also, Gilbert Ryle, "G. E. Moore's 'The Nature of Judgment'," *G. E. Moore: Essays in Retrospect* (London, 1970), pp. 89-101.

Bertrand Russell, *A Critical Exposition of the Philosophy of Leibniz* (Cambridge, 1900).

G. E. Moore, "Mr. McTaggart's 'Studies in Hegelian Cosmology'," *Proceedings of the Aristotelian Society*, v. 2, (1902), pp. 177-214; "Mr. McTaggart's Ethics," *International Journal of Ethics*, v. 13 (1903), pp. 341-70.

[2] Bertrand Russell, *The Principles of Mathematics* (Cambridge, 1903). Also, Morton Grosser, *The Discovery of Neptune* (Cambridge, Mass., 1962).

G. E. Moore, *Principia Ethica* (Cambridge, 1903); Bertrand Russell, "Determinism and Morals," *Hibbert Journal*, v. 7 (1908), pp. 113-21, reprinted as "The Elements of Ethics" in *Philosophical Essays* (London, 1910). Mary Warnock, *Ethics since 1900* (London, 1960), Chapter 2; George C. Kerner, *The Revolution in Ethical Theory* (Oxford, 1966), Chapter 1; Ronald Jager, "Analyticity and Necessity in Moore's Early Work," *Journal of the History of Philosophy*, v. 7 (1969), pp. 441-58. Also, Joseph Butler, *The Analogy of Religion* (London, 1736).

[3] G. E. Moore, "The Refutation of Idealism," *Mind*, v. 12 (1903), pp. 433-53; Bertrand Russell, "G. E. Moore's *Principia Ethica*," *The Independent Review*, v. 11 (1904), pp. 328-33; "Ethics," *New Quarterly*, v. 3 (1910), pp. 21-34; "Free Man's Worship," *The Independent Review*, v. 1 (1903), pp. 415-24, first reprinted in *Philosophical Essays*.

CHAPTER FOURTEEN

[1] Bertrand Russell, "Alfred North Whitehead," *Portraits from Memory* (New York, 1956), pp. 99-104. G. D. Bowne, *The Philosophy of Logic 1880-1908* (The Hague, 1966).

Bertrand Russell, "On Denoting," *Mind*, v. 14 (1905), pp. 479-93; "Les Paradoxes de la Logique," *Revue de Metaphysique et de Morale*, v. 14 (1906), pp.

627-650; "Mathematical Logic as Based on the Theory of Type," *American Journal of Mathematics*, v. 30 (1908), pp. 222-62. Also, Norwood Russell Hanson, "Leverrier: the Zenith and Nadir of Newtonian Mechanics," *Isis*, v. 53 (1962), pp. 359-78; Bertrand Russell, "Letter to Frege," printed in *From Frege to Godel*, ed. Jean Van Heijenoort (Cambridge, Mass., 1967), pp. 124-5.

² Bertrand Russell, "The Study of Mathematics," *New Quarterly*, November, 1907, first reprinted in *Philosophical Essays*.

G. E. Moore, "George Santayana, *The Life of Reason*," *International Journal of Ethics*, v. 17 (1907), pp. 248-53; "W. R. Boyce Gibson, *A Philosophical Introduction to Ethics*," *International Journal of Ethics*, v. 15 (1905), pp. 370-9; "The Nature and Reality of Objects of Perception," *Proc. Arist. Soc.*, v. 6 (1906), pp. 68-127.

³ Bertrand Russell and Alfred North Whitehead, *Principia Mathematica* (Cambridge, 1910, 1912, 1913), 3 vols.; Bertrand Russell, *An Introduction to Mathematical Philosophy* (London, 1919), p. 135.

⁴ George Santayana, *The Life of Reason* (London, 1905-6); *Three Philosophical Poets* (Cambridge, Mass., 1910); "The Philosophy of Mr. Bertrand Russell," *Winds of Doctrine* (New York, 1913), pp. 110-54.

⁵ Bertrand Russell, *Our Knowledge of the External World* (Chicago, 1914); *The Problems of Philosophy* (London, 1912), p. 20. Also, Charles Fritz, *Bertrand Russell's Construction of the External World* (London, 1952), pp. 78-117; James Feibleman, *Inside the Great Mirror* (The Hague, 1958), Chapter 1.

Bertrand Russell, "George Santayana," *Portraits from Memory*, pp. 92-8; George Santayana, *The Letters of George Santayana*, ed. Daniel Cory (New York, 1955), pp. 137, 181.

CHAPTER FIFTEEN

¹ Bertrand Russell, *German Social Democracy* (London, 1896); "On Justice in War-Time. An Appeal to the Intellectuals of Europe," *Independent Review*, v. 1 (1915), pp. 145-51, 223-30, reprinted in *Justice in War-Time* (Chicago, 1916); "Is a Permanent Peace Possible," *Atlantic Monthly*, v. 115 (1915), pp. 367-76, reprinted in *Justice in War-Time*.

² Alfred North Whitehead, *An Introduction to Mathematics* (London, 1911). Victor Lowe, "The Development of Whitehead's Philosophy," *The Philosophy of Alfred North Whitehead*, ed. P. A. Schlipp (New York, 1941), pp. 17-64.

Alfred Whitehead, "The Aim of Education," *Mathematical Gazette*, v. 8 (1916), pp. 191-203, first reprinted in *The Organisation of Thought* (London, 1917); "A Polytechnic in War-Time," *The Organisation of Thought*; "Graphical Solution for High Angle Fire," *Proceedings of the Royal Society of London*, Series A, v. 94 (1918), pp. 301-7. Also, Whitehead, "Memories," *Atlantic Monthly*, v. 157 (1936), pp. 672-9; *Dialogues of Alfred North Whitehead as Recorded by Lucien Price* (Boston, 1954).

Alfred Whitehead, "A Revolution in Science," *Nation and Athenaeum*, v. 26 (1919), pp. 232-33; Albert Einstein, "What is the Theory of Relativity," "Paradise Lost," *Ideas and Opinions* (New York, 1954).

³ Alfred North Whitehead, *An Enquiry Concerning the Principles of Natural Knowledge* (Cambridge, 1919). Harry Kohlsatt Wells, *Process and Unreality* (New York, 1950), Part I.

⁴ Alfred North Whitehead, "Symposium:—Time, Space, and Material: Are they, and if so in what sense, the ultimate data of science?," *Aristotelian Society Supplementary Volume 2* (1919), pp. 44-57; *The Concept of Nature* (Cambridge, 1920); *The Principle of Relativity* (Cambridge, 1922). Nathaniel Lawrence, *Whitehead's Philosophical Development* (Berkeley, 1956), Part II.

⁵ John Ellis McTaggart, *The Nature of Existence* (Cambridge, 1921, 1928),

2 vols. S. V. Keeling, "Introduction," John Ellis McTaggart, *Philosophical Studies* (London, 1934), pp. 9-33.

C. D. Broad, *An Examination of McTaggart's Philosophy* (Cambridge, 1933, 1938, 1938), 3 vols. Also, Broad, "An Autobiography," *The Philosophy of C. D. Broad*, ed. P. A. Schlipp (New York, 1959), pp. 3-68; "Newton," *Ethics and the History of Philosophy* (London, 1952), pp. 3-28.

CHAPTER SIXTEEN

[1] Alfred North Whitehead, *Science and the Modern World* (New York, 1925). Mary A. Wyman, *The Lure for Feeling* (New York, 1960).

[2] Alfred North Whitehead, *Process and Reality* (New York, 1929). Dorothy Emmet, *Whitehead's Philosophy of Organism* (London, 1932); Stephen Lee Ely, *The Religious Availability of Whitehead's God* (Madison, 1942); Craig R. Eisendrath, *The Unifying Moment* (Cambridge, Mass., 1971), pp. 199-202. Also, "Corrigenda for *Process and Reality*," *Alfred North Whitehead: Essays on his Philosophy*, ed. George L. Kline (Englewood Cliffs, N.J., 1963), pp. 200-7.

[3] Alfred North Whitehead, *Religion in the Making* (New York, 1926); G. E. Moore, "A. N. Whitehead, *Religion in the Making*," *The Nation and Athenaeum* (1927), p. 664.

Bertrand Russell, *The Analysis of Mind* (London, 1921); G. E. Moore, "Bertrand Russell, *The Analysis of Mind*," *The Times Literary Supplement* (1921), p. 622.

G. E. Moore, "Is Goodness a Quality," *Aristotelian Society Supplementary Volume 11* (1932), pp. 116-31 (henceforth to be cited *Arist. Soc. Suppl. Vol.*—); "Are the Characteristics of Particular Things Universal or Particular," *Arist. Soc. Suppl. Vol. 3* (1923), pp. 95-113; "Symposium: Imaginary Objects," *Arist. Soc. Suppl. Vol. 12* (1933), pp. 18-70; "Symposium: Is Existence a Predicate," *Arist. Soc. Suppl. Vol. 15* (1936), pp. 175-88; "The Death of Dr. McTaggart," *Mind*, v. 34 (1925), pp. 269-71. Richard Braithwaite, "George Edward Moore, 1873-1958," *Proceedings of the British Academy*, v. 47 (1961), pp. 293-309.

G. E. Moore, "A Defence of Common Sense," *Contemporary British Philosophy*, ed. J. H. Muirhead (London, 1925), pp. 193-223; "Proof of an External World," *Proceedings of the British Academy*, v. 25 (1939), pp. 273-300. Norman Malcolm, *Knowledge and Certainty* (Englewood Cliffs, N.J., 1963), pp. 163-83; Alice Ambrose, "Moore's Proof of an External World," *The Philosophy of G. E. Moore*, pp. 397-417; Morris Lazerowitz, "Moore and Linguistic Philosophy," *G. E. Moore: Essays in Retrospect*, pp. 102-21.

[4] Alfred North Whitehead, "Immortality," *The Harvard Divinity School Bulletin*, v. 39 (1941), pp. 5-21; also printed in *The Philosophy of Alfred North Whitehead*, pp. 682-700.

G. E. Moore, "A Reply to My Critics," *The Philosophy of G. E. Moore*, p. 677. Also, Rudolph Metz, *A Hundred Years of British Philosophy* (London, 1938), p. 540; L. Susan Stebbing, "Moore's Influence," *The Philosophy of G. E. Moore*, pp. 517-32.

Bertrand Russell, *Human Knowledge: its Scope and Limits* (New York, 1948).

SUBJECT INDEX

INDEX OF NAMES